COUNTERBLASTS

COUNTERBLASTS is a series of short, polemical titles that aims to revive a tradition inaugurated by Puritan and Leveller pamphleteers in the seventeenth century, when, in the words of one of their number, Gerard Winstanley, the old world was "running up like parchment in the fire." From 1640 to 1663, a leading bookseller and publisher, George Thomason, recorded that his collection alone contained over twenty thousand pamphlets. Such polemics reappeared both before and during the French, Russian, Chinese and Cuban revolutions of the last century.

In a period where politicians, media barons and their ideological hirelings rarely challenge the basis of existing society, it is time to revive the tradition. Verso's Counterblasts will challenge the apologists of Empire and Capital.

The Imperial Messenger:
Thomas Friedman
at Work

Bélen Fernández

VERSO

London • New York

for my amazing parents, with love and gratitude

First published by Verso 2011
© Bélen Fernández 2011

The moral rights of the author have been asserted

1 3 5 7 9 10 8 6 4 2

Verso
UK: 6 Meard Street, London W1F 0EG
US: 20 Jay Street, Suite 1010, Brooklyn, NY 11201
www.versobooks.com

Verso is the imprint of New Left Books

ISBN-13: 978-1-84467-749-8

British Library Cataloguing in Publication Data
A catalogue record for this book is available from the British Library

Library of Congress Cataloging-in-Publication Data
A catalog record for this book is available from the Library of Congress

Typeset in Minion Pro by MJ Gavan, Cornwall
Printed in the US by Maple Vail

CONTENTS

INTRODUCING FRIEDMAN

The House Republicans don't seem to have noticed that today's U.N. is not the U.N. of the 1970's when the Soviets and their pals could pass a resolution that the world was flat.

—Thomas Friedman, 1995

The World Is Flat: A Brief History of the Twenty-first Century
—Thomas Friedman, 2005

In the first chapter of his bestseller on globalization, *The World Is Flat*, three-time Pulitzer Prize–winning foreign affairs columnist for the *New York Times* Thomas Friedman suggests that his repertoire of achievements also includes being heir to Christopher Columbus. According to Friedman, he has followed in the footsteps of the fifteenth-century icon by making an unexpected discovery regarding the shape of the world during an encounter with "people called Indians."[1]

Friedman's Indians reside in India proper, of course, not in the Caribbean, and include among their ranks CEO Nandan Nilekani of Infosys Technologies Limited in Bangalore, where Friedman has come in the early twenty-first century to investigate phenomena such as outsourcing and to exult over the globalization-era instructions he receives at the KGA Golf Club downtown: "Aim at either Microsoft or IBM."[2] Nilekani unwittingly plants the flat world seed in Friedman's mind by commenting, in reference to technological advancements enabling other countries to challenge presumed American hegemony in certain business sectors: "Tom, the playing field is being leveled."[3]

The Columbus-like discovery process culminates with Friedman's conversion of one of the components of Nilekani's idiomatic expression into a more convenient synonym: "What Nandan is saying, I thought to myself, is that the playing field is being flattened ... Flattened? Flattened? I rolled that word around in my head for a while and then, in the chemical way that these things happen, it just popped out: My God, he's telling me the world is flat!"[4]

The viability of the new metaphor has already been called into question by Friedman's assessment two pages prior to the flat-world discovery that the Infosys campus is in fact "a different world," given that the rest of India is not characterized by things like a "massive resort-size swimming pool" and a "fabulous health club."[5] No attention is meanwhile paid to the possibility that a normal, round earth—on which all circumferential points are equidistant from the center—might more effectively convey the notion of the global network Friedman maintains is increasingly equalizing human opportunity.

An array of disclaimers and metaphorical qualifications begins to surface around page 536, such that it ultimately appears that the book might have been more appropriately titled *The World Is Sometimes Indefinitely Maybe Partially Flat—But Don't Worry, I Know It's Not*, or perhaps *The World Is Flat, Except for the Part That Is Unflat and the Twilight Zone Where Half-Flat People Live*. As for his announcement that "unlike Columbus, I didn't stop with India,"[6] Friedman intends this as an affirmation of his continued exploration of various parts of the globe and not as an admission of his continuing tendency to err—which he does first and foremost by incorrectly attributing the discovery that the earth is round to the geographically misguided Italian voyager.

Leaving aside for the moment the blunders that plague

Friedman's writing, the comparison with Columbus is actually quite apt in other ways, as well. For instance, both characters might be accused of transmitting a similar brand of hubris, nurtured by their respective societies, according to which "the Other" is permitted existence only via the discoverer-hero himself. While Columbus is credited with enabling preexisting populations on the American continent to enter the realm of true existence by reporting them to European civilization, Friedman assumes responsibility for the earth's inhabitants in general without literally having to encounter them.

As the world becomes ever more interconnected, Friedman appears to be under the impression that he is licensed to extrapolate observations of select demographic groups, such as Indian call center employees pleased with the opportunities provided them by U.S. corporations, and to issue pronouncements like the following on behalf of humanity: "Three United States are better than one, and five would be better than three."[7] Not surprisingly, Friedman does not respond favorably when elements of humanity fail to internalize the aspirations he has assigned them, resulting in anthropological revelations such as that one of the impediments to freedom in the Arab world is "the wall in the Arab mind."[8] Friedman explains in 2003 that "I hit my head against that wall" while conversing with Egyptian journalists who "could see nothing good coming from the U.S. 'occupation' of Iraq" and who are thus written off as proponents of "Saddamism."[9]

Friedman initially hocks the possibility of a democratizing war on Iraq as "the most important task worth doing and worth debating,"[10] based on a variety of fluctuating reasons, such as that "install[ing] a decent, tolerant, pluralistic, multireligious government in Iraq ... would be the best answer and antidote to both Saddam and Osama."[11] However, Friedman himself reiterates that the real threat to "open, Western, liberal societies today" consists not of "the deterrables, like Saddam, but the undeterrables—the boys who did 9/11, who hate us more than they love life. It's these human missiles of mass destruction that could really destroy our open society."[12] No compelling justification is ever provided for how a war against deterrables whose weapons are not the problem will solve the problem of undeterrables who *are* the weapons and who by definition cannot be deterred anyway. As for Friedman's speculation in a 1997 column that "Saddam Hussein is the reason God created cruise missiles," this is not entirely reconcilable with his suggestion in the very same article that Saddam be eliminated via "a head shot"—not generally a setting on such weaponry.[13]

Though he never disputes the idea that war on Iraq was a "legitimate choice,"[14] Friedman gradually downgrades his war aims to "salvag[ing] something decent"[15] in said country, while appearing to forget for varying stretches of time that the U.S. military is also still involved in a war in Afghanistan. Given the prominence of Friedman's perch at the *New York Times*, from which he is permitted to promote—and to disguise as pedagogical in nature—bellicose projects resulting in over one million Iraqi deaths to date,[16] it is not at all far-fetched to resurrect the comparison with Columbus in order to suggest that the designated heir is also complicit in the decimation of foreign populations standing in the way of civilization's demands.

The foundations of Friedman's journalistic education consist of a tenth-grade introductory course taught by Hattie M. Steinberg at St. Louis Park High School in a suburb of Minneapolis in 1969, after which Friedman claims to have "never needed, or taken, another course in journalism."[17] Following a BA from Brandeis University and a Master of Philosophy degree in Modern Middle East studies from Oxford, Friedman worked briefly for United Press International and was hired by the *New York Times* in 1981. He served as bureau chief in both Beirut and Jerusalem in the 1980s before becoming the *New York Times*' chief diplomatic correspondent in Washington, D.C., and then, in 1995, its foreign affairs columnist. He has written five bestselling books, dealing variously with the Middle East, globalization, and the clean energy quest: *From Beirut to Jerusalem* (1989), *The Lexus and the Olive Tree:*

Understanding Globalization (1999), *Longitudes and Attitudes: Exploring the World After September 11* (2002), *The World Is Flat: A Brief History of the Twenty-first Century* (2005), and *Hot, Flat and Crowded: Why We Need a Green Revolution—And How It Can Renew America* (2008).[18]

Friedman's writing is characterized by a reduction of complex international phenomena to simplistic rhetoric and theorems that rarely withstand the test of reality. His vacuous but much-publicized "First Law of Petropolitics"—which Friedman devises by plotting a handful of historical incidents on a napkin and which states that the price of oil is inversely related to the pace of freedom—does not even withstand the test of the very Freedom House reports that Friedman invokes as evidence in support of the alleged law.[19] The tendency toward rampant reductionism has become such a Friedman trademark that one finds oneself wondering whether he is not intentionally parodying himself when he introduces "A Theory of Everything" to explain anti-American sentiment in the world and states his hope "that people will write in with comments or catcalls so I can continue to refine [the theory], turn it into a quick book and pay my daughter's college tuition."[20]

In the case of Friedman's musings on the Arab/Muslim world, the reduction process produces decontextualized and often patronizing or blatantly racist generalizations, such as that suicide bombing in Israel indicates a "collective madness"[21] on the part of the Palestinians, whom Friedman has determined it is permissible to refer to collectively as "Ahmed."[22] Criticism of Israeli crimes is largely restricted to the issue of settlement-building; generalizations about the United States meanwhile often arrive in the form of observations along the lines of: "Is this a great country or what?"[23] This does not mean, however, that the United States is not in perennial danger of descending into decisive non-greatness if it does not abide by Friedman's diktats on oil dependence and other matters, such as the need to expand U.S. embassy libraries across the globe because "you'd be amazed at how many young people abroad had their first contact with America through an embassy library."[24]

Complementing his reductionist habit is Friedman's insistence on imbuing trivial experiences abroad with undue or false significance, often in support of whatever "meta-story" he is peddling at the moment. The "tiny Vietnamese woman crouched on the sidewalk with her bathroom scale" in Hanoi in 1995, to whom Friedman gives a dollar to weigh himself each morning of his visit, thus becomes proof that "globalization emerges from below, from street level, from people's very souls and from their very deepest aspirations."[25] The Pakistani youth wearing a jacket imprinted with the word "Titanic" on Friedman's Emirates Air flight in 2001 becomes a sign that Pakistan is either the *Titanic* or the iceberg.[26] The presence of pork chops at Friedman's cousin Giora's bar mitzvah in Israel prompts deep reflection: "I thought about the meaning of Giora's pork chops for several days. They seemed to contain a larger message."[27]

Friedman begins *The Lexus and the Olive Tree* with a detailed recounting of a 1994 experience in a Tokyo hotel in which his room service request for four oranges results first in four glasses of orange juice and then in four peeled and diced oranges, all transported by a Japanese serviceperson unable to correctly pronounce the word "orange." Only after almost two pages do we learn that the point of this citrus saga, plus another one in a Hanoi hotel dining room involving tangerines, is that Friedman "would find a lot of things on my plate and outside my door that I wasn't planning to find as I traveled the globe for the *Times*."[28]

That these extensive travels have not produced a more relevant introductory anecdote to a book about globalization is curious, especially since Friedman boasts in *Longitudes and Attitudes* that he has "total freedom, and an almost unlimited budget, to explore,"[29] and especially since he criticizes writers who eschew shoe-leather reporting in favor of "sitting at home in their pajamas firing off digital mortars."[30] It perhaps does not occur to our foreign affairs columnist that, in the era of online publications, most writers do not have access to the funds that would enable them to fire off digital mortars about the "Russian breakfast" option on the room service menu at the five-star Meliá Cohiba in Havana,[31] or to arrive at conclusions regarding the root causes of poverty in Africa by going on safari in Botswana.[32] It should be noted, however, that Friedman's coverage of the Lebanese civil war and the first Palestinian Intifada—though often plagued by untruths as well—was more readily classifiable as shoe-leather reporting, perhaps because he did not define his job at the time as "tourist with an attitude."[33]

Friedman additionally reveals in *Longitudes and Attitudes* that the "only person who sees my two columns each week before they show up in the newspaper is a copy editor who edits them for grammar and spelling," and that for the duration of his columnist career up to this point he has "never had a conversation with the publisher of *The New York Times* about any opinion I've adopted—before or after any column I've written."[34] It comes as no surprise, of course, that said publisher feels no need to reign in an employee whose last failure to toe the paper's editorial line appears to have occurred in 1982, when Friedman's reference to indiscriminate Israeli shelling of West Beirut as indiscriminate launches a battle ultimately resulting in a $5,000 raise and an "emotional lunch" with *New York Times* executive editor A. M. (Abe) Rosenthal, who "threw his arms around me in a big Abe bear hug, told me all was forgiven and then whispered in my ear: 'Now listen, you clever little !%#@: don't you ever do that again.'"[35] Friedman's confirmed immunity from most kinds of editing meanwhile explains his continued ability to churn out incoherent metaphors, the terms of which he himself tends to lose track.

Consider, for example, his pre–Iraq war advice to George W. Bush to throw his steering wheel out the window in a vehicular game of chicken with Saddam Hussein, immediately followed by the warning that "if Saddam swerves aside by accepting unconditional [weapons] inspections," the Bush team cannot "also swerve off the road, chase [Saddam's] car and crash into it anyway"—an option that would seem to have been obviated by removal of the Bush team's navigational instrument.[36] A different sort of metaphorical pile-up occurs when Friedman visits Afghanistan, and readers are bombarded with an image of Kabul as a smashed cake-like Liberia-esque Ground Zero East covered with snow, ice, and aspects of Dresden, the Beirut Green Line, and Hiroshima.[37]

Alas, the point of this book is not to laugh at Friedman's bungled metaphors, or the number of times he devises foreign policy prescriptions based on experiences in hotel rooms, restaurants, and airplanes. Rather, it is to demonstrate the defectiveness in form and in substance of his disjointed discourse, and in doing so offer a testament to the degenerate state of the mainstream media in the United States.

Friedman's reporting is replete with hollow analyses (e.g., an American victory in Afghanistan is possible as long as it recognizes that "Dorothy, this ain't Kansas"[38]) and factual inaccuracies, ranging from the relatively trivial (Chile shares a border with Russia but Poland does not[39]) to the sort of deliberate obfuscation of fact that is condoned by the establishment (the Palestinians were offered 95 percent of what they wanted at Camp David). Self-contradictions abound, and, two hundred pages into *The World Is Flat*, Friedman defines Globalization 1.0 as the era in which he was required to physically visit an airline ticket office in order to make his travel arrangements—whereas, according to the definition he provides at the start of the book, Globalization 1.0 ended around the year 1800.[40]

As for contradictions in matters of greater geopolitical consequence, these include the aforementioned continuous adding and subtracting of motives for the Iraq war, which is alternately characterized as evidence of the moral clarity of the Bush administration, evidence of the U.S. military's ability to make Iraqis "Suck. On. This,"[41] and simultaneously a neoconservative project and "the most radical-liberal revolutionary war the U.S. has ever launched"[42]—indicating that "the left needs to get beyond its opposition to the war and start pitching in with its own ideas and moral support to try to make lemons into lemonade in Baghdad."[43] The supremely liberal nature of the war is especially confounding given that Friedman also defines himself as "a liberal on every issue other than this war."[44]

Whatever era of globalization we are currently in, it is one in which news professionals are increasingly poised to influence the outcomes of the very world events they are reporting. Friedman's contributions are not limited to Iraq, as is clear from the following passage from veteran British reporter Robert Fisk's *The Great War for Civilisation: The Conquest of the Middle East*:

> How many journalists encouraged the Israelis—by their report-ing or by their willfully given, foolish advice—to undertake the brutal assaults on the Palestinians? On 31 March 2002—just three days before the assault on Jenin—Tom Friedman wrote in *The New York Times* that "Israel needs to deliver a military blow that clearly shows terror will not pay." Well, thanks, Tom, I said to myself when I read this piece of lethal journalism a few days later. The Israelis certainly followed Friedman's advice.[45]

That Friedman discredits himself as a journalist by championing the killing of civilians has not prevented him from being hailed as a master of the trade, an objective commentator on the Middle East, and a foreign policy sage sought out by Barack Obama in times of international uncertainty (such as the 2011 Arab uprisings, when Obama is presumably pleased to discover that he himself is one of the catalysts of the very uprisings he is seeking to understand[46]). Friedman appears as required reading on university syllabi and receives compensation in the form of $75,000 for public speak-ing appearances.[47] He occupies slot No. 33 on *Foreign Policy*'s Top 100 Global Thinkers of 2010, accompanied by the reminder that "Friedman doesn't just report on events; he helps shape them"—despite minor setbacks such as the disastrous fate recently met by his thoughts on the Irish economy.[48]

Friedman's latest incarnation as award-winning conservationist has spawned a whole new level of irony as he has endeavored to reconcile this identity with preceding ones: "The neocon strategy may have been necessary to trigger reform in Iraq and the wider

Arab world, but it will not be sufficient unless it is followed up by what I call a 'geo-green' strategy."[49] Readers may question how many true "geo-greens" would advocate the tactical contamination of the earth's soil with depleted uranium munitions. Why not introduce a doctrine of neoconservationism?

A more critical question, of course, is how a journalist whose professional qualifications include rhetorical incoherence has nonetheless ascended to an internationally recognized position as media icon. (Friedman even suggests at one point that Osama bin Laden has been perusing his column.[50]) Hardly a fluke, Friedman's accumulation of influence is a direct result of his service as mouthpiece for empire and capital, i.e., as resident apologist for U.S. military excess and punishing economic policies.

Naturally, Friedman is far from alone when it comes to co-opted media figures providing a veneer of independent validation to state and corporate hegemonic endeavors in which they are entirely complicit. Friedman's exceptionalism lies simply in the extent of his symbiosis with centers of power. Let us briefly reconsider the evolution of *The World Is Flat*, which begins with Friedman's hobnobbing with the Infosys CEO in Bangalore.

A favorable profile of Friedman from a 2006 edition of the *Washingtonian* specifies that Friedman's flat-world theory was developed in collaboration with the vice president of corporate strategy at IBM, and that—in addition to remaining on *The New York Times* bestseller list for over a year—the book "jump-started a national debate over American competitiveness that was picked up in President Bush's State of the Union address."[51] An article from the *Financial Times* website the previous year meanwhile announces Friedman's receipt of the first annual £30,000 *Financial Times* and Goldman Sachs Business Book of the Year Award for *The World Is Flat*; Friedman is quoted as repaying the compliment by declaring the *Financial Times* and Goldman Sachs "two such classy organizations, who take business and business reporting seriously. I'm thrilled and honoured because the judges who made this award are such an esteemed group."[52]

Among the "esteemed" components of the "classy" Wall Street firm is executive Lloyd Blankfein, a member of the judge's panel for Friedman's award who, in the aftermath of the 2008 financial meltdown, reiterated his commitment to serious business by lying under oath to Congress about Goldman's classy defrauding of clients. In an indispensable exposé for *Rolling Stone*, investigative journalist Matt Taibbi provides the following analogy about the firm's self-enriching exploitation, "at the expense of society," of the meltdown it helped to create:

> Goldman, to get $1.2 billion in crap off its books, dumps a huge lot of deadly mortgages on its clients, lies about where that crap came from and claims it believes in the product even as it's betting $2 billion against it. When its victims try to run out of the burning house, Goldman stands in the doorway, blasts them all with gasoline before they can escape, and then has the balls to send a bill overcharging its victims for the pleasure of getting fried.[53]

Friedman, despite criticizing U.S. investment banks in 2008 for deviating from the corporate ethics set forth in his friend Dov Seidman's book How: *Why How We Do Anything Means Everything … in Business (and in Life)*, by bundling together risky mortgage bonds in order to "engineer money from money,"[54] continues throughout 2008 and 2009 to quote Goldman Sachs executives and analysts on how the U.S. government should respond to the financial crisis—namely by throwing more billions at banks.[55] It is not until 2010 that Friedman directly denounces Goldman as "the poster boy for banks behaving by 'situational values'—exploiting whatever the situation, or rules that it helped to write, allowed."[56] Another Seidman concept, situational values are the opposite of "sustainable values" and are consistently decried by Friedman, who fails to explain how intermittent denunciation of Goldman Sachs is indicative of a sustainable value system. He meanwhile continues to campaign against entitlements and to encourage the slashing of corporate and payroll taxes,[57] policies obviously not designed to punish the poster boy.

Aside from Blankfein, the judging panel for the 2005 FT–Goldman Sachs award also happens to include the Chairman and Chief Mentor of Infosys, star of *The World Is Flat*. Though £30,000 may be an insignificant sum for a character who accumulates at least seven figures of annual income on top of having married into one of the hundred wealthiest families in the United States,[58] the award is a useful example of the potentially incestuous nature of the relationship between business and business reporting. The process of mutual aggrandizement in this case is straightforward: Friedman writes book about globalization under guidance of corporate executives, corporate executives hail book as ingenious blueprint for world, accolades propel Friedman's fame, Friedman exploits fame to further reinforce elite power structures while occasionally attributing his project to more sentimental motivations such as those cited in *The World Is Flat*:

> When done right and in a sustained manner, globalization has a huge potential to lift large numbers of people out of poverty. And when I see large numbers of people escaping poverty in places like India, China, or Ireland, well, yes, I get a little emotional.[59]

As for Friedman's genuine motivations, he regularly advertises his subscription to billionaire investor Warren Buffett's theory that everything he has achieved in life is a result of having been born in the United States, and reiterates his duty to pass his situation on to his children. Given that the overwhelming majority of offspring produced in the United States—not to mention the world—cannot aspire to situations that involve belonging to one of the country's hundred richest families, it goes without saying that Friedman fully endorses the perpetuation of a system of institutionalized economic inequality.

As he himself notes in *The Lexus and the Olive Tree* with regard to the "Darwinian brutality" of free-market capitalism: "Other systems may be able to distribute and divide income more efficiently and equitably, but none can generate income to distribute as efficiently."[60] Friedman's tendency to convert victims of imposed economic systems into victims of natural selection is symptomatic of his categorical dismissal of the realities affecting the global poor (see, for example, his response to Nobel prize-winning economist Joseph Stiglitz's observation in 2006 that "The number of people living in poverty in Africa in the last 20 years has doubled" with the statement: "But India matters"[61]). Such tendencies are meanwhile rendered all the more grating by Friedman's occasional assumption of the role of capitalist victim himself, as in the following scenario from 1998:

> While waiting to see if the U.N. Secretary General's 11th-hour visit to Iraq can avert a war, I sought some diversion by catching up on the sports news. Talk about depressing. If you want to see how the other great superpower at work in the world today—the unfettered markets—is reshaping our lives and uprooting communities, turn to sports.[62]

The superior depressiveness in this case is in part a result of adverse effects of unfettered markets on Friedman's NBA season tickets, such as that "teams are being forced to trade away high-priced stars left and right."[63]

Friedman's prophecies and directives do not all emerge from the depths of corporate libido. He is also equipped with a "brain trust,"[64] a group of academics, experts, and rabbis with predictable views who are personal friends of Friedman and are quoted so regularly at times that one finds oneself wondering, for example, if Johns Hopkins professor Michael Mandelbaum, Middle East expert Stephen P. Cohen, and Israeli political theorist Yaron Ezrahi might not be nominated honorary *New York Times* columnists. Mandelbaum and Cohen also share the distinction of being Friedman's "soul mates and constant intellectual companions,"[65] while Cohen is graced with the additional denomination "soul brother."[66]

As late Palestinian American scholar Edward Said notes in his 1989 essay "The Orientalist Express: Thomas Friedman Wraps Up the Middle East"—in reference to Friedman's blissful reductions of Arabo-Islamic peoples in *From Beirut to Jerusalem*—Friedman "palms off his opinions (and those of his sources) as reasonable, uncontested, secure. In fact they are minority views and have been under severe attack for several decades now."[67] Other passages from Said's essay are useful for comprehending the triumph of the persona of Thomas Friedman on the journalistic stage:

> It is not just the comic philistinism of Friedman's ideas that I find so remarkably jejune, or his sassy and unbeguiling manner … It is rather the special combination of disarming incoherence and unearned egoism that gives him his cockily alarming plausibility— qualities that may explain [*From Beirut to Jerusalem*]'s startling commercial success. It's as if … what scholars, poets, historians, fighters, and statesmen have done is not as important or as central as what Friedman himself thinks.[68]

As for what happens when Friedman himself thinks that Iraqis should "Suck. On. This" as compensation for 9/11, we can only assume that haughty refrains of sexual-military domination find resonance among audiences seeking to defy feelings of individual and/or national inadequacy. It is meanwhile not clear why Friedman subsequently purports to be scandalized by the sexual-military goings-on at Abu Ghraib.

In this book, I draw primarily from Friedman's dispatches as *New York Times* foreign affairs columnist (1995–present) and his five books. I draw to a lesser extent from his pre-1995 articles and from select interviews and public appearances.[69] (Iraqis may be interested to know, however, that contemporary inciters of bloodshed have in past decades pursued more innocuous subjects, such as how "Iowa Beef Revolutionized Meat-Packing Industry."[70]) Section I of the book, "America," will focus on Friedman's view of the role of the United States on this earth. Section II, "The

Arab/Muslim World," will address Friedman's commitment to Orientalist traditions, with a focus on his post-9/11 radicalization and the war on terror. Section III, "The Special Relationship," will deal with Friedman's double standards vis-à-vis Israel.

Regarding the future of the Friedman phenomenon, a television anchor from Israel's Channel 2 informs him during a 2010 interview that he is an "endangered species" and poses the question: "Ten years from now, will an institution like Thomas Friedman be possible?"[71] She is referring not to the possibility that by the year 2020 journalists who assign "moral clarity" to George W. Bush will no longer receive Pulitzer Prizes for "clarity of vision," but rather to current trends away from print media.[72]

Friedman laughs and suggests that the substance of his work will ensure his continued relevance. But you never know. After all, as Friedman himself has reasoned, it would be crazy to pay a lot of money for a belt if you already have suspenders, "especially if that belt makes it more likely your pants will fall down."[73]

1 AMERICA

I didn't start globalization, I can't stop it—except at a huge cost to human development.
　　　　　　　　　　　—Thomas Friedman, *The Lexus and the Olive Tree*

With all due respect to 1960's revolutionary ideology, the wretched of the earth want to go to Disney World, not to the barricades—if they're given half a chance. If not, they will eat their rain forest, whatever it might be.
　　　　　　　　　　　　　　　　　　　　—Thomas Friedman, 1998

May 31, 2010. Israeli commandos slaughter nine Turkish humanitarian activists on board the Freedom Flotilla endeavoring to deliver aid to besieged Gaza. The event takes place in international waters. Thomas Friedman's reaction is to put the word humanitarian in quotation marks and to announce that Turkish "concern for Gaza and Israel's blockade is so out of balance with ... other horrific cases in the region" that Turkey is risking its "historic role as a country that can be Muslim, modern, democratic."[1]

One of the horrific cases cited by Friedman is the recent destruction by "pro-Hamas gunmen"[2] of facilities at a U.N.-sponsored summer camp in Gaza. It thus appears that, if the Turks do indeed wish to "get back in balance,"[3] they will have to ignore not only Hamas' official condemnation of the destruction in question but also Israel's history of attacks on regional U.N. institutions, which—unlike Friedman's preferred "horrific case"—have not been casualty-free.[4]

Two weeks after the flotilla assault, Friedman travels to Turkey to deliver a scheduled presentation at Istanbul's Özyeğin University about his latest book, *Hot, Flat, and Crowded: Why We Need a Green Revolution—And How It Can Renew America*.[5] Although he mercifully refrains from discussing his audience's lack of balance, it seems more than slightly ironic that an American columnist who has just written off the elimination of nine Turkish activists by a U.S.-funded army as a "setup"[6] is now lecturing an auditorium full of Turks on how "a lot of bad stuff happens in the world without America, but not a lot of good stuff."[7] As for Friedman's ejaculation that "green is the new red, white, and blue, oh yes it is, baby," this is only subsequently amended to reflect the geographical circumstances: "And it's the new red and white in Turkey."[8]

Near the end of his two-hour lecture, our columnist stumbles into revealing that the book he is promoting "is really about America. It's not about energy," and that both *The World Is Flat* and *Hot, Flat, and Crowded* "have nothing to do with technology or environment at heart" but are instead "basically cries of the heart to get my country focused on fixing itself."[9] Lest said country misinterpret these cries as encompassing genuine concern for biodiversity or the possibility that the Internet can lift the global poor out of poverty, Friedman subsequently embarks on the even more transparently focused mouthful *That Used to Be Us: How America Fell Behind in the World We Invented—And How We Can Come Back*, which he manages to describe in a 2011 Fox Business interview as "the first book I've really written about America."[10]

As for Friedman's qualifications as overseer of the U.S. return to glory, it is helpful to review some of his signature theories and policy prescriptions from past years and to make note of how these have ultimately fared. Given space constraints, it is impossible to devote much analysis to more short-lived gems, such as Friedman's 1996 suggestion that "the U.S. should flood Iraq with counterfeit Iraqi dinars. It would wreak havoc. Because the U.S.

has blocked the sale of money-printing presses, ink and paper to Iraq, Washington can already print better Iraqi money than Baghdad can,"[11] or his post-9/11 recommendation regarding potential U.S. partners in the struggle against Osama bin Laden: "The Cali cartel doesn't operate in Afghanistan. But the Russian mafia sure does, as do various Afghan factions, drug rings and Pakistani secret agents."[12]

One of the best-known components of Friedman's résumé is the Golden Arches Theory of Conflict Prevention, the birth of which he describes in *The Lexus and the Olive Tree*:

> For all I know, I have eaten McDonald's burgers and fries in more countries in the world than anyone, and I can testify that they all really do taste the same. But as I Quarter-Poundered my way around the world in recent years, I began to notice something intriguing. I don't know when the insight struck me. It was a bolt out of the blue that must have hit somewhere between the McDonald's in Tiananmen Square in Beijing, the McDonald's in Tahrir Square in Cairo and the McDonald's off Zion Square in Jerusalem. And it was this: No two countries that both had McDonald's had fought a war against each other since each got its McDonald's.[13]

The Lebanese McDonald's is invoked as proof of the theory's validity, with no regard for the fact that Israel is at the time of writing engaged in a continuing military occupation of south Lebanon punctuated by deadly bombing campaigns. Friedman deals with other theoretical complications that have arisen since the release of the first edition of *The Lexus* in 1999—namely the war by nineteen McDonald's-possessing NATO countries on McDonald's-possessing Yugoslavia—by arguing that the outcome of the conflict demonstrates that citizens of nations that have developed economically to the point of being able to host McDonald's establishments prefer American fast food over wars. Serbia's capitulation is cast as a result of its citizens' decision that "they wanted to stand in line for burgers, much more than they wanted to stand in line for Kosovo."[14]

Friedman's additional excuse that "the Kosovo war wasn't even a real war"[15] is meanwhile called into question by such things as his own article from 1999 stating that "Like it or not, we are at war with the Serbian nation."[16] That Friedman's regular consumption of McDonald's, designated symbol of the globalization and economic integration that are supposedly "having a restraining effect on aggressive nations,"[17] has not had a similar effect on his personal propensities is clear from his encouragement of NATO's air campaign ("Give war a chance"[18]) and his repeated entreaties for "sustained," "unreasonable," and "less than surgical bombing"[19] to prevent the inhabitants of Belgrade from continuing to partake in "Sunday merry-go-round rides, while their fellow Serbs are 'cleansing' Kosovo."[20]

Decreeing the need for "a new Serbian ethic that understands how to live in 21st-century Europe,"[21] Friedman threatens the Serbs: "Every week you ravage Kosovo is another decade we will set your country back by pulverizing you. You want 1950? We can do 1950. You want 1389? We can do 1389 too."[22] This leap onto the bandwagon of ethic-inducing pulverization in a war partly undertaken to expand and empower NATO in the post–Cold War world is difficult to reconcile with Friedman's own definition of himself as "a long and cranky opponent of NATO expansion."[23]

Readers of Friedman's column are often reminded that *New York Times* columnists are not permitted to endorse U.S. presidential candidates. The blatant endorsement of war crimes like collective punishment, however, is apparently less polemical, even when columnists cannot keep track of their own reasons for said punishment. In separate reflections on the war with Serbia published two months apart in 1999, Friedman writes in the former that "once the [Kosovar] refugee evictions began … using a huge air war for a limited objective was the only thing that made sense."[24] He then lets slip in the latter that he may indeed understand the true sequence of events: "NATO bombed, and

[Slobodan] Milosevic began ruthlessly killing and evicting Kosovar Albanians."[25]

When it comes time for McDonald's installation in the Baghdad Green Zone, the Golden Arches Theory of Conflict Prevention is abandoned in favor of concoctions like Friedman's Tilt Theory of History, which applies to situations in which "you take a country, a culture, or a region that has been tilted in the wrong direction and tilt it in the right direction."[26] Friedman subsequently offers the Dell Theory of Conflict Prevention in *The World Is Flat*, according to which "no two countries that are both part of a major global supply chain, like Dell's, will ever fight a war against each other as long as they are both part of the same global supply chain."[27] We are left to assume that pre-war Iraqi oil exports to the United States did not constitute part of a major global supply chain.

Another overly simplistic theory that somehow continues to elude the very minimal amount of scrutiny that is required to debunk it is Friedman's First Law of Petropolitics, which I will refer to by its convenient acronym. The FLOP, which debuted in *Foreign Policy* magazine in 2006, posits that "in oil-rich petrolist states, the price of oil and the pace of freedom tend to move in opposite directions."[28] According to *Hot, Flat, and Crowded*, the thought process culminating in the discovery of the FLOP began after 9/11 when, allegedly emboldened by the high price of oil, Venezuelan President Hugo Chávez announced that British Prime Minister Tony Blair as well as U.S.-sponsored free trade coalitions could "go to hell."[29]

Additional oil-related coincidences accrue over the years, as Friedman observes that Bahrain, the first Persian Gulf oil state to start running out of oil, is not only "the first Gulf state to hold a free and fair parliamentary election, in which women could run and vote" but also "the first Gulf state to hire [consulting firm] McKinsey & Company to design an overhaul of its labor laws … and the first Gulf state to sign a free-trade agreement with the United States."[30] The evidence of the correlation between the price of oil and the pace of freedom becomes insurmountable one afternoon in 2006 over lunch with *Foreign Policy* editor Moisés Naím, and—after sketching a graph to this effect on his napkin—Friedman woos Naím with such statistics as that "when oil was $25–$30 a barrel, George W. Bush looked into Russian president Vladimir Putin's soul and saw a friend of America there," but that the current view consists of oil companies and democratic institutions "that Putin has swallowed courtesy of $100-a-barrel oil."[31]

Friedman fails to mention that, around the same time that Bush was reading Putin's soul, Friedman himself was encouraging his readership to "keep rootin' for Putin," whom he touted as "for real," "Russia's first Deng Xiaoping," and the architect of the country's transition from "Das Kapital to DOS capital."[32] As for Friedman's assertion in *The World Is Flat* that the primary cause of the demise of the Soviet Union "was the information revolution that began in the early to mid-1980s,"[33] this notion is discarded in favor of the new FLOP-friendly argument that high oil prices in the 1970s followed by $10-a-barrel oil prompted the Soviet collapse.

That the 2007 edition of *The World Is Flat*, released the year after the FLOP's birth, is not amended to reflect the new thinking could be construed as a sign that manuscript size and frequency of publication may sometimes trump content and conviction. Undeterred by the possibility that the abandonment of past predictions might encumber one's current credibility as foreign affairs sage, Friedman is tasked by Naím with turning his napkin into an article.

Hot, Flat, and Crowded outlines the expansion of the napkin into four separate graphs:

> On one axis, I plotted the average global price of crude oil going back to 1979, and along the other axis I plotted the pace of expanding or contracting freedoms, both economic and political—as measured by the Freedom House "Freedom in the World" report and the Fraser Institute's "Economic Freedom of the World Report"—for Russia, Venezuela, Iran, and Nigeria.[34]

According to Friedman, the resulting four graphs indicate that

> as oil prices went down in the early 1990s, competition, transparency, political participation, and accountability of those in office all tended to go up in these countries—as measured by free elections held, newspapers opened, reformers elected, economic reform projects started, and companies privatized. But as oil prices started to soar after 2000, free speech, free press, fair elections and freedom to form political parties and NGOs tended to erode in these countries.[35]

This correlation sounds delightful, especially when it is compounded by compelling evidence such as that "a Westernized Iranian woman reporter in Tehran once said to me as we were walking down the street: 'If only we didn't have oil, we could be just like Japan.'"[36] The project's flaws, however, are numerous, and cannot be compensated for via Friedman's simple disclaimer that "this is not a scientific lab experiment."[37]

First of all, the graphs do not take into account the wide range of freedom indicators listed by Friedman.[38] The graph on Iran, for example, plots crude oil prices against "Freedom to Trade Internationally," which in the Iranian context is presumably a reflection of the intensity of sanctions by international actors. It is difficult to argue that this specific category is at all representative of the general level of domestic freedom.

The Nigeria graph plots oil prices against "Legal System and Property Rights," while the Venezuela graph plots oil prices against the country's Freedom House rankings. All of the graphs indicate an inverse relationship, but a glance at the Freedom House "Freedom in the World" data from 1973 to 2010[39] turns up contradictions such as these:

1. Following a string of "Partly Free" years, Nigeria's Freedom Status switches to "Not Free" in 1993. This is precisely the year of the Nigerian oil field privatization that appears on Friedman's

cumulative FLOP graph as one of three global historical events signifying an increase in the pace of freedom.

2. Venezuela has maintained a "Partly Free" status since 1999, even when Chávez was telling various international entities to go to hell.

3. Bahrain transforms from "Partly Free" to "Not Free" in 2009, despite Friedman's insistence—undeterred by his own discussion in *The World Is Flat* of the Bahraini regime's Internet censorship and reliance on walled palaces and Sunni dominance—that dwindling oil reserves have forced the country's democratization.

More important than any of these contradictions, however, is Friedman's cheerleading of the U.S. war on Iraq "to create a free, open and progressive model in the heart of the Arab-Muslim world to promote the ideas of tolerance, pluralism and democratization"[40] when he is already convinced in 2002 that unless the United States "encourage[s] alternative energies that will slowly bring the price of oil down and force [Arab/Muslim] countries to open up and adapt to modernity—we can invade Iraq once a week and it's not going to unleash democracy in the Arab world."[41] This same year he nonetheless classifies the invasion of Iraq as "the most important task worth doing and worth debating," even while admitting that it "would be a huge, long, costly task—if it is doable at all, and I am not embarrassed to say that I don't know if it is."[42]

Taking into account the speculation by oil economist and World Bank adviser Dr. Mamdouh Salameh in 2008 that the invasion of Iraq has thus far trebled the price of crude oil,[43] Friedman's 2006 proposal for a Geo-Green party in the United States to "advanc[e] political and economic reform in the Arab-Muslim world, without another war"[44] acquires an even more tragicomic hue. According to Friedman, "however the Iraq war ends," the Geo-Green party will stimulate alternatives to oil and thus "gradually bring down the price, possibly as low as $25 to $30 a barrel"—i.e., the approximate price of oil in 2002.[45]

Recent years have seen a surge in Friedman's insistence on the need for "nation-building at home,"[46] in order to resolve issues ranging from the United States' "mounting education deficit, energy deficit, budget deficit, health care deficit and ambition deficit"[47] to Penn Station's "disgusting track-side platforms [that] apparently have not been cleaned since World War II"[48] to the fact that, while China spent the post-9/11 period enhancing its national infrastructure in preparation for the Beijing Olympics, "we've been building better metal detectors, armored Humvees and pilotless drones."[49] Friedman's fury over funding cuts to the National Science Foundation might be more understandable, however, had:

1. The NSF appeared somewhere on the 2002 hierarchy of most-important-even-if-impossible-tasks.
2. He specified that the Iraq war be fought without Humvees.
3. He not advised Democratic presidential candidate John Kerry in 2004 to "connect up with that gut fear in the American soul and pass a simple threshold test: 'Does this man understand that we have real enemies?'" by "drop[ping] everything else—health care, deficits and middle-class tax cuts—and focus[ing] on this issue. Everything else is secondary."[50]

Consider for a moment that over half of U.S. government spending goes to the military,[51] an institution Friedman lauds as the protector of American economic hegemony in *The Lexus*:

Indeed, McDonald's cannot flourish without McDonnell Douglas, the designer of the U.S. Air Force F-15. And the hidden fist that keeps the world safe for Silicon Valley's technologies to flourish is called the U.S. Army, Air Force, Navy and Marine Corps. And these fighting forces and institutions are paid for by American taxpayer dollars.[52]

Consider, then, the 2007 estimate by the American Friends Service Committee that the hidden fist's not-so-hidden maneuverings in Iraq were costing $720 million a day. The *Washington Post* reports that this sum alone "could buy homes for almost 6,500 families or health care for 423,529 children, or could outfit 1.27 million homes with renewable electricity," as well as making substantial contributions to the U.S. education system, which Friedman has categorized as one of the many areas in which the country "has been swimming buck naked."[53]

This is not to imply, of course, that had these funds not been used on war they would have been used on these specific domestic nation-building projects, but rather to point out the sort of self-contradictions one invites by maintaining unwavering commitment to few principles aside from the idea that America should dominate the world.

Despite Friedman's newfound annoyance that the United States is preoccupied with nation-building abroad and that "the Cheneyites want to make fighting Al Qaeda our Sputnik"[54] while "China is doing moon shots"[55] and turning from red to green, he credits the U.S. army with "outgreening al-Qaeda"[56] in Iraq. In *Hot, Flat, and Crowded*, we learn that this has been achieved via a combination of insulation foam and renewable energy sources, reducing the amount of fuel required to air condition troop accommodations in certain locations.

After speaking with army energy consultant Dan Nolan—whom he "couldn't help but ask, 'Is anybody in the military saying, "Oh gosh, poor Dan has gone green—has he gone girly-man on us now?" '"[57]—Friedman announces that the outgreening of Al Qaeda constitutes a typical example

of what happens when you try to solve a problem by outgreening the competition—you buy one and you get four free. In Nolan's case, you save lives by getting [fuel transportation] convoys off the road, save money by lowering fuel costs [from the quoted "hundreds of dollars per gallon"[58] often required to cover delivery], and maybe have some power left over to give the local mosque's imam so his community might even toss a flower at you one day, rather than a grenade.[59]

The fourth benefit, courtesy of Nolan, is that soldiers will be so inspired by green efforts at their bases in Iraq that they will "come back to America and demand the same thing for their community or from their factory," which Friedman reports as unquestioningly as he does the allegation that the U.S. army prompted the desegregation of America by "show[ing] blacks and whites that they could work together."[60] As for the first three benefits gotten for "free" with the Al Qaeda outgreening purchase, it should be recalled that the very appearance of Al Qaeda in Iraq was itself no more than a free benefit of the U.S. invasion, as were convoy fatalities, heightened fuel costs for the U.S. military, and grenades. A deal indeed.

It is no less than remarkable that, in a matter of six pages in a book purporting to serve as an environmental wakeup call, Friedman has managed to greenwash the institution that holds the distinction of being the top polluter in the world.[61] The feat is especially noteworthy given that, smatterings of insulation foam and solar panels notwithstanding, the U.S. military's overwhelming reliance on fuel means that its presence in Iraq is not at all reconcilable with Friedman's insistence that dependence on foreign oil reserves is one of the greatest threats to U.S. security. The greenwashing incidentally also occurs *after* Friedman has decreed that the United States should cease operations in Iraq so as not to "throw more good lives after good lives."[62]

In 2010 it is then revealed that certain branches of the armed forces are strategizing to outgreen not only Al Qaeda but also the Taliban and the world's petro-dictators. Friedman exults over the existence of aviation biofuel made from pressed mustard seeds and the existence of a green forward-operating Marine base in Helmand Province, Afghanistan, offering encouragement such as "Go Navy!" and "God bless them: 'The Few. The Proud. The Green.' Semper Fi."[63] It is not clear whether Friedman has forgotten that he is vehemently opposed to the military escalation in Afghanistan.

Returning to the subject of the hidden fist's role as safeguard of McDonald's and Silicon Valley, Friedman worries in the 1990s that the fact that "America truly is the ultimate benign hegemon and reluctant enforcer"[64] might impede the exploitation of the post–Cold War international system, which has been summed up as follows: "Globalization is us."[65] A list of hegemonic achievements from this time period would thus appear to include benignly dispatched cruise missiles, the benign elimination of half a million Iraqi children via sanctions,[66] benign support for various dictators, and benign economic policies that Friedman himself acknowledges have had "enormously socially disruptive" effects, such as widening gaps in income distribution.[67] Rather than encourage any sort of in-depth consideration of these effects, however, Friedman prefers to focus attention superficially on the salary discrepancy among professional basketball players, devoting approximately nine pages of *The Lexus* to the idea that "you can learn everything you need to know about [the socially disruptive impact of globalization] by studying just one group of people—the National Basketball Association and, in particular, the bench of the 1997–98 World Champion Chicago Bulls."[68]

In the introduction to *The Lexus*, Friedman responds to allegations that he "loves globalization" by comparing his feelings for the phenomenon to his feelings about the dawn: "It does more good than harm, especially if you wear sunscreen and sunglasses."[69] He protests that he is "a journalist, not a salesman for globalization,"[70] although readers might be forgiven for mistaking vacuous corporate name-dropping formulas like "Attention Kmart shoppers: Without America on duty, there will be no America Online"[71] for something other than journalism.

As for Friedman's assertion that "globalization is bringing more people out of poverty faster than ever before in the history of the world,"[72] this is slightly irreconcilable with such details as Russia's post-communist transition from a country with less than 2 million people living under the international poverty line to a country with 74 million living under the same line.[73] That Friedman is not completely oblivious to the utility of the democratic alibi in globalizing economic oppression is clear from his announcement in 1995 that "I now understand that graffito that reportedly appeared on a wall in Poland last year. It said: 'We wanted democracy but we ended up with capitalism.'"[74]

In *The World Is Flat* we learn that there is "only one right direction"[75] that states can pursue, and Friedman professes to "get a little lump in my throat when I see countries like China, India, or Ireland adopting a basically proglobalization strategy, adapting it to their own political, social, and economic conditions, and reaping the benefits."[76] The lump merits some additional examination for several reasons.

For starters, it is only after 546 pages of manuscript, many of which are devoted to India's reaping of globalization benefits—Friedman even spends two pages transcribing sound bytes from an Indian call center, such as: "Woman operator in Bangalore after someone has just slammed down the phone on her: 'Hello? Hello?'"[77]—that we are instructed to "have no illusions" and that the Indian high-tech sector "accounts for 0.2 percent of employment in India."[78]

Curiously, Friedman appears to have abandoned his *Lexus*-era claim that he is not "particularly happy"[79] about the adoption of Western names and accents by Indian call center operators, and he reports after participating in an "accent neutralization" class in 2004 that watching young Indians "earnestly trying to soften their t's and roll their r's … is an uplifting experience."[80] Reviewing how many of these workers now have credit cards and can purchase American goods, Friedman determines that "there is nothing more positive than the self-confidence, dignity and optimism that comes from a society knowing it is producing wealth by tapping its own brains—men's and women's—as opposed to one just tapping its own oil, let alone one that is so lost it can find dignity only through suicide and 'martyrdom.'"[81]

The drawbacks of lost societies are illustrated through Friedman's recollection of a previous encounter with three young Palestinians in Ramallah who "talked about having no hope, no jobs and no dignity, and they each nodded when one of them said they were all 'suicide bombers in waiting.'"[82] This confirmation allows Friedman to defend the outsourcing of American jobs "to places like India or Pakistan" as a means of "mak[ing] not only a more prosperous world, but a safer world for our own 20-year-olds," who will presumably then only have to worry about potential suicide bombings conducted by the 99.8 percent of Indians not employed in the high-tech sector.[83]

As for India's unique historical circumstances, such as its freedom from occupation by Israel, the version of Friedman's Ramallah encounter provided in *The World Is Flat* reveals that the young Palestinian who speaks of his brethren as "martyrs in waiting" specifies that this is due in large part to Israeli treatment of Palestinians at checkpoints.[84] Friedman also notes in this case that one of the other two young men is an engineering student whose dream of attending the University of Memphis has been thwarted by the difficulty of obtaining a U.S. visa, another situation that will not be rectified by the transfer of "low-wage, low-prestige jobs"[85] to India. As author Naomi Klein points out in response to Friedman's promotion of call centers to the frontlines of World War III, simpler and more relevant solutions to terrorist proliferation at the time might have included ending the Israeli occupation and recognizing that the exploitation of Iraqi reconstruction as "a vast job-creation program for Americans" was fueling the insurgency in Iraq.[86]

Friedman's portrayal of India as a model for the globalization era is meanwhile hardly consistent. For example, in *The Lexus* he categorizes India as a "budding kleptocracy."[87] Then in 2002 he credits Indian "democracy" with the fact that "rioting didn't spread anywhere" after what he acknowledges was a pogrom incited by the Hindu nationalist government of the state of Gujarat, in which several thousand Muslims were massacred.[88] In this same article— perplexingly titled "Where Freedom Reigns," in spite of the massacre of Muslims—he announces that "50 years of Indian democracy ... and 15 years of economic liberalization" have resulted in "all this positive energy" in Bangalore, "where the traffic is now congested by all the young Indian techies ... who have gotten jobs, apartments—and motor scooters—by providing the brainpower for the world's biggest corporations."[89]

In 2004, however, we learn that the Bangalore government is "rife with corruption," that the public school system is dysfunctional, and that infrastructure is falling apart while "beggars dart in and out of the traffic"—a scene contrasted with the "beautiful, walled campuses" of the high-tech firms that "thrive by defying their political-economic environment, not by emerging from it."[90] This, of course, is the exact inverse of the argument from 2002, and is not compatible with the idea that free markets reduce poverty or, obviously, walls—which are supposed to be being blown down by Friedman's "flat-world platform."[91]

In 2006 Friedman promotes India as "a beacon of tolerance and stability" and encourages "finding a creative way to bring [it] into the world's nuclear family," i.e., to violate the Nuclear Nonproliferation Treaty via the Bush team's arms deal with New Delhi without losing the ability to invoke the NPT against other nations: "India deserves to be treated differently than Iran."[92] It is not clear how nuclear deals with India are congruent with Friedman's goal of defusing anti-Americanism in Pakistan. Indian author and activist Arundhati Roy has meanwhile pointed out Friedman's curious choice of the adjective *tolerant* given, for example, the thousands of Indian political prisoners, the caste system pitted against the indigenous and the poor, and India's insistence on perpetuating "one of the most brutal military occupations in the world" in Kashmir.[93]

In 2011 Indian Muslims resurface in Friedman's seemingly platitudinous but actually nonsensical assertion that "they are, on the whole, integrated into India's democracy because it is a democracy," followed by the proof: "There are no Indian Muslims in Guantánamo Bay."[94] If the current standard for judging whether democracies are really democracies is whether or not any nationals have been held in illegal U.S. detention centers, Friedman should perhaps reconsider the democratic credentials of Britain and Australia.[95]

As for the issue of traffic congestion in Bangalore, for years Friedman pushes the idea that the earth should host as many "Americas" as possible, encouraging his readership to "imagine how beneficial it would be for the world, and for America, if rural China, India, and Africa were to grow into little Americas or European Unions in economic and opportunity terms."[96] He then decides that "there are too many Americans in the world today"—"in American-sized homes, driving American-sized cars, eating American-sized Big Macs"—and that "the good lord didn't design our little planet for this many Americans."[97] Rather than revisit his own past recommendations—such as that, in the interest of Balkan stability, "Bosnia needs big tanks, big roads and Big Macs,"[98] or that the proliferation of the Golden Arches is the key to global conflict prevention—Friedman announces the latest solution to the world's problems and the means by which "we can get our groove back": the United States must be the leader in a clean energy revolution necessitated by U.S. planetary leadership in the first place.[99]

In *Hot, Flat, and Crowded*, Friedman expresses his annoyance for the claim that a green revolution is already under way in the United States: "Really? Really? A green revolution? Have you ever seen a revolution where no one got hurt?"[100] It is not clear who is supposed to be getting hurt when Friedman's argument that the "old system … has reached its financial and environmental limits"[101] is juxtaposed with his 2008 response to the U.S. government bailout of the very banks and corporations Friedman accuses of financially and environmentally unsustainable behavior: "You have to save the system."[102]

Friedman's wish that "America could be China for a day—just one day. *Just one day!*"[103] is meanwhile a reference to the advantages of systems free of such obstacles as permanent presidential campaigns and gerrymandered congressional districts, which according to Friedman have inhibited the launch of the required revolution in the United States. His fear that China is going to "clean our clock"[104] via its "Green Leap Forward"[105] suggests that he was perhaps naïve to welcome Chinese globalization strategies with the aforementioned lump in his throat.[106] It also confirms the baselessness of his 2003 ultimatum to China that, unless the country begins fulfilling its duties as part of "the World of Order"—i.e., signing off on American military schemes to "manage the World of Disorder"—it risks a reduction to "only exporting duct tape."[107]

The third of the three listed recipients of the globalization throat lump is Ireland, where Friedman's lump-related exuberance has spawned economic prophesies ending in dismal failure. Friedman first celebrates Irish passage from potato famine fame to hub for U.S. corporations like Dell during a visit in 2001, when he somehow determines that his experience trying to check out of his hotel—"a real stone castle" whose computer system has just crashed, preventing Friedman from retrieving his bill—"pretty well sums up the conflicting trends in … the European country that has been the biggest beneficiary of globalization and the one that is most ambivalent about those benefits."[108]

Ambivalence disappears in honor of Friedman's next visit in 2005, and he instructs his audience to "Follow the Leapin' Leprechaun":

> It is obvious to me that the Irish-British [economic] model is the way of the future, and the only question is when Germany and France will face reality: either they become Ireland or they become museums. That is their real choice over the next few years—it's either the leprechaun way or the Louvre.[109]

The French are regularly targeted by Friedman for a litany of perceived abuses, among them transforming from "our annoying ally" to "our enemy" who "wants America to fail in Iraq"[110] while in the meantime "trying to preserve a 35-hour work week in a world where Indian engineers are ready to work a 35-hour day."[111] Friedman appears to find nothing contradictory in advocating for impossibly extended workdays when he has both reported the confirmation by an Indian call center worker that when one works through the night one's "biological clock goes haywire"[112] and has himself asserted that "the problem is that human beings simply are not designed to be like computer servers. For one thing, they are designed to sleep eight hours a night."[113]

As for Friedman's self-described "poking fun at France" via personalized pep talks to Chirac—"Yo, Jacques, what world do you think you're livin' in, pal? Get with the program! It's called Anglo-American capitalism, mon ami"—and references to "anti-globalist Gaullist Luddites," there is a decided double standard that Friedman maintains with regard to the technologies he insists are necessary to achieve wealth and productivity.[114] Quoted in *Foreign Policy* as saying "I talk the talk of technology, but I don't walk the walk,"[115] Friedman elsewhere admits to not knowing how to program his VCR,[116] and announces to the graduating class of Williams College in 2005: "And don't leave me a [mobile phone] message, because I still don't know how to retrieve them and I have no intention of learning."[117]

That Friedman is exempt from the get-wired-or-die options he bestows on the rest of the world, with the accompanying warning that "the fast eat the slow," is thus clear.[118] What is not clear is how he feels entitled to complain about the effects of the very technological ubiquity he has demanded. On the one hand, he condemns the lack of wireless infrastructure in the New York subway, expresses extreme displeasure at the number of times his phone calls get dropped on "America's sorry excuse for a bullet train" (a.k.a. the Acela),[119] and devises a hypothetical election campaign based "on a one-issue platform: I promise, if elected, that within four years America will have cellphone service as good as Ghana's."[120] On the other, he announces he cannot "wait for the day that Motorola comes out with a device that enables you to jam all the cell phones around you"[121] so that his restaurant meals are not tainted by other people's conversations, and laments his inability to interact with Paris cab drivers and passengers on Colorado ski lifts thanks to the monopoly on their attention by technological gadgets.[122]

It is meanwhile important to recall that, as tough as conditions may be on the ski lift, the level of personal suffering involved
undoubtedly pales in comparison to that experienced in other
venues on the receiving end of Friedman-sanctioned modernization crusades. Iraq comes to mind, where citizens perish by the
hundreds of thousands while Friedman unearths encouraging
indications of the possibility that democracy-resistant Arab political culture can change ("Consider what was the most talked-about
story in the Arab world in recent weeks. Iraq? No. Palestine? No
… It was the Arab version of 'American Idol'!"[123]). Other candidates include the countless numbers of people across the globe
whose health and livelihoods have been adversely affected by
the business practices of biotech giant Monsanto and Canadian
gold-mining company Goldcorp Inc., the CEOs of which appear
in *The Lexus* and *The World Is Flat*, respectively—the former as a
humble, principled, and environmentally conscious businessman,
the latter as the source of ingenious ways of using the Internet to
find gold.

Monsanto holds the distinction of being a Vietnam-era
manufacturer of the lethal defoliant Agent Orange, now special-
izing in genetically engineered crops and the infamous herbicide
Roundup, which is toxic to soil, animals, and humans alike.
Goldcorp, for its part, is responsible for things like open-pit
cyanide leach mining in Guatemala, which results in arsenic-
contaminated rivers, deforestation, and a host of physical afflic-
tions for the local population, among them persistent skin rashes
and an increase in spontaneous abortions.[124] It is fairly obvious
that there should be no words of praise for either of these corporations anywhere on the résumé of anyone who feels comfortable
beginning sentences with the words "As an environmentalist."[125] It
is also fairly obvious that such a person should not announce two
months after the 2011 Fukushima Daiichi disaster that "I have no
problem with more nuclear power, if you can find a utility ready to
put up the money,"[126] or dismiss European aversion to genetically
modified organisms—the cultivation of which is environmentally

destructive—as merely another example of the "Euro-whining" that characterizes opposition to war on Iraq.[127]

Dining at the Hotel Schweizerhof in Davos, Switzerland, in 2003, Friedman is irked to discover a "tiny asterisk"[128] on the menu indicating the potential presence of GMOs in meat imported from the United States. The combination of the asterisk and the fact that Europeans continue to smoke cigarettes permits Friedman to arrive at the conclusion that arguments against war by the leaders of Germany and France are "deeply unserious" and that said countries are merely pursuing "an assertion of identity by trying to be whatever the Americans are not."[129] The reason for this behavior is that "being weak after being powerful is a terrible thing. It can make you stupid."[130]

The tone of this analysis signals a marked departure from Friedman's pro-European jubilation of 2001: "I am now officially declaring my total affection and support for the European Union. I love the E.U. I wish there were two. May it go from strength to strength."[131] Acknowledging that the European "version of capitalism will always stress social welfare more than ours," Friedman argues that it is nonetheless hugely valuable, "in this world of increasingly messy states, for us to have another version of the United States across the Atlantic."[132]

This brings us back to the subject of Ireland in 2005, a country that has apparently avoided stupidity by going from potato famine to Dell rather than from strength to weakness, and has proven itself a more loyal replica of the United States by favoring corporations over workers. Friedman informs us: "The Irish have a plan. They are focused. They have mobilized business, labor and government around a common agenda. They are playing offense."[133] Outlining the "leprechaun way" that must now be adopted by Germany and France if they want to avoid economic irrelevance and decline, he states: "One of the first reforms Ireland instituted was to make it easier to fire people."[134]

Friedman, whose views on labor rights include that "the most important thing [Ronald] Reagan did was break the 1981 air traffic controllers' strike, which helped break the hold of organized labor over the U.S. economy,"[135] has long seen job security as an impediment to innovation and progress because "the easier it is to fire people, the more willing companies are to hire people."[136]

Actually, the easier it is to fire people, the easier it is for Dell to close its manufacturing center in Limerick, lay off 1,900 employees, and transfer major operations to Poland in 2009, invalidating do-it-yourself guides by *New York Times* columnists on how to "become one of the richest countries in Europe" through globalization.[137] As Sean Kay, chair of the International Studies Program at Ohio Wesleyan University, notes in an article on *Foreign Policy*'s website, Friedman might have avoided his premature leprechaun celebration had he relied on more thorough investigative techniques than, for example, emailing with Michael Dell about the perks of Irish industrial and tax policies.[138]

Responding to Friedman's "wildly inaccurate" statement that, "because of all the tax revenue and employment the global companies are generating in Ireland, Dublin has been able to increase spending on health care, schools and infrastructure," Kay writes: "In reality, the government at the time was not only *not* generating revenue, its investment in education was declining and it was beginning to accumulate massive debt. Today, Ireland's deficit is at 32% of GDP—the highest in the Eurozone."[139] Kay concludes that Friedman "owes it to both the people of Ireland and his readers to correct the record," given that his flawed theorizing was "embraced and celebrated by an Irish government that was reveling in excess and deeply entangled with corrupt bankers" and that it "reinforced a doubling down on damaging economic and political actions in a small and vulnerable country that is now suffering deep pain"—which will presumably only intensify in accordance with the EU-IMF bank bailout.[140]

Admitting when one has erred certainly enhances one's overall credibility and coherence as a journalist and economic commentator, even when one might prefer to distance oneself from past analyses such as that "there is never going to be any European monetary union. Forget it. Buy German marks. They're all you'll ever need."[141] It also aids in the recuperation of one's license to criticize others for pursuing the very policies or ideas one previously promoted. The obstacles to a Friedman apology in the case of Ireland, however, are threefold.

First of all, Friedman has a knack for putting optimistic spins on "deep pain." See, for example, his reaction to the 1997 Asian financial crisis: "Yes, many Thais are now hurting. But at least the country is finally building some of the regulatory institutions it needs to insure that global funds cascading into Thailand are not so easily misallocated … That's no crisis in my book."[142] The real cause of the crisis, of course, was not the Asian misallocation of funds but rather the machinations of the neoliberal international economic institutions now tasked with rectifying the crisis via an intensification of the same policies encouraging unregulated financial speculation and permanent "hurting" of the non-elite.[143] Undeterred, Friedman announces: "I wish everyone could come to democracy by reading Madison, but sometimes the push has to come from Merrill Lynch."[144]

That systems imposed by Wall Street investment firms do not by definition qualify as democracy becomes all the more apparent when popular opposition to the IMF drives the outcome of the 2001 Thai elections, despite Friedman's previous quote from a Thai newspaper editor who assures him that "We do not see the IMF as the enemy."[145] It is meanwhile unclear why Friedman is concerned with combating corruption in Asia and introducing financial responsibility and the rule of law when he is at the same time making such arguments as that "some of Italy's vices during the cold war—its weak governments, its epidemic of tax evasion, the penchant of Italians to work around the state rather than through it—have become virtues in this era of globalization."[146]

As for Friedman's assessment in 1998 that "the turmoil and pain in Indonesia are obviously tragic, but they are not the fault of currency traders," this occurs in the same article in which he explains that, when the "huge electronic herd of traders … stampedes, small and large countries that have opened their economies up to it can be crushed—far beyond what they deserve."[147] Friedman additionally reasons that, because the hammering of Indonesia by the markets has "exposed and helped topple possibly the most corrupt regime in the world today, led by President Suharto," the turmoil and pain are—as in Thailand—"no crisis in my book."[148] This is the same Suharto regime, of course, that is defended by Friedman the previous year when the U.S. Congress moves to block the sale of certain fighter jets to Indonesia and to freeze the training of Indonesian military officers in the United States on account of the Indonesian occupation of East Timor, where one-third of the population was eliminated in the invasion of 1975 that was also conducted by the Suharto regime. (Friedman opines: "Indonesia is too complex to be a pariah."[149])

The second obstacle to an apology from Friedman for his failed prognostications on Ireland is thus that, given his views on the utility of pain, it is unlikely he detects any fundamental conceptual errors on his part. That the Irish system is, as Kay points out, already clearly failing when Friedman pens his extended ode suggests that reality is accorded minimal importance in Friedmanomics. His reaction to its decisive failure would presumably entail prescriptions for the "Root Canal politics" he urges in 2010 as the necessary response to the global financial recession and the profligacy of the baby boomer generation—defined simultaneously as the offspring of "The Greatest Generation" and the offspring of "the Tooth Fairy."[150]

Writing in the context of the hung parliament in the UK and the Greek riots in opposition to forthcoming draconian austerity measures, Friedman declares:

> Britain and Greece are today's poster children for the wrenching new post–Tooth Fairy politics, where baby boomers will have to accept deep cuts to their benefits and pensions today so their kids can have jobs and not be saddled with debts tomorrow. Otherwise, we're headed for intergenerational conflict throughout the West.[151]

Friedman does not delve into the details of what exactly a Western intergenerational conflict would involve or why it is more worrisome than an inter-class conflict or an international "war of choice"[152] on Iraq costing the United States an estimated $3 trillion. As journalist Joshua Holland points out, Friedman's proclaimed "meta-story" explaining why the events in the UK and Greece may soon be "coming to a theater near you" fails to consider the possibility that 90 percent of U.S. public debt results from past military spending.[153]

Instead, we learn that the Tooth Fairy is to blame for engaging in "bogus accounting" and for "deluding us into thinking that by borrowing from China or Germany, or against our rising home values, or by creating exotic financial instruments to trade with each other, we were actually creating wealth."[154] However, because we are now in a situation in which "that Tooth Fairy, she be dead," it apparently follows that the blame for Western debt must be reassigned:

> In Britain, everyone over 60 gets an annual allowance to pay heating bills and can ride any local bus for free. That's really sweet—if you can afford it. But Britain, where 25 percent of the government's budget is now borrowed, can't anymore.[155]

Aside from elderly bus riders, other culprits requiring retaliation include Greeks employed in hazardous professions who have been permitted early retirement with full pensions.[156] As for those persons and firms who physically carried out the Tooth Fairy's bogus accounting and false creation of wealth, financial speculators are rehabilitated into "lords of discipline, the Electronic Herd of bond traders," also referred to as "Mr. Bond Market of Wall Street and the City of London."[157] Mr. Bond Market is the Tooth Fairy's sole surviving sibling and the appointed custodian of her progeny—i.e., the overseer of the job cuts, pay cuts, benefit cuts, education cuts, and entitlement cuts that will supposedly spare baby boomers the wrath of their own children.

Friedman's insistence on the necessity of these punitive measures would not seem to be entirely congruent with his definition
of himself as an "Integrationist-Social-Safety-Netter," one of four
identity options contained within the "Friedman matrix of globalization politics" devised in the 1990s.[158] The "matrix" consists
of two perpendicular lines, the "globalization line" and the "distribution axis." Friedman invites readers to discover their own
compound identities by plotting whether they are Separatists or
Integrationists on the first line and whether they are Social-Safety-
Netters or Let-Them-Eat-Cakers on the second.[159]

The metaphor-heavy discussion of the matrix in the (already
metaphor-reliant) *Lexus* results in a cluttered scene of trampo-
lines, trapezes, wheels, and turtles thrown in among Japanese
luxury automobiles and olive trees. Suffice it to say that
Integrationist-Social-Safety-Netters believe that "we still need
traditional safety nets—social security, Medicare, Medicaid, food
stamps and welfare—to catch those who simply will never be fast
enough or educated enough to deal with the Fast World, but who
you don't want just falling onto the pavement," since this would
inhibit globalization.[160] Let-Them-Eat-Cakers meanwhile believe
that "globalization is essentially winner take all, loser take care of
yourself."[161]

Flash forward to 2009 and Friedman's recognition of the fact
that the recession-inducing capitalist system wrongfully "relied
upon the risks to the Market and to Mother Nature being under-
priced and to profits being privatized in good times and losses
socialized in bad times."[162] That Friedman decides that the proper
response to this scenario is to *further* socialize losses suggests the
potential utility of a new matrix category such as the "Have-Your-
Cake-And-Eat-It-Too-ers," especially given that Friedman has
been aware at least since 1999 of the hazards of the system:

Global financial crises will be the norm in this coming era. With
the speed of change going on today, and with so many countries
in different stages of adjustment to this new globalization system,

crises will be endemic. So, dear reader, let me leave you with one piece of advice: Fasten your seat belts and put your seat backs and tray tables into a fixed and upright position. Because both the booms and the busts will be coming faster. Get used to it, and just try to make sure that the leverage in the system doesn't become so great in any one area that it can make the whole system go boom or bust.[163]

Several years before determining that elderly patrons of the British public transportation system should absorb the fallout from the neoliberal airplane ride, Friedman announces his belief that "history will rank [Tony] Blair as one of the most important British prime ministers ever" for making British liberalism "about embracing, managing and cushioning globalization, about embracing and expanding freedom—through muscular diplomacy where possible and force where necessary—and about embracing fiscal discipline."[164] Blair is alternately praised as the only adult in the room during UN deliberations about Iraq and as someone who is "always leav[ing] you with the impression that for him the Iraq war is just one hammer and one nail in an effort to do tikkun olam," a Kabbalah concept meaning "to repair the world."[165]

The socialization of losses incurred via the adult-like forcible expansion of world-repairing freedom becomes a dubious business, however, when the columnist proposing it acknowledges that "in deciding to throw in Britain's lot with President Bush on the Iraq war, Mr. Blair not only defied the overwhelming antiwar sentiment of his own party, but public opinion in Britain generally."[166] What is even more intriguing is that Friedman intends this as a reason Blair should be enshrined in history as a top British leader, and salutes his tenacity: "He had no real support group to fall back on. I'm not even sure his wife supported him on the Iraq war. (I know the feeling!)"[167]

The resulting argument is that it is laudable to promote democracy abroad by anti-democratically taking your country to war.

Despite initially throwing in the towel on Iraq in 2006, Friedman continues in the midst of global recession to churn out justifications for the price tag of military excess, and announces in 2009 that, "as outrageously expensive and as uncertain the outcome, trying to build decent, pluralistic societies in places like Iraq is not as crazy as it seems."[168] The evidence is that "few, if any, Indian Muslims are known to have joined Al Qaeda,"[169] which once again highlights how much better Friedman's time would be spent were he to cease repeatedly questioning whether Saddam's personality is a result of the nature of Iraqi society or vice versa and to instead focus his chicken-or-egg philosophical musings on what came first, the U.S. war or Al Qaeda in Iraq.

This brings us to the third impediment to a Friedman apology on Ireland, which is that, in cases where he does accept some degree of personal miscalculation, he still appears to be under the impression that continuous self-contradiction suffices in lieu of a straightforward admission of error. Following his declaration of 9/11 as the onset of World War III, Friedman complains that the United States has become "the United States of Fighting Terrorism,"[170] an entity that makes Friedman check his tweezers at the airport;[171] he later surmises that he overreacted to 9/11,[172] but nonetheless reaffirms the worthwhile nature of the part of the overreaction that involved outrageously expensive and uncertain pluralism-building experiments resulting in the deaths of over a million Iraqis. Reasoning that "if Disney World can remain an open, welcoming place, with increased but invisible security, why can't America?," Friedman announces: "We can't afford to keep being this stupid! We have got to get our groove back."[173] He meanwhile goes from declaring in April 2003 that "One hopes Americans will now stop overreacting to 9/11. Al Qaeda is not the Soviet Union. Saddam was not Stalin. And terrorism is not communism"[174] to warning, less than nine months later, that "as dangerous as the Soviet Union was, it was always deterrable with a wall of containment and with nukes of our own. Because, at the end of the day, the Soviets loved life more than they hated us."[175]

No apology ever accompanies acknowledgement of overreaction, nor does Friedman resurrect the details of his prolonged warmongering effort based on "fight[ing] the terrorists as if there were no rules,"[176] "us[ing] whatever tactics will make the terrorists feel bad, not make us feel good,"[177] and recognizing the occasional Arab need for a "2-by-4 across the side of the head."[178] None of these sentiments is in turn affected by his warning in 2001 that "if we are going to be stomping around the world wiping out terrorist cells from Kabul to Manila, we'd better make sure that we are the best country, and the best global citizens, we can be. Otherwise, we are going to lose the rest of the world."[179] Initial suggestions to Bush regarding the pursuit of optimal U.S. behavior abroad include launching a program for energy independence and donating solar-powered light bulbs with American flag decals on them to African villages, "so when those kids grew up they would remember who lit up their nights."[180]

Bush's response on the global citizen front is, needless to say, largely unsatisfactory, though he does pull through in other areas: "All hail to President Bush for how he has conducted the war against Osama bin Laden."[181] The ensuing upsurge in global anti-Americanism is described as the result of a range of factors, not only the 9/11 transformation of "Puff the Magic Dragon—a benign U.S. hegemon touching everyone economically and culturally … into Godzilla, a wounded, angry, raging beast touching people militarily,"[182] but also the tendency of Arab/Muslim leaders to deflect popular discontent from themselves onto America, as well as "the real reason … that so many people in the world dislike President Bush so intensely," which is that "they feel that he has taken away something very dear to them—an America that exports hope, not fear."[183]

It is debatable, of course, what percentage of people being "militarily touched" by Godzilla have come to the realization that what they are really disgruntled about is Bush's destruction of their idyllic conception of America. As for European anti-American sentiment, Friedman discovers in 2005 that this is indeed not entirely reducible to "classic Eurowhining," and that some of the current European discourse vis-à-vis the United States is "very heartfelt, even touching."[184] The following analysis is offered after a round of interviews conducted at a "trendy bar/beauty parlor" in East Berlin: "Europeans love to make fun of naïve American optimism, but deep down, they envy it and they want America to be that open, foreigner-embracing, carefree, goofily enthusiastic place that cynical old Europe can never be."[185]

Again, it is impossible to determine the percentage of U.S. inhabitants who would define even pre-9/11 existence in the country as one of goofily carefree enthusiasm. Severe discrepancies in the distribution of wealth and opportunities, for example, are hinted at in Friedman's scattered mentioning of things like American "inner cities where way too many black males are failing."[186] This occurs as a side note in an article about his younger daughter's Maryland high school graduation ceremony in which he transcribes thirty-four student names to highlight their "stunning diversity—race, religion, ethnicity" and announces that he is "not yet ready to cede the 21st century to China" because "our Chinese will still beat their Chinese."[187]

Friedman is slightly more subdued the following year when Asian names dominate the Rensselaer Polytechnic Institute commencement at which he is speaking, and he warns that "if we can't educate enough of our own kids to compete at this level, we'd better make sure we can import someone else's, otherwise we will not maintain our standard of living."[188] Friedman sees the "foreigner-embracing"[189] nature of the United States, endangered by 9/11, as ensuring continued power and innovative advantage in the midst of the flat-world dichotomy between "high- and low-imagination-enabling countries,"[190] and regularly stresses the importance of America's ability to "skim the cream off the first-round intellectual draft choices from around the world."[191] He rues the fact that green cards are not being stapled to the diplomas of foreign students who obtain advanced degrees at U.S. universities, although his magnanimous immigration policy is not limited to the hypereducated: "I would never turn back a single Haitian boat person."[192]

As for black males who have managed to elude failure in inner cities, one of these stars in the concluding paragraphs of *The Lexus* as proof that "America is not at its best every day, but when it's good, it's very, very good."[193] The year is 1994, and Friedman has just attended a Christmastime performance by local elementary school choruses, among them his older daughter's, which kicked off with the Hanukkah classic "Maoztzur":

> Watching this scene, and hearing that song, brought tears to my eyes. When I got home, my wife, Ann, asked me how it was. And I said to her: "Honey, I just saw a black man dressed up as Santa Claus directing four hundred elementary-school kids singing 'Maoztzur' in the town square of Bethesda, Maryland. God Bless America."[194]

I highlight such passages not so much to catalog instances of clichéd feel-good nationalism on Friedman's part but rather because America's multiethnic identity serves, in his view, as one of the reasons the country is entitled to its position as global role model and educator—in both its Puff the Magic Dragon and Godzilla incarnations.

Friedman's first tears over 9/11 are incidentally shed, we are told in the "Diary" section of *Longitudes and Attitudes*, at yet another national appreciation moment taking place in the context of his daughters' academic and musical formation. This time the event is Back to School Night at Natalie's junior high, which features "a Noah's Ark of black, white, and Hispanic kids, singing 'God Bless America' and the school orchestra plucking out the National Anthem."[195] Friedman concludes that "Natalie's school and the World Trade Center actually have a lot in common—both are temples of America's civic religion," which is defined as being anchored in the "faith" that everyone can aspire to come to the United States and make of themselves whatever they want.[196]

The need for a civic religion is, it appears, a result of the failure of "bin Laden & Sons"[197] to appreciate that America is not godless and materialistic and that "we are rich and powerful precisely *because* of our values—freedom of thought, respect for the individual, the rule of law, entrepreneurship, women's equality, philanthropy, social mobility, self-criticism, experimentation, religious pluralism —not despite them."[198] The similarity between Natalie's school and the Trade Center, "a place where thousands of people were practicing this civic religion—kissing their spouses good-bye each morning, going off to work, and applying their individual energy in a way that added up to something much larger," is a function of the number of different nationalities contained therein.[199]

Potential drawbacks to American values such as freedom of thought are underscored a bit further along in the *Longitudes* diary when Friedman takes on the "political correctness"[200] of college campuses in the United States shortly after 9/11. Making college rounds, he confronts the grim reality that some U.S. academics do indeed disagree with analyses of delicate anthropological phenomena by columnists who end their first post-9/11 dispatch with the words "Semper Fi."[201] However, rather than cast said disagreement as a manifestation of the freedom of ideas, Friedman does exactly the opposite. Proclaiming an "intellectual hijacking" under way that is being conducted by persons disingenuously assigning their own preferred motives to Al Qaeda, such as a concern for Palestinians or a dislike of U.S. military presence in Saudi Arabia— the latter motive which Friedman himself incidentally invokes at times—he testifies: "The idea that there are radical Muslims who hate us because they see us as 'infidels' and blame us for all the ills that plague their own societies is simply not allowed to be said on most college campuses. Sorry, but this is true."[202]

At one campus, Friedman finds his sole ally in the security guard that has been provided him: "He was an off-duty fireman or policeman—I forget. Anyway, he was a wonderfully earthy guy, the sort of cop or fireman America is built on."[203] The issue of freedom of thought meanwhile once again comes into play when, presumably in response to self-flagellating college faculty overcome by the "impulse to blame America first,"[204] Friedman declares that his college visits "prompted me to turn to my daughters at the dinner table one evening and tell them, 'Girls, you can have any view you want—left, right, or center. You can come home with someone black, white, or purple. But you will never come in this house and not love your country and not thank God every day that you were born an American.'"[205]

Another advantage to the civic religion of the United States is that, whenever its "bedrock values are threatened," various civically religious individuals can be mobilized "into a fist."[206] The multicolored composition of the fist is such that, while on a post-9/11 jaunt to Afghanistan, Friedman experiences a "flash of déjà vu" at Bagram Air Base:

> I felt like I was back at Natalie's Eastern Middle School. I looked around the room at the Special Forces A-teams that were there and could see America's strength hiding in plain sight. It wasn't smart missiles or night-fighting equipment. It was the fact that these Special Forces teams each seemed to be made up of a collection of black, Asian, Hispanic, and white Americans.[207]

The melting pot that is the U.S. military is marveled at time and again, as are the opportunities the institution provides for showcasing the superior U.S. commitment to dismantling traditional gender barriers. At Bagram, for example, Friedman engages in Orientalist exultation over the "mind-bending experience" offered to POWs who have gone from "being in Al Qaeda, living, as James Michener put it, 'in this cruel land of recurring ugliness, where only men were seen,' and then suddenly being guarded by a woman with blond locks spilling out from under her helmet and an M16 hanging from her side."[208] In another instance, Friedman advertises a "fascinating article"[209] in *The Atlantic Monthly* about a U.S. F-15 jet fighter with a female bombardier who drops a 500-pound bomb onto a Taliban truck caravan. Friedman summarizes:

"As the caravan is vaporized, the F-15 pilot shouts down at the Taliban—as if they could hear him from 20,000 feet—'You have just been killed by a girl.'"[210]

Gender-conscious ejaculations by F-15 pilots seemingly unaware that life is not a video game are not, of course, remotely indicative of female empowerment. Undeterred, Friedman collects additional evidence during a visit in 2005 to the U.S.S. *Chosin*, a guided-missile cruiser in the Persian Gulf that contains not only "blacks, whites, Hispanics, Christians, Jews, atheists, [and] Muslims" but also various women officers.[211] After speculating as to what local Arab fishermen must think hearing female voices over the *Chosin*'s loudspeaker and radio, Friedman boasts of U.S. military accomplishments in Iraq: "In effect, we are promoting two revolutions at once: Jefferson versus Saddam and Sinbad versus the Little Mermaids—who turn out to be captains of ships."[212]

The fact that the female crew is still conceived of by non-Iraqis in terms of "Little Mermaids" who are simultaneously permitted to serve as ship captains suggests that fundamental obstacles to gender equality still exist in supposedly post-revolutionary societies. Other obstacles to the U.S. army-as-vehicle-for-women's-rights model include *Time Magazine* articles that begin: "What does it tell us that female soldiers deployed overseas stop drinking water after 7 p.m. to reduce the odds of being raped if they have to use the bathroom at night?"[213] According to the 2010 article, the Pentagon estimates that the number of female soldiers sexually assaulted by their male counterparts while serving in Iraq and Afghanistan rose 25 percent from fiscal year 2007–8, and that 80 to 90 percent of sexual assaults in the military go unreported.

Friedman, however, prefers to focus on the cheery cohesion of the armed forces, while devising new ways for America to simultaneously engage in military destruction and societal improvement abroad. Among the most bizarre of these is his "new rule of thumb" proposed in 2010 following a visit to Yemen: "For every Predator missile we fire at an Al Qaeda target here, we should help Yemen build 50 new modern schools that teach science and math and critical thinking — to boys and girls."[214]

The new rule of thumb is the product of Friedman's experience chewing *qat*—"the mildly hallucinogenic leaf drug that Yemeni men stuff in their cheek after work"[215]—at a meeting with Yemeni officials, lawmakers, and businessmen, primarily U.S.-educated or with children currently studying in the United States, who complain about the Yemeni education system. Having thus swiftly and scientifically analyzed a country he has never before visited, Friedman urges: "If we stick to something close to that ratio of targeted killings to targeted kindergartens, we have a chance to prevent Yemen from becoming an Al Qaeda breeding ground."[216] It is not explained whether the kindergartens will teach children not to feel anger when Yemeni civilians are killed by U.S. drones.

Friedman's frequent inclination toward specific cohorts abroad, especially in the Arab/Muslim world, can also be observed in his 2002 publicizing of the existence of "a secularized, U.S.-educated, pro-American elite and middle class in Saudi Arabia, who are not America's enemies. They are good people, and you can't visit Saudi Arabia without meeting them."[217] What is implied by such sentence structures is that religious, non-U.S.-educated, and non-elite Saudis *are* America's enemies and are not good people, which automatically obliterates the hope that any fragments of human reality might survive Friedman's prattle.

As for other varieties of U.S.-administered education, Friedman's solution for quelling the Abu Ghraib torture scandal is to "close this prison immediately and reopen it in a month as the Abu Ghraib Technical College for Computer Training."[218] He meanwhile swears his commitment to "dismantling Guantánamo Bay and replacing it with a free field hospital for poor Cubans," a curious solution in a country that already offers free universal health care.[219] The real tragedy of Abu Ghraib and Guantánamo in Friedman's view is, of course, that they have exacerbated the lack of "moral authority" on the part of the Bush-Cheney team, which is nonetheless still described in 2007 as possessing "moral clarity."[220]

It is important to emphasize that Friedman *is* often critical of the United States. However, criticism is levied solely to discourage behavior Friedman sees as jeopardizing U.S. power, the maintenance of which remains his supreme goal. For example, his berating of U.S. administrations for failing to launch a green revolution is a result of his conviction that "making America the world's greenest country is not a selfless act of charity or naïve moral indulgence. It is now a core national security and economic interest," necessary for restoring the United States to global preeminence.[221]

As one might expect, Friedman's view of what qualifies as proper environmentalism is in constant flux. He alternately: demands a Manhattan Project for renewable energy;[222] advocates for the import of Brazilian sugar ethanol;[223] demands that Europe abandon its opposition to GMOs, "which will be critically important if we want to grow more of our fuel—à la corn ethanol or soy biodiesel";[224] warns against "end[ing] up in a very bad place, like in a crazy rush into corn ethanol, and palm oil for biodiesel";[225] declares that he is "wary of biofuels" and that "what makes sense in Brazil does not make sense in the United States";[226] announces that "all environmentalists have their favorite 'green' energy source" and that his is "called coal";[227] cautions: "Let's make sure that we aren't just chasing the fantasy that we can 'clean up' coal";[228] resurrects the "heretofore specious notion of 'clean coal'";[229] characterizes a Manhattan Project for clean energy as an "easy sound bite" for politicians and a "cop-out";[230] and advises the Tea Party to improve its image by becoming the Green Tea Party ("I'd be happy to design the T-shirt logo and write the manifesto").[231] Additionally, he goes from harping on Bush for Kyoto Protocol–related unilateralism, "selfishness and hubris"[232] to deciding that Kyoto is unfeasible and that if the United States simply unilaterally stages a green revolution, the world will forget its resentment and follow.

In *Hot, Flat, and Crowded*, Friedman proposes, "with tongue only slightly in cheek," the following bumper sticker formula to express the goal of a Clean Energy System: "REEFIGDCPEERPC < TTCOBCOG."[233] This stands for "a renewable energy ecosystem for innovating, generating, and deploying clean power, energy efficiency, resource productivity, and conservation < the true cost of burning coal, oil, and gas."[234] A response to Google's proposed formula of "RE < C—renewable energy cheaper than coal," it is a rare example of an instance in which Friedman's normal tendency toward reductionism might have proved more effective.[235]

As for the Friedman formula according to which "the only engine big enough to impact Mother Nature is Father Greed: the Market," the idea that a system that runs on greed and the exploitation of resources and humans in the interest of profit can somehow provide a solution to the very ills it creates is fanciful, to say the least. In 2006 Friedman reasons that "there is nothing wrong about" China's (not Mother-Nature-friendly) extraction of natural resources from Latin America because "America and Spain did the same for years—and often rapaciously" and because China's "voracious appetite … is helping to fuel a worldwide boom in commodity prices that is enabling a poor, low-industrialized country like Peru to grow at 5 percent."[236] For an example of what can happen when commodity booms do not benefit poor people who also possess appetites, see the Arab uprisings of 2011.

Friedman applies the logic of greed in his tirade against the "ridiculous" World Trade Organization protests of 1999, entitled "Senseless in Seattle."[237] Praising the conditions of a particular Victoria's Secret underwear factory in Sri Lanka that "I would let my own daughters work in," Friedman lectures the opponents of globalization:

> You make a difference today by using globalization—by mobilizing the power of trade, the power of the Internet and the power of consumers to persuade, or embarrass, global corporations and nations to upgrade their standards. You change the world when you get the big players to do the right things for the wrong reasons.[238]

This particular strategy has already been test-driven in Brazil, where Friedman discovers in 1998 a "global triple threat" to the Pantanal region from "external forces of globalization," such as international energy companies.[239] Ford Motors' financing of various initiatives in the region by Conservation International is cast as being based on the calculation that "they can sell a lot more Jaguar cars if they are seen as saving the jaguars of the Pantanal," and Friedman concludes that "if that's what it takes to save this incredibly beautiful ecosystem and way of life, then God bless Henry Ford and the Internet."[240] There is no detectable concern for the fact that the initiatives do not reverse any of the listed threats or Ford's contributions to global pollution.[241]

"Senseless in Seattle II" is meanwhile penned as a follow-up to the original article, which elicits a response from his "environmentalist allies" regarding its depiction of the WTO protests as wholly unserious.[242] In the sequel, Friedman permits that "there were some serious groups there raising serious points" but still maintains that it is wrong to oppose the WTO when serious activism can be accomplished by simply ignoring the organization in order to save Flipper and make the Mexicans save him too:

> Sure, the W.T.O. ruled against the U.S. laws banning tuna caught in nets that also catch dolphins. But I just went to my Giant supermarket and checked every can of tuna. They all said: "Dolphin safe." Now how could that be? Because the smart activists ignored the W.T.O. ruling, mobilized consumers to pressure the tuna companies, the tuna companies pressured the fishermen and Flipper got saved. That's how you change the world. If we didn't have free trade with Mexican fishermen, would we have been able to pressure them into using dolphin-safe nets on the tuna they sell us? Not a chance.[243]

Friedman categorizes himself in 2006 as no longer just a free trader but a "radical free trader."[244] His recognition that free trade is inherently not free comes through in his writing on occasion, such as when he demands an abolishment of the "crazy 54-cent tariff" in order to make Brazil the "Saudi Arabia of sugar"[245] (which, it has been pointed out, is not at all congruent with his goal of U.S. energy independence[246]). As for the biased nature of U.S. agricultural subsidies, which have been ruled against by the WTO,[247] this is highlighted by Friedman's detection of the following hypothetical sequence of events in 2003:

> The Pakistani farmer we've put out of business with our farm subsidies then sends his sons to the Wahhabi school because it is tuition-free and offers a hot lunch. His sons grow up getting only a Koranic education, so they are totally unprepared for modernity, but they are taught one thing: that America is the source of all their troubles.[248]

That such conclusions might be arrived at independent of the Koran, such as among Central American families put out of business by "free trade" with the United States, is disregarded by Friedman, who determines that by allowing Central America to engage in "labor-intensive sewing" we will "help consolidate these fragile democracies by locking in a trading relationship with the U.S. that is critical for their development."[249] Accusing members of the U.S. Congress of antiglobalist behavior worthy of the French for threatening to reject the Central American Free Trade Agreement in 2005, Friedman subsequently boasts in reference to the article: "I wrote a column supporting the CAFTA, the Caribbean Free Trade initiative [sic]. I didn't even know what was in it. I just knew two words: free trade."[250]

A testament to the amount of research that consistently goes into the *New York Times* foreign affairs column, such admissions tend also to deprive their makers of credibility in accusing others of being unserious. Friedman, who has been described by noted economist and media analyst Edward S. Herman as a "media-based ideologue for corporate expansion abroad,"[251] nonetheless continues to churn out disparaging analyses of the opponents of his corporate vision. These are variously written off as "a rogues' gallery of Communists, anarchists, protectionist unions and over-fed Yuppies out for their 1960's fix"²⁵² and "pampered American college kids, wearing their branded clothing, [who] began to get interested in sweatshops as a way of expiating their guilt"²⁵³ over the incredible wealth of the United States.

It is not entirely clear why we are supposed to view the college kids with distaste when Friedman himself invokes collegiate anti-sweatshop efforts as proof of globalization's effectiveness in improving worker conditions.²⁵⁴ It would not be farfetched to assume, however, that the students' crime is a failure to appreciate their pampered status, given the frequency with which Friedman paraphrases Warren Buffett's theory that "everything I got in life was because I was born in this country, America, at this time, with these opportunities and these institutions." ²⁵⁵ At his 2010 talk in Istanbul, Friedman defines himself politically as a believer in this theory rather than as a Democrat or Republican, and reiterates that it is his duty to pass on a similar situation to his children. Non-billionaires and foreign audiences might be forgiven for a lack of complete sympathy.

Here it is useful to draw attention to a socioeconomic obser-vation by author Norman Solomon, made in 2006 but especially valid at a time when Friedman is advocating for planet-wide enti-tlement cuts. Writing in the aftermath of the profile of Friedman in the *Washingtonian*, which reports his annual seven-figure income and 11,400-square-foot house then valued at $9.3 million, Solomon argues that, while Friedman's astronomical wealth of course does not automatically invalidate what he writes, it pro-vides a necessary context for "how he is accustomed to moving through the world":

> It's reasonable to ask whether Friedman—perhaps the richest jour-nalist in the United States—might be less zealously evangelical for "globalization" if he hadn't been so wealthy for the last quarter of a century. Meanwhile, it's worth noting that the corporate forces

avidly promoting his analysis of economic options are reaping massive profits from the systems of trade and commerce that he champions.[256]

Similar points have been made by Herman, who offers the following bit of trivia on the subject of Friedman's far-reaching influence: "It is not hard to understand why, in a letter of March 31, 1999, former Enron CEO Kenneth Lay recommended a Friedman article on globalization to his friend George Bush as 'an excellent account of most of the basic issues.'"[257] Other CEOs are presumably grateful for the covert advertising Friedman conducts on their behalf (e.g., "when I was done interviewing the mayor, I thanked him and started to pack up my IBM ThinkPad laptop"[258]). As for the 2008 news that the family trusts of Friedman's wife Ann, heiress of shopping mall developer General Growth Properties, had declined in value from $3.6 billion to less than $25 million as a result of the housing crisis, this sort of information is useful when interpreting Friedman's criticism of the practice of socializing losses in the U.S. financial system.[259]

As noted previously, the ideal response in Friedman's view to the socialization of losses is to direct them on to the lower echelons of society. Declaring that "we are entering an era where to be a leader will mean, on balance, to take things away from people," he praises the cutting of pensions in Atlanta in defiance of unions, underscoring once again the disingenuous nature of his rallying to cast the taking away of things as collective national sacrifice for the purpose of creating a "Re-generation"[260] to replace the "Subprime Generation."[261] As for those whose profligacy is directly to thank for the recession, Friedman observes in 2008 that "unfortunately, some people who don't deserve it will be rescued" by the government bailout of the financial system.[262] Directly prior to the bailout, Friedman manages to cast the recession-inducing system itself as the magical restorer of order: "The market is now consolidating [the financial] industry, with the strong eating the weak, which will impose its own fiscal discipline. Good."[263]

The socioeconomic milieu in which Friedman operates has been clear at least since *From Beirut to Jerusalem*, where he composes a list of seven things that define the real civil war–era Beirut for outsiders viewing it as a place of continuous massacres. The list consists of "the par-5 first hole at the Beirut Golf and Country Club, where Ann and I were members in good standing"; a note on the golf course bulletin board announcing the postponement of the club championship in 1982; an ad in an English-language weekly; a sign on a bridge; a television commercial; a gourmet supermarket offering "*foie gras* flown in daily from Paris"; and the Summerland Hotel.[264] That Friedman recognizes the highly stratified nature of Lebanese society, and the fact that most Lebanese do not survive the brutal civil war with the help of country clubs and *foie gras*, is blatantly obvious from the rest of the book. That he has nonetheless chosen to define Beirut as such on behalf of the Lebanese is thus all the more disappointing.

Friedman repeatedly argues that sustained globalization is the best cure for poverty, and that "the world's poor do not resent the rich anywhere nearly as much as the left-wing parties in the developed world imagine."[265] Coincidentally, it is also America "that benefits most from today's global integration—as the country whose people, products, values, technologies and ideas are being most globalized."[266] Friedman supports his argument that the global poor are demanding more globalization, not less, by alternately encouraging readers to "just ask any Indian villager"[267] and by informing them that "Africans themselves will tell you that their problem with globalization is not that they are getting too much of it, but too little."[268]

The problem, of course, is that Friedman himself rarely seeks the opinion of the very people for whom he is claiming to speak, despite admitting to having an essentially unlimited travel budget.[269] The "Africans themselves" he mentions in his 2001 article datelined "Accra," for example, end up consisting of the director of Ghana's Institute for Economic Affairs, an Indian trade economist, and Harvard's neoliberal shock therapist Jeffrey

Sachs.[270] No Africans real or honorary are meanwhile quoted in Friedman's 2009 article datelined "Chief's Island, Botswana," in which he manages a 121-word description of a leopard eating an antelope in a tree, confirms from the Grameen Foundation's Eric Cantor that cell phone- and Internet-equipped African teenagers will use the technology to research STDs, and concludes that the outcome of Robert Mugabe's dictatorship in Zimbabwe is that "both its people and wildlife are endangered species."[271]

Let us now revisit Friedman's determination that "the 'wretched of the earth' want to go to Disney World—not to the barricades. They want the Magic Kingdom, not *Les Misérables*."[272] He explains in *The Lexus* that he learned this "little secret" by talking to people such as "a little old lady with a scale in Hanoi,"[273] to whom he gives a dollar every morning to weigh himself. However, if one flips sixteen pages back to the original mention of Friedman's self-described "contribution to the globalization of Vietnam" via scale payments, one learns that he did not actually talk to the little old lady: "To me, her unspoken motto was: 'Whatever you've got, no matter how big or small—sell it, trade it, barter it, leverage it, rent it, but do something with it to turn a profit, improve your standard of living and get into the game.'"[274]

This is not to say that the poor are never allowed their own voices in Friedman's writings. In March of 1995, for example, the opening line of a Friedman column stars a sixty-year-old Mexican peasant named Ricarda Martinez, who "says she's never heard of Wall Street and doesn't know anything about dollar-linked peso bonds, George Soros or Merrill Lynch's emerging markets fund"—which have just launched what Friedman refers to as a "financial neutron bomb" on Mexico.[275] Curiously, the columnist who will soon denounce antiglobalists as "The Coalition to Keep Poor People Poor"[276] here reports that Martinez can no longer afford to purchase meat and quotes her as saying: "Mexico is now different—now we are poor."[277]

Martinez is promptly forgotten, and Friedman moves on to promoting the $20 billion U.S.–Mexico bailout as the "truly populist thing to do," given that "Robin Hood and Billionaire Bob have a joint peso account."[278] He then turns his attention to more distant shores and only returns to Mexico in 2004, whereupon "it definitely caught my ear when I started to hear two non-Spanish words on this trip that I'd never heard here before: 'China' and 'India.'"[279] Mexicans are reported to be hearing a "giant sucking sound" as their jobs and markets are appropriated by the two words[280]; conspicuously lacking from Friedman's subsequent article is a correction to the tune of "In my last column I reported that 'China' and 'India' are not Spanish words. They are."

Undeterred, Friedman is back once again in 2010 with the news that, although "40 percent of [Mexicans] live below the poverty line" after sixteen years of NAFTA, political and economic headway can still be achieved via pro-NAFTA reforms such as the privatization of the state-owned oil company Pemex.[281] The only person consulted for the article, it appears, is Mexican economist—and, Friedman fails to mention, former Trade and NAFTA Minister at the Mexican embassy in Washington, D.C.—Luis de la Calle, whose study of the top fifty Mexican baby names of 2008 Friedman cites: "The most popular for girls, [de la Calle] said, included 'Elizabeth, Evelyn, Abigail, Karen, Marilyn and Jaqueline, and for boys Alexander, Jonathan, Kevin, Christian and Bryan.' Not only Juans."[282] This is, of course, an indisputably compelling and nonracist indication of the correlation between free trade and societal improvement.[283]

Generic English names are not always synonymous with progress, however, and Friedman condemns the U.S. Congress in 2004 for being "out to lunch—or, worse, obsessed with trying to keep Susie Smith's job at the local pillow factory that is moving to the Caribbean" rather than "thinking about a national competitiveness strategy."[284] Statements like these call into question the sincerity of his claim elsewhere that "I'd feel better about America's economy if I knew we were prospering as one country, not as two,"[285] and reinforce the notion that there is a hierarchy of respectable professions, as previously suggested in *The Lexus*:

"Yes, not everybody has a great job—some people are flipping hamburgers and others are designing web pages."[286]

The hamburger judgment is especially curious, given that it occurs in the same book in which Friedman is advertising McDonald's as the key to world peace, and not so long after he has boasted of eating Big Macs in fourteen different countries in a single year.[287] A decade later, we learn that hamburger flippers are in fact to blame, along with currency speculators, for U.S. decadence, and that "even before the current financial crisis, we were already in a deep competitive hole—a long period in which too many people were making money from money, or money from flipping houses or hamburgers."[288]

Additional blame is distributed in Friedman's 2010 dispatch "Too Many Hamburgers?," inspired by a Chinese television skit about an American child who loses a race to his Chinese, Indian, and Brazilian counterparts on account of obesity. Friedman emphasizes that there is no reason "our *right* system ... should not be able to generate the kind of focus, legitimacy, unity and stick-to-it-iveness to do big things—democratically—that China does autocratically," but that this objective is being hampered "because too many of our poll-driven, toxically partisan, cable-TV-addicted, money-corrupted political class are more interested in what keeps them in power than what would again make America powerful, more interested in defeating each other than saving the country."[289] This is not an enormously surprising state of affairs when Friedman himself has consistently defined human greed as the driving factor in the economic system he endorses.

Friedman's exact thoughts on the *right*ness of the U.S. political system are meanwhile unclear, given that he pronounces it "dysfunctional" in an article the following month.[290] Such inconsistencies are, of course, simply the latest additions to a history defined by failure to keep track of the terms of arguments. Take, for example, Friedman's explanation in *The Lexus* that his concept of Integrationist-Social-Safety-Nettism "is actually the *only* way for a country to thrive and survive in this new system [of globalization]. There is no Third Way. There is only one way."[291] Juxtapose this with the explanation of the same phenomenon offered during Friedman's *New York Times*–sponsored discussion with Joseph Stiglitz: "You know, my motto, historically, is people said, you know, there's no third way. And my answer is that the only way is the third way."[292]

As for how to go about saving a system that may or may not be right, Friedman summarizes the "gut thesis" of his forthcoming book on the decline of the United States during his 2011 phone interview with Fox's Don Imus: "It's not a man on horseback we need, Don, it's a different horse right now, and a different horse that demands a different kind of politics that drives the country in a different direction."[293] He refrains from advertising the animal as the latest engine not only for American renewal but for global renewal, as well—as might be expected from Friedman-crafted scenarios—or from urging other countries to get their own horses and head for the racetrack (but not to win).

The horse is at least more environmentally friendly than former metaphorical models, such as Friedman's "five gas stations theory of the world," which posits that globalization is pushing the entire planet toward the adoption of the "American gas station."[294] Writes Friedman in *The Lexus*:

> First there is the Japanese gas station. Gas is $5 a gallon. Four men in uniforms and white gloves, with lifetime employment contracts, wait on you. They pump your gas. They change your oil. They wash your windows, and they wave at you with a friendly smile as you drive away in peace. Second is the American gas station. Gas costs only $1 a gallon, but you pump it yourself. You wash your own windows. You fill your own tires. And when you drive around the corner four homeless people try to steal your hubcaps.[295]

And so on.

Whatever new kind of politics the horse demands from the United States in order to drive the country in a new direction, it is safe to assume that its blinders will remain firmly in place when it comes to the issue of the inherent superiority of a system of institutionalized inequality. And in case it forgets, Friedman will always be there with reminders like: "You win the presidency by connecting with the American people's gut insecurities and aspirations. You win with a concept. The concept I'd argue for is 'neoliberalism.'"[296]

As for potential role models for the U.S. equine renaissance, these include autocratic Singapore, the star of an article Friedman produces during the forty-six days following the 2010 uprising in Tunisia in which he refrains from mentioning the democratic revolts sweeping the region from which he has consistently demanded democracy. Given that Singapore's "top bureaucrats and cabinet ministers have their pay linked to top private sector wages, so most make well over $1 million a year," we are told, the country has "something to teach [the United States] about 'attitude'—*about taking governing seriously*."[297]

2 THE ARAB/MUSLIM WORLD

When it comes to discussing the Middle East, people go temporarily insane, so if you are planning to talk to an audience of more than two, you'd better have mastered the subject.
— *From Beirut to Jerusalem*

Colonel Oliver North thought he was dealing with Iranian "moderates" when he was really dealing with Iranian grocers; he had no idea how to bargain with the original rug merchants. He should have taken business lessons from Libyan leader Muammar Qaddafi.
— *From Beirut to Jerusalem*

In a 2004 article entitled "In My Next Life," Friedman offers a satirical commentary on various sectors of the U.S. citizenry that have in his view committed ethical infractions. The article begins with the declaration: "In my next life, I want to be Tom DeLay, the House majority leader." Among the reasons produced is that "I want to have the gall to sully American democracy at a time when young American soldiers are fighting in Iraq so we can enjoy a law-based society here and, maybe, extend it to others."[1]

In his defense, DeLay may not be aware that the purpose of devastating Iraq is to consolidate U.S. democracy. Undeterred, Friedman expands his list of reincarnation aspirations to include "gutless Republican House members" who have abetted DeLay's democratic sullying, the guard of the Minnesota Timberwolves basketball team, and "any American college or professional athlete."[2] The last group is selected based on unethical overreactions to first-down runs and similar feats: "For the smallest, most routine bit of success in my sport, I want to be able to get in your face—I want to know who's your daddy, I want to be able to high-five, low-five, thump my chest and dance on your grave. You talkin' to me?"[3]

Let us compare for a moment the tone of the prototypical athletic grave-dancer with the tone of the featured guest of talk show host Charlie Rose on May 30, 2003. This guest announces that he now understands that the real reason for the war on Iraq was to burst the "terrorism bubble" that had emerged in "that part of the world" and that—as "we learned on 9/11, in a gut way"[4]—posed a "fundamental threat to our open society":

> *Thomas Friedman [to Rose]*: We needed to go over there, basically, um, and … take out a very big stick, um, right in the heart of, of that world … What they needed to see was American boys *and girls* going house to house from Basra to Baghdad, um, and basically saying: "Which part of this sentence don't you understand? You don't think, you know, we care about our open society; you think this bubble fantasy, we're just gonna let it grow? Well. Suck. On. This."[5]

This particular bout of grave-dancing is revealing for a number of reasons aside from its crude imagery. For one thing, Friedman's announcement that he has only in retrospect understood the real reason for the war signals that widely read columnists who bleated from their *New York Times* perches in 2002 that a democratizing invasion was the "most important task worth doing" are not required to have a solid grasp of what they themselves think the purpose of the operation is.[6] For another, Friedman himself criticizes the Bush administration for trying to imply a link between Osama bin Laden and Saddam Hussein,[7] who nonetheless appear here to inhabit the same "bubble fantasy."

Friedman meanwhile quotes the bubble as warning America: "We've got you … because we don't care about life, we're ready to sacrifice, and all you care about are your stock options and your Hummers."[8] He proceeds to note that the United States "coulda hit Saudi Arabia. It was part of that bubble. Coulda hit Pakistan. We hit Iraq because we could. That's the real truth."[9] This argument is reiterated in an article published shortly after the Rose interview: "Smashing Saudi Arabia or Syria would have been fine. But we hit Saddam for one simple reason: because we could, and because he deserved it and because he was right in the heart of that world."[10] As for why the smashing of Afghanistan is not a sufficient response to the bubble, Friedman explains: "Afghanistan wasn't enough."[11]

Keeping in mind the above comments, let us return to the next item in Friedman's list of reincarnation options: the owner of a Hummer decorated with American flag decals, "because Hummer owners are, on average, a little more patriotic than you and me."[12] Friedman elaborates:

Yes, I want to drive my Hummer and never have to think that by consuming so much oil, I am making transfer payments to the worst Arab regimes that transfer money to Islamic charities that transfer money to madrassas that teach children intolerance, antipluralism and how to hate the infidels.

And when one day one of those madrassa graduates goes off and joins the jihad in Falluja and kills my neighbor's son, who is in the U.S. Army Rangers, I want to drive to his funeral in my Hummer. Yes, I want to curse his killers in front of his mother and wail aloud, "If there was only something I could do …" And then I want to drive home in my Hummer, stopping at two gas stations along the way.[13]

Ironically, Friedman's own behavior is even more riddled with ethical complications than that of the imaginary Hummer driver. In fact, he appears to be an ideal candidate for his own list. The Friedman reincarnation option might be summarized as follows:

In my next life I want to be Thomas Friedman. Yes, I want to tell Charlie Rose that the real reason we smashed Iraq was because we could. Then, four days later, I want to write an article entitled "Because We Could," in which I specify that there were three additional reasons for the war aside from the real reason, but at no point do I mention oil.

Jump ahead to 2004. I want to harangue Donald Rumsfeld for his doctrine of "Just enough troops to lose."[14] After that, I want to decide that the war *is* about oil and that American Hummer owners are to blame for the Fallujah deaths of their neighbors' sons. Yes, I want to rail against these Hummer people even though I cannot think of a single one of them who presides over a biweekly *New York Times* column that has for the past several years been devoted to funneling American soldiers to Iraq.

I want them to assume direct responsibility for the jihadist-production cycle that begins with Hummer gas pump transfer payments to the Saudis, who live in the same terrorism bubble as now-devastated Iraq, except that Saudi Arabia produced fifteen of the 9/11 hijackers and Saddam produced none. I, on the other hand, want to continue to be able to write things like: "Frankly, I have a soft spot for the de facto Saudi ruler, Crown Prince Abdullah, who is a man of decency and moderation"[15] and "Of course, we must protect the Saudis."[16] A year after suggesting that George Bush reduce U.S. financing of terrorists and set a geo-green example by renouncing his limo,[17] I want to report that I am being chauffeured around Budapest in one, and I even want to provide the driver's website—www.fclimo.hu—so that everyone can witness the capitalist evolution and integration into the global economy of a "Communist-era-engineer-turned-limo-proprietor."[18]

Yes, I want to be Thomas Friedman in my next life, and throughout my lectures I want to remain oblivious to the fact that I do not require hypothetical reincarnation as the owner of a luxury SUV in order share the blame for U.S. war deaths.

As for the question of whether telling Arab populations to suck on things constitutes acceptable journalistic etiquette, the sucking order must be interpreted not as a slip of the tongue or heat-of-the-moment discharge but rather as a logical occurrence in the context of Friedman's career and journalistic identity. In order to gain a better contextual understanding, it is helpful to review certain defining characteristics of Friedman's writing, as well as key historical events—namely 9/11—that have influenced his perspective.

For starters, Friedman's reliance on overly simplistic and baseless analyses of international phenomena has led to a range of bizarre prescriptions, such as his proposal in 2004 that, if the United States simply lowers its profile in the Arab world, the Arabs will suddenly realize that their children are being outperformed academically by "many of their maids' children—from India, China, Sri Lanka and the Philippines."[19] The latest short-lived ultimatum on the issue of how to achieve reform in the Arab/Muslim world thus becomes: "Only when the Arabs focus on how their maids' children are doing in the world, not what the Americans are doing in their region, will they revisit one of the most famous sayings of the Prophet Muhammad: 'Seek knowledge, even unto China. That is the duty for every Muslim.'"[20] It is not clear how the United States is supposed to go about waging low-profile regional wars, or why the elimination of the United States as a distraction would cause wealthy Arabs to suddenly envy the scholastic exploits of the offspring of their domestic servants.

This same tendency toward baseless reductionism is amply showcased in Friedman's assertion that the crashing of planes into the World Trade Center and the blowing up of Israelis in pizza parlors necessitates door-to-door U.S. army-administered sucking from Basra to Baghdad.[21] The jingoistic bombast and sense of vicarious delight in military punishment contained in such outbursts is meanwhile not unexpected from a columnist who variously emits the following announcements:

1. "I loved Don Rumsfeld's briefings during the Afghan war. They were no-nonsense tough, with a dose of American nationalism that resonated with me."[22]
2. "Mr. Obama's gift for outreach would be so much more effective with a Dick Cheney standing over his right shoulder, quietly pounding a baseball bat into his palm."[23]
3. "I have a confession to make. Right after 9/11, I was given a CD by the Mormon Tabernacle Choir, which included its rendition of 'The Battle Hymn of the Republic.' I put it in my car's CD player and played that song over and over, often singing along as I drove."[24]

Curiously, Friedman qualifies his affection for Rumsfeld's no-nonsense Afghan briefings with an expression of concern that the Pentagon is now emitting "a certain degree of imperial contempt for the rest of the world, especially the Arab-Muslim world," that this is "not healthy," and that "it is too bad that Mr. Bush's instinctive humility has given way lately to Texas cowboy lingo when talking about Iraq."[25] Declarations of Arab/Muslim "backwardness"[26] and the use of suction-related lingo implying sexual humiliation, on the other hand, are evidently less problematic.

Tied up with Friedman's habit of reductionism is his tendency to downplay the importance of the historical milieu in which populations exist and events occur. Near the beginning of *The Lexus and the Olive Tree*, Friedman admits to having engaged in "two-dimensional" journalism while covering "'Mother of all Tribal Wars'—the Arab-Israeli conflict" in Beirut and Jerusalem in the 1980s:

> [Journalism] was about politics and culture, because in the Middle East your culture pretty much defined your politics. Or, to put it another way, the world for me was all about watching people clinging to their own roots and uprooting their neighbors' olive trees.[27]

It is quite a stretch, of course, to suggest that opposition to the erection of a Jewish state on Arab land might somehow be reducible to a matter of culture, or that the Arab–Israeli conflict's "tribal" nature signifies its automatic exemption from analysis within standard historical parameters and against a backdrop of imperialism, colonialism, and ethnic cleansing.[28] The blanket application of olive tree imagery is additionally misleading given that Israel is the regional figure most associated with uprooting other people's agricultural livelihoods.[29]

Though Friedman does on occasion mention the post-WWI partitioning of the Middle East by the British and French and the resulting difficulties for affected populations, the relationship of Zionism to such projects is never truly explored. In *From Beirut to Jerusalem*, for example—in which the chapter entitled "Whose Country Is This, Anyway?" merely deals with competition in Israel between religious and secular Jews—relevant bits of Zionist history are found lodged among oddly conceived observations on the centrality of the "biblical super story" to Western existence, despite the inferior size of the Sea of Galilee:

> As Lloyd George, the British Prime Minister when the 1917 Balfour Declaration promising the Jews a homeland was issued, once told the Zionist leader Chaim Weizmann, the names Judea, Samaria, and Jerusalem "are more familiar to me than the names of Welsh villages of my own childhood." Indeed, every American is familiar with a place like the Sea of Galilee—even though many states in the United States have lakes which are much bigger.[30]

That British–Zionist collusion against Palestine was far more sinister than Lloyd George's expressions of Orientalist nostalgia would imply is clear from Weizmann's musings on the population of Palestine prior to the establishment of the state of Israel, cited here by historian David Hirst: "'The British told us,' [Weizmann] confided to a colleague, 'that there are some hundred thousands of negroes and for those there is no value'; they were like 'the rocks of Judea, obstacles that had to be cleared on a difficult path.'"[31] Friedman's relationship with Israel will be discussed in detail in the next section; what must be emphasized at the moment is that the Arab/Muslim world cannot be credibly analyzed by someone who refuses to question the legitimacy of Zionism or to consider the extent to which its destructive legacy continues to influence current events.

Ironically, Friedman manages to highlight his propensity for historical decontextualization in the very section of *The Lexus* in which he is supposed to be outlining his transformation from a two-dimensional to a six-dimensional view of the world—in other words, in which he is ostensibly *adding* layers of context. The need for more dimensions initially becomes apparent, we are told, thanks to certain complications during the 1989 confirmation hearing before the U.S. Senate of Secretary of State James Baker, which is Friedman's first assignment as the *New York Times'* chief diplomatic correspondent:

> I am embarrassed to say that since both my B.A. and M.A. were in Arabic and Middle Eastern Studies, and since I had spent almost my entire journalistic career up to that point covering the Middle East, I really did not know very much about any other parts of the world, and I certainly did not know anything about most of the issues the senators were quizzing Mr. Baker about, such as the START treaty, the Contras, Angola, the CFE (Conventional Forces in Europe) arms control negotiations and NATO … I couldn't keep straight whether the Contras were our guys or their guys, and I thought CFE was a typo and was actually "café" without the "a."[32]

Apparently unconcerned that this admission does not reflect very favorably on *New York Times* standards for selecting diplomatic correspondents, Friedman goes on to claim that, as a result of his four-year stint, he "managed to add a new dimension to politics and culture—the national security, balance-of-power dimension."[33] The third of the six dimensions in which Friedman now sees the world, he explains that it "comprises the whole nexus of issues revolving around arms control, superpower competition, Cold War alliance management and power geopolitics."[34]

It would thus seem that it has taken the former *New York Times* bureau chief in Beirut and Jerusalem until the end of the Cold War to discover balance-of-power theory and other basic international relations concepts—which, it should be stressed, apply to the Middle East just as they do to the rest of the world. Equally remarkable is that the evidence Friedman provides of his newfound dimensional sophistication is a revelation he has on a flight to Israel, according to which the epicenter of tension between the United States and the Arab/Muslim world is in fact geopolitically irrelevant: "I found myself looking out the window of the Secretary of State's airplane, down at the West Bank, and thinking, 'You know, in raw power terms, this place really isn't very important anymore. Interesting, yes. But geopolitically important, no.'"[35]

As for Friedman's professed lack of knowledge about Angola prior to the 1989 Senate hearing, the addition of the balance-of-power dimension to his outlook enables him to proclaim in 1996 with regard to the Angolan civil war: "This is, quite simply, the stupidest war in Africa."[36] The reason it is so stupid is that "most of the people caught up in it don't even know what it's about anymore."[37] Fortunately, Friedman knows—thanks to his brief descent upon the country as part of the entourage of U.S. Ambassador to the U.N. Madeleine Albright—that, since other methods of putting a stop to the war have not worked, "we're going to have to do it the old-fashioned way. That is for one side to win and for the other to lose, and the quicker that happens the better off the Angolan people will be."[38]

What is particularly interesting about Friedman's charitable intervention on behalf of the Angolans is that he does in this case include some background information on the civil war, such as its origins in the war of independence from Portugal and the Cold War superpower battle by proxy for the "prize" of oil- and diamond-rich Angola.[39] Such contextual details do not, however, prevent him from assigning the adjectives "stupid" and "senseless"[40] to the conflict. It is as if the only truly applicable event in the timeline of African history is the end of the Cold War, after which Angolans are supposed to recognize the altered geopolitical landscape and strike the tumult of past decades from collective memory. It would presumably behoove them to ignore the fact that Friedman's touted "benign hegemon"[41] of the post–Cold War era is the very country that he is currently urging to switch sides on its former Angolan client in order to enable an "old-fashioned" routing.[42]

Especially clear in Friedman's dealings with the Arab/Muslim world is the idea that, just because America is "not always at our best in how we act toward the world"[43]—which he intermittently admits without delving into the details of murderous campaigns in southeast Asia, Latin America, and elsewhere—this should not have a sustained negative impact on its global image or arouse undue suspicion about its present motives. Consider Friedman's acknowledgement prior to the start of the war on Iraq that only after 9/11 "did the U.S. begin to call for democracy in the Arab world—but only to get rid of Yasir Arafat and to punish those Arab regimes it did not like, namely Saddam Hussein's."[44] Six months later and five months into the Iraq war, the global superpower is fully rehabilitated into democratic conscientiousness with Friedman's announcement that "Iraqis and other Arabs are now being treated to something radically new: our ideas, the revolutionary side of American power."[45]

Given that the radical new treat is *still* only being used to punish the regime of Saddam Hussein, and that it is being delivered via illegal military attack on a sovereign nation,[46] the "many leftists" Friedman subsequently accuses of not understanding the war for democracy may be forgiven for their confusion.[47] Baathists and Arab dictators, on the other hand, have somehow managed to correctly interpret America's spontaneous revolutionary transformation, and Friedman informs us that "they understand that U.S. power is not being used in Iraq for oil, or imperialism, or to shore up a corrupt status quo," and that is instead "the most radical-liberal revolutionary war the U.S. has ever launched."[48]

Friedman himself, of course, states this very same year that the war is "partly for oil."[49] The previous year, he also incidentally explains that the "rage" that caused 9/11 "is due in part to anger at U.S. support for anything Israel does" and in part to "the way too many Arab regimes, backed by America, have kept their young people without a voice or the tools to succeed in the modern world."[50] Friedman's ability to leap from such admissions into claiming that an effective way of radically, liberally, and revolutionarily combating the regional "terrorism bubble" is to make the citizens of a regime *not* backed by America "Suck. On. This" is merely a testament to the advantages of having a news job in which one is not required to maintain a coherent discourse.

The advantages are further underscored in 2010 when Friedman concludes that the "short answer" for why the United States invaded Iraq and Afghanistan in response to 9/11 "is because Pakistan has nukes that we fear and Saudi Arabia has oil that we crave."[51] That Friedman is never forced to formally retract or even informally amend indisputably offensive and racist statements meanwhile permits him to divert attention from the role of Israel in generating regional rage by accusing the Palestinians of "a collective madness."[52]

Friedman's reaction to 9/11 merits examination, as it is this event that propels his condescension vis-à-vis Arabs and Muslims to new heights and further convinces him of his own pedagogical role in the world. This conviction is highlighted in its earlier, less overtly bellicose stages by Edward Said, who notes in his 1989 essay "The Orientalist Express" that "Friedman has internalized the norms, if not the powers, of the secretary of state not just of the United States, but of all humanity" in *From Beirut to Jerusalem*, and that, with an air of "unearned egoism," he "offers advice to everyone about how much better they could be doing if they paid attention to him."[53]

The details of Friedman's 9/11 experience are found in the "Diary" section of *Longitudes and Attitudes*. He learns of the attacks while in the Tel Aviv suburbs, where he is in the process of retrieving his bathing suit from his taxicab after conducting an interview with Tel Aviv University President Itamar Rabinovich. Returning to Rabinovich's office, Friedman watches CNN footage for several hours with female university staff, who "kept asking what it would mean for Israel. 'I don't know,' I snapped. 'It's World War III,' I thought to myself. 'It's much bigger than Israel.'"[54]

It would appear from the paragraphs that follow, however, that World War III is in fact not much bigger than Friedman himself. Feeling "suffocated," Friedman leaves the office, procures a room at the beachfront Tel Aviv Hilton, refuses his friends' invitation to dinner, and ultimately goes into labor during a late-night walk by the sea: "It was there, massaged by the Mediterranean breeze, that my head started to clear and I finally gave birth to the thought that had been bothering me most: 'What kind of world are my two girls going to grow up in?'"[55]

Friedman identifies this as the point at which "I first started to get angry."[56] The anger progresses into "outrage" when his daughter Orly's county youth orchestra trip to Italy is cancelled on account of 9/11 after she had "practice[d] extra-hard all summer in order to retain her chair in the violin section."[57] Obstacles are then erected to his daughter Natalie's class trip to New York, while Friedman battles the "new world knocking" by "insist[ing] on going to concerts and Baltimore Orioles games[,] chaf[ing] at the extra searches suddenly imposed at Camden Yards [baseball stadium], and [getting] enraged while standing in long security lines at Dulles Airport."[58] None of this prevents him from hyping an impending war of civilizations,[59] or from later criticizing Bush for simultaneously discussing the Iraq threat and playing golf[60]—despite Friedman's recent publication of ten reasons the Golf Channel is preferable to Middle East news,[61] and his announcement that "the only survival purchase I've made since Code Orange is a new set of Ben Hogan Apex irons."[62]

This is a good place to point out just how convenient is Friedman's failure to unambiguously address or unreservedly condemn the "very stupid and bad things [the U.S. has done] over the years in just about every corner of the world,"[63] for which he compensates with statements ranging from "Without a strong America holding the world together, and doing the right thing more often than not, the world really would be a Hobbesian jungle"[64] to "America, at its best, is not just a country. It's a spiritual value and role model."[65] Slightly more colorful examples of U.S. influence occur in *The Lexus*: "The Malaysians go to Kentucky Fried Chicken and the Qataris go to Taco Bell for the same reason Americans go to Universal Studios—to see the source of their fantasies."[66]

By glossing over the recent history of the United States, a country aptly characterized by Martin Luther King, Jr. as "the greatest purveyor of violence in the world,"[67] Friedman is able to declare that "the U.S. is not a predatory power"[68] and to propose that Barack Obama share the 2009 Nobel Peace Prize with "the most important peacekeepers in the world for the last century— the men and women of the U.S. Army, Navy, Air Force and Marine Corps."[69] In the hypothetical acceptance speech to the Nobel committee that he drafts for Obama, Friedman does not list as one of the century's notable peacekeeping efforts the secret unleashing of the equivalent of five Hiroshimas on neutral Cambodia in the 1970s,[70] although he does cite present U.S. operations in Iraq and Afghanistan despite, for example, massive civilian casualties and continued attacks by U.S. helicopter gunships on Afghan children gathering wood.[71]

It is presumably thanks in part to contextual amputation that Friedman is able to avoid pondering how "outraged" he would feel if Orly and Natalie, as opposed to having their travels to Europe and New York temporarily curtailed by security concerns, were instead obliterated by an airborne component of the U.S. military or its adopted Israeli counterpart. He meanwhile acknowledges that his anger over 9/11, "to be honest … wasn't only about my kids," but rather about the violation of the idea that "no matter how crazy the world was out there, America was my cocoon that I could always crawl back into."[72] As for populations that dare not desire their own cocoons, it is useful to mention such statistics as that over seven hundred Pakistani civilians were killed in 2009 alone by U.S. drone strikes[73], which Friedman has previously proclaimed are "sometimes … the only way justice gets done."[74]

Given that Friedman inhabits a political and journalistic circle in which the denomination "bad guys"[75] is deemed a valid component of wartime discourse, it is logical that the term "civilians" may at times be found to be unnecessarily specific. However, Arab and Muslim civilian casualties generally have a higher chance of being advertised as such if their demise has been wrought by other Arabs and Muslims, especially if the wringing can be invoked to prove that "a death cult has taken root in the bosom" of Islam and that "this cancer is erasing basic norms of civilization."[76] The monopoly that Friedman and his ilk enjoy over derivatives of the Latin root "civ" means that he is not required to explain how it is that events like the Israeli slaughter of Palestinian civilians in Jenin in 2002—which Friedman quite literally encourages[77]—does not infringe on civilizational norms.

Instead, he uses a post-Jenin dispatch to argue that, because a book by a Chinese mother about how to get your child into Harvard has sold more than 1.1 million copies in China while the "normally intelligent" Saudi ambassador to the U.K. has merely published a poem praising an eighteen-year-old female Palestinian suicide bomber, China "will eventually build Harvards of its own," while Saudi "priorities will be too messed up."[78] Where Tiananmen Square lies on the continuum of civilization is not addressed.

Friedman's classification of Al Qaeda as "enemies of civilization" in an article in 2001 meanwhile enables him to defend the selective curtailment of civil liberties in the United States: "Attorney General John Ashcroft is not completely crazy in his impulse to adopt unprecedented, draconian measures and military courts to deal with suspected terrorists."[79] Friedman does not appear to detect any sort of irony in denouncing terrorist flaunting of the American legal system while he himself is engaged in deliberate fear-mongering on behalf of the subversion of justice: "Let's not forget what was surely the smile on those hijackers' faces as they gunned the engines on our passenger planes to kill as many Americans as possible in the World Trade Center. Let's not forget what they would do had they had access to even bigger weapons. And let's not forget how long they lived among us and how little they absorbed—how they went to their deaths believing that American laws were only something to be eluded."[80]

That it is not always easy to tell who is and is not a civilian is clear from Friedman's assessment at the start of the U.S. war on terror:

> Think of all the nonsense written in the press—particularly the European and Arab media—about the concern for "civilian casualties" in Afghanistan. It turns out many of those Afghan "civilians" were praying for another dose of B-52's to liberate them from the Taliban, casualties or not.[81]

By allegedly sanctioning their own immolation, then, Afghan civilians earn the right to appear in quotation marks. (What they might be in unpunctuated form is debatable. Martyrs, perhaps?) Our columnist does not explain how he has obtained this particular insight into Afghan prayers, although seasoned readers might expect him to credit Middle East expert—and Friedman's designated "soul brother"—Stephen P. Cohen,[82] or else to excerpt a lengthy passage translated by "the invaluable MEMRI research service,"[83] the Zionist propaganda arm[84] upon which Friedman relies for quotes from enlightened Arab and Muslim scholars confirming Arab and Muslim defects. In the end Friedman cites both Cohen and MEMRI, but not in reference to the prayers; Cohen remarks on Friedman's insistence on a war of ideas in the Arab/Muslim world, and MEMRI translates a "remarkable essay" by a Kuwaiti professor, according to which Arab Muslims are variously masters of terrorism, the ignorant and intolerant laughingstock of the world, and the recipients of the following "clear" message from the West: "mend your ways or else."[85]

Friedman's incessant repetition of the mantra that "people do not change when you tell them they should, but when they tell themselves they must," occasionally attributed to his "intellectual soul mate" Michael Mandelbaum[86], has not inhibited the steady issuance of his own personal threats to the Arab/Muslim world. These range from anti–suicide terrorism lectures such as "No matter how bad, your life is sacred"[87]—although apparently less so when on the receiving end of prayer-answering B-52s—to the pronouncement in 2005 that, unless the "moral vacuum in the Sunni Arab world" is rectified and Iraqi Sunnis cease engaging in ethnic cleansing, an unsurprising result of the U.S. invasion,[88] the United States "should arm the Shiites and Kurds and leave the Sunnis of Iraq to reap the wind."[89]

The latter threat, accompanied by the assessment that "maybe this neighborhood is just beyond transformation,"[90] occurs a mere two and a half years into Friedman's war for democracy, which he has repeatedly warned will be an extremely long and difficult process.[91] In keeping with his optimistic nature, however—which, Friedman tells us, has been attributed by Israeli general Uzi Dayan to his diminutive stature and the fact that he can "only see that part of the glass that's half full"[92]—Friedman strives to maintain an upbeat outlook in the face of mounting evidence of Arab failure to internalize the proper aspirations, and lauds Iraqi exposure to the "melting pot of U.S. soldiers" whose "million acts of kindness and ... profound example of how much people of different backgrounds can accomplish when they work together" are deemed to more than compensate for crimes of torture and Abu Ghraib.[93] As late as 2010, Friedman defends the smashing of the country on the grounds that "Bush's gut instinct that this region craved and needed democracy was always right," and that democracy simply "was never going to have a virgin birth in a place like Iraq."[94]

As is clear from U.S. Secretary of State Condoleezza Rice's suggestion in July 2006 that the current Israeli bombardment of Lebanon constitutes "the birth pangs of a new Middle East",[95] Western envoys to the region are often under the impression that, despite a presumed history of Arab animosity to democracy, democratic orientation can be forged with the right amount of fire power, civilian casualties, and references to the birthing process. Gestational irregularities arising from such assumptions, however, are observable in Friedman's discovery, shortly after Rice's detection of Middle Eastern birth pangs, that "we are not midwifing democracy in Iraq. We are baby-sitting a civil war."[96]

Friedman's intermittent reliance on infant terminology to analyze parts of the Arab/Muslim world, which reaches unprecedented levels in 2009 when Friedman refers to Afghanistan as "a special needs baby" that the United States has decided to adopt,[97] is merely one manifestation of a tradition of unabashed Orientalism that discredits Arabs and Muslims as agents capable of managing their own destinies and sets up a power scheme in which the United States and its military simultaneously occupy the positions of killer/torturer, liberator, educator, and parent/babysitter. Friedman, the self-appointed overseer of the relationship, is tasked with interpreting the intricacies of Arab and Muslim populations for uninitiated observers and reducing over 20 percent of humanity and fifty-seven distinct countries to a more readily digestible "Other."

It could be argued that Friedman's credentials for such a position date back to his first trip to Israel at age fifteen, described in *From Beirut*, during which he discovers the relative ease with which historical claims to Jerusalem can be established:

Indeed, from the first day I walked through the walled Old City of Jerusalem, inhaled its spices, and lost myself in the multicolored river of humanity that flowed through its maze of alleyways, I felt at home. Surely in some previous incarnation, I must have been a bazaar merchant, a Frankish soldier perhaps, a pasha, or at least a medieval Jewish chronicler. It may have been my first trip abroad, but in 1968 I knew then and there that I was really more Middle East than Minnesota.[98]

Armed with his appropriated identity, the teenage Friedman returns to the United States, where his high school experience proceeds to consist, "I am now embarrassed to say, [of] one big celebration of Israel's victory in the Six-Day War," and where "I became so knowledgeable about the military geography of the Middle East that when my high-school geography class had a teaching intern from the University of Minnesota for a month, he got so tired of my correcting him that he asked me to give the talk about the Golan Heights and the Sinai Peninsula while he sat at my desk."[99] In 1972 Friedman expands his scope of expertise by visiting Cairo, which was "crowded, filthy, exotic, impossible—and I loved it … I even loved my [golf] caddy at the Gezira Sporting Club."[100]

In the decades prior to 9/11, Friedman exhibits a subtle tendency toward ethnic stereotyping of Arabs and Muslims, visible in references to "buxom, Cleopatra-eyed Lebanese girls" who cause Israeli soldiers to realize during their invasion of Lebanon in 1982 that "this was not the Sinai, filled with cross-eyed Bedouins and shoeless Egyptian soldiers."[101] Consider also the choice of demeaning language in, for example, Friedman's depiction in *From Beirut* of the "wild-eyed Muslim sheik" he encounters in the company of Lebanese Prime Minister Saeb Salam.[102] According to Friedman, when Salam informs the sheikh that Friedman has won a Pulitzer Prize, speaks Arabic, and is Jewish, "this poor little sheik's eyes bulged out. I thought his beard might fall off … After a limp handshake he scurried out the door."[103]

As for the lexicon of popular images aside from Cleopatra to which the Middle East is often reduced, Friedman draws from this in later years to produce such assessments as that "the willingness of some Egyptians to demand to run against Hosni Mubarak when he seeks a fifth—unopposed—term" is the equivalent, in terms of unusualness, of "watching camels fly."[104] The assessment that Iran's Mahmoud Ahmadinejad is "nothing more than a shah with a turban" meanwhile highlights once again the potential advantages to assigning more than a copy editor to Friedman, or to alerting the existing copy editor to the fact that Ahmadinejad does not wear a headpiece.[105]

Edward Said has challenged Friedman's superimposition of desert scenery onto the contemporary Middle East in his explanation of the Hama massacre of 1982, which Friedman attributes in part to the notion that Syrian President Hafez al-Assad viewed the Sunnis of Hama as "members of an alien tribe—strangers in the desert—who were trying to take his turkey," something we are told happens in Bedouin legends.[106] Said comments:

> So astonishing a jump, from modern, predominantly urban Syria to the prehistoric desert, is of course the purest Orientalism, and is of a piece with the moronic and hopelessly false dictum offered later in the book that the Arab political tradition has produced only two types: the merchant and the messiah.[107]

It should be noted, however, that Said's original conception of Orientalism as Eurocentric prejudice must be amended slightly in Friedman's case to incorporate his generalizations about Europeans themselves,[108] collectively denounced as "Eurowimps"[109] when they do not exhibit sufficient enthusiasm for U.S. military endeavors against Arabo-Islamic peoples. Friedman alternately cajoles particularly intransigent language groups with persuasive slogans like "Ich bin ein New Yorker,"[110] advocates removing France from the U.N. Security Council because, "as they say in kindergarten, [it] does not play well with others,"[111] and warns Spain that a withdrawal from Iraq in the aftermath of the Madrid bombings of 2004 is a potential modern-day equivalent of the European appeasement of Adolf Hitler.[112]

The Arab merchant/messiah dichotomy criticized by Said meanwhile expands in complexity with Friedman's detection in the 1990s of the latest, most immediate threat to America and the world, the "Super-Empowered Angry Man," who is both angry at American hegemony and empowered by globalization and technology to wreak large-scale havoc in response.[113] The Super-

Empowered Angry Man is not bound by ethnic specifications, although it quickly becomes apparent that his most probable incarnation is as an Arab Muslim, and in 2000 Friedman offers the example of Osama bin Laden, said to be the proprietor of a "sort of Jihad Online (JOL)."[114]

Friedman occasionally drops roundabout hints as to the role of the United States in the creation of such networks, such as "It seems likely that some of the Saudi hijackers first came in contact with Al Qaeda and went through Terrorism 101 when they signed up for the jihad in Afghanistan against the Soviets,"[115] or his note in *The World Is Flat* that, once bin Laden and his jihadi companions had forced the Soviet Union out of Afghanistan in 1989 "(with some help from U.S. and Pakistani forces) … bin Laden looked around and found that the other superpower, the United States, had a huge presence in his own native land, Saudi Arabia, the home of the two holiest cities in Islam. And he did not like it."[116] In 2010, meanwhile, Friedman admits that:

> the Middle East we are dealing with today is the product of long-term trends dating back to 1979. And have no illusions, we propelled those trends. America looked the other way when Saudi Arabia Wahabi-fied itself. Ronald Reagan glorified the Afghan mujahedeen and the Europeans hailed the Khomeini revolution in Iran as a "liberation" event.[117]

Of course, not only did the United States fund, train, and equip the mujahedeen to fight the Soviets in Afghanistan,[118] the Pentagon was also instrumental in transporting thousands of Islamic fighters to Bosnia in the 1990s to aid the Bosnian Muslims in the war against the Serbs, once again sanctioning the notion of intercontinental jihad.[119] However, Friedman's rare acknowledgement that Al Qaeda and similar phenomena might have logical and readily detectable foundations in U.S. foreign policy choices is decisively overwhelmed by his predilection for identifying endemic Arab/Muslim deficiencies.

Consider, for example, his explanation in *Longitudes* of the "cognitive dissonance" among young Muslim males in Europe "that is the original spark for all their rage."[120] Undeterred by the fact that he possesses no qualifications in any of the behavioral sciences, Friedman packages his faux expertise in language easily comprehensible to the average computer-savvy Westerner:

> They [the cognitively dissonant Muslims] must be saying to them-selves: If Islam is God 3.0 and Christianity is God 2.0 and Judaism is God 1.0, how could it be that those living in countries dominated by God 2.0 and God 1.0 are, on average, doing so much better—politically, economically, and educationally—than those living in countries practicing God 3.0?[121]

According to Friedman, young Islamists answer their own question by assigning blame to Europe, the United States, and Israel, while refusing to understand that "much of Christianity is really God 2.0.1—it is the updated version that has gone through the Enlightenment. The same goes for much of Judaism, which is actu-ally God 1.0.1. Islam would benefit so much from a reformation of its own, a version of God 3.0.1," which would permit the faith to "embrace modernity."[122] Evidence of Islam's incompatibility with the modern world ranges from a lack of separation of mosque and state to a "minority" of Saudi preachers who invoke Qur'anic verses to justify 9/11, while Friedman claims that "there was no Christian or Jewish terrorist leader I knew of who was citing … references [to Christian and Jewish holy books] as justification for going and killing non-Jews or non-Christians."[123] That Friedman continues to attribute George W. Bush's murderous military campaigns to "moral clarity"[124] suggests that the church/state separation is not fundamentally threatened when god instructs U.S. presidents to go to war against mainly non-Jews and non-Christians.[125] The relentless invocation of the Bible by Jewish leaders and Christian Zionists to justify ethnic cleansing of Palestinians meanwhile underscores the relatively lenient Enlightenment standards to which Gods 1.0 and 2.0 are held.

The Islamic "struggle with modernity" temporarily becomes the sole dominion of Sunni Muslims in 2005, when Friedman relates the following quandary in an article:

> There are a lot of angry people in the world. Angry Mexicans. Angry Africans. Angry Norwegians. But the only ones who seem to feel entitled and motivated to kill themselves and totally innocent people, including other Muslims, over their anger are young Sunni radicals. What is going on?[126]

Friedman's sectarian selectiveness in this case is presumably due in large part to the current failure of Iraqi Sunnis to cooperate with Friedman's various decrees, among them: "You cannot imagine how much distress there is among certain Arab elites that the people of Iraq preferred liberation by America to more defiance [of the West] under Saddam."[127] One simple answer to the question of "What is going on?" might incorporate the fact that the United States has not, in the past two years, engaged in a full-fledged military occupation of Mexico, Africa, or Norway while simultaneously spawning a civil war. As for Friedman's portrayal of suicide bombing as a distinct characteristic of "Sunni Islamic civilization"—a result of young Sunnis being "on the one hand, tempted by Western society, and ashamed of being tempted" and "on the other hand ... humiliated by Western society" and the superior "spirit of innovation" fostered by Christianity, Judaism, and Hinduism (which has debuted as God 0.0[128])—ambidextrous Sunni humiliation is merely the latest manifestation of Friedman's failure to keep abreast of his own views on certain issues.[129]

Consider his pronouncement three years earlier, in March of 2002, according to which "every day for the past six months, Palestinian men and women—many of them secular, not religious [i.e., not Sunni]—have strapped dynamite around their waists and blown themselves up against Israeli targets."[130] The following week, Friedman declares a threat to the security of "all of civilization ... because Palestinians are testing out a whole new form of warfare, using suicide bombers ... to achieve their political aims," and denounces as "a huge lie" the argument that Palestinian suicide bombing is an effect of "desperation" under the Israeli occupation, since "a lot of other people in the world are desperate, yet they have not gone around strapping dynamite to themselves."[131]

A little over four months later, in August of 2002, Friedman surfaces in Sri Lanka with the following lede: "It's often forgotten that while suicide bombing started in the Middle East, the people who perfected suicide as a weapon of war were the Tamil Tigers militia."[132] It thus appears that suicide bombing is not in fact a "whole new form of warfare" and that Palestinians are not the only ones blowing themselves up, although Friedman still fails to mention other relevant precedents, such as suicide attacks conducted against the Israeli occupation in Lebanon prior to Israel's withdrawal. It also bears emphasizing that neither the Tamil Tigers, the Lebanese suicide bombers of Shia, Christian, and Communist background, or the Japanese kamikaze pilots of World War II were Sunni.

Regarding the "huge lie" that desperation has led Palestinians to strap dynamite to themselves, Friedman meanwhile backtracks into acknowledging in 2004 that "I don't buy it myself, but one can plausibly argue that 37 years of Israeli occupation of the West Bank have made Palestinians so crazy that scores of them would have volunteered for suicide bombing missions over the last few years."[133] Another rare reference to possible causality occurs in 1997: "The reason Israel's security chiefs warned Mr. Netanyahu that his [settlement building] in Jerusalem could trigger violence was because they understood that the Palestinians, having no other means to stop Israeli bulldozers, would resort to terrorism."[134]

As University of Chicago professor Robert Pape points out in an interview, published in *The American Conservative* three days after Friedman poses the question of why young Sunni males are "so willing to blow up themselves and others in the name of their religion":

> The central fact is that overwhelmingly suicide-terrorist attacks are not driven by religion as much as they are by a clear strategic objective: to compel modern democracies to withdraw military forces from the territory that the terrorists view as their homeland. From Lebanon to Sri Lanka to Chechnya to Kashmir to the West Bank, every major suicide-terrorist campaign—over 95 percent of all the incidents—has had as its central objective to compel a democratic state to withdraw.[135]

Pape is speaking in the interview about his book *Dying to Win: The Strategic Logic of Suicide Terrorism*, which—interestingly enough—appears on the recommended reading list that Friedman composes on his short-lived *New York Times* blog in 2005 (though he does specify that the list is composed of "books that I have read, read about or read parts of").[136] Pape's reminder that, prior to the U.S. invasion, "Iraq never had a suicide-terrorist attack in its history. Never"[137] goes unheeded by Friedman, who prefers to rely on the analysis of his biographer/translator friend Raymond Stock, "a long-time resident of Cairo," who informs Friedman that Sunni suicide attacks in general are "the modern incarnation of several deeply rooted and interlocking wars" dating back to the seventh century.[138] The prudence of Friedman's decision to temporarily exempt the Shia faith from the "struggle with modernity" is meanwhile called into question when he subsequently discovers that the "cold war" between the United States and Iran is "the real umbrella story in the Middle East today—the struggle for influence across the region, with America and its Sunni Arab allies (and Israel) versus Iran, Syria and their non-state allies, Hamas and Hezbollah."[139]

The Orientalist tendency to anchor Oriental subjects in antiquity, where they remain in perpetual need of civilization by the West and its militaries, is viewable time and again in Friedman's discourse—from his outright insistence that Arabs and Muslims are "backward"[140] and intent on maintaining a situation in which "the past buries the future,"[141] to his more refined anthropological assessments, such as one made during his foray into Umm Qasr, Iraq, a month following the 2003 invasion: "It would be idiotic to even ask Iraqis here how they felt about politics. They are in a pre-political, primordial state of nature."[142] Shaping the Iraqi primordial mush proves a daunting task for the United States, despite various assistance from Friedman, ranging from his encouragement of national cohesion via articles like "Are There Any Iraqis in Iraq?" (answer: there is an Iraqi silent majority, but it is being outperformed by the Iraqi Khmer Rouge posing as the Iraqi Viet Cong[143]), to advice regarding treatment of elected Iraqi leaders: "We should lock them in a room and not let them out until they either produce a national unity government, so Americans will want to stay in Iraq, or fail to produce that government, which would signal that it's time to warm up the bus."[144]

In 2010 Friedman once again brings up the "simple but gnawing question" that has yet to be resolved concerning Iraq's prewar incarnation: "Was Iraq the way Iraq was (a dictatorship) because Saddam was the way Saddam was, or was Saddam the way Saddam was because Iraq was the way Iraq was ... incapable of self-rule and only governable by an iron fist?"[145] The disingenuous irony of championing a war-based "democracy experiment in the Arab-Muslim world"[146] when one admits to not knowing whether the *demos* on the receiving end of the war is interested in the sort of democracy that one intends to install is even better highlighted in Friedman's previous explanation that, "unlike in Eastern Europe [in the late 1980s]—where a democratic majority was already present and crying to get out, and all we needed to do was remove the wall—in Iraq we first need to create that democratic majority."[147] As for the limits that govern disingenuous experiments in democracy, Friedman hints at these with such statements as "While we would like an Iraqi national movement—binding Shiites, Kurds and Sunnis—to coalesce, we don't want it coalescing in opposition to us."[148]

An examination of Friedman's treatment of the subject of women in the Arab/Muslim world is meanwhile integral to any study of his *mission civilisatrice*, given that he invokes reasons such as that Mideast rulers "keep their women backward"[149] to justify U.S.-guided regional rectification. Friedman provides confirmation of the righteousness of his mission in *Longitudes*, where he excerpts a personal email received from a young Saudi female in 2002: "I dream of having all my rights as a human being. Saudi women need your pen, Mr. Friedman."[150]

Leaving aside for the moment the fact that Friedman's pen is during this very same time period also known for producing such statements as "I don't want to see the Saudi regime destabilized"[151]—and that it goes as far as to include the homeland of bin Laden and fifteen of the 9/11 hijackers in "The World of Order" alongside the West and other esteemed company[152]—let us review some of the interventions on behalf of Arab/Muslim females by Friedman's writing utensil. These include an article from 1999 in which we are told that, although the first two Arabic sentences Friedman learned in college were "The Nile River is the biggest and longest river in the world" and "Women are half the nation," only one of these "is actually believed in today's Arab world," as opposed to Singapore where "Miss Internet Singapore" has just been chosen "on the basis of how well she could design a Web page."[153]

In *Longitudes*, meanwhile, Friedman comments in reference to the jeans-clad Saudi passenger seated next to him on a British Airways[154] flight to Riyadh: "What a waste! What a waste that such a lovely woman had to be covered," but promptly announces on the following page his belief that, even if the veil were no longer mandatory in Saudi Arabia, a lot of women, "particularly [those] age thirty and older," would continue to wear it: "It is not an Islamic thing—there is nothing in the Koran that dictates that women have to be veiled—it is a cultural thing, a conservative desert Bedouin thing."[155] The fundamentally inferior and archaic nature of certain cultures is underscored in the very next paragraph when Friedman describes his visit to a Riyadh hospital where he observes an elderly heart attack victim: "She had the oxygen mask covering her mouth and then had put her black face veil over the oxygen mask. It was scary even to look at, and struck me as almost medieval."[156]

Oddly, some of the most Orientalist gender-related musings captured by Friedman's pen occur in his alleged tour de force on environmentalism. Eighty-two pages into *Hot, Flat, and Crowded*, Friedman asserts that the most important geopolitical trend to emerge from the "onset of the Energy-Climate Era"[157]—defined as the historical epoch that is being "giv[en] birth to" by the "convergence of global warming, global flattening, and global crowding"[158]—may be a "shift in the center of gravity of Islam—away from a Cairo-Istanbul-Casablanca-Damascus urban/Mediterranean center ... toward a Salafi Saudi/desert-centered Islam, which [is] much more puritanical, restrictive toward women, and hostile to other faiths."[159] It appears that the Mediterranean-vs.-desert reduction—which fails to account for a host of landscapes, such as the world's most populous Muslim nation, Indonesia, and vast deserts in the proximity of Cairo, Casablanca, and Damascus—may have been appropriated from the little-known "writer William G. Ridgeway, who penned a thoughtful and provocative series of 'Letters from Arabia'" containing the idea of a struggle between "Desert Islam" and "Urban Islam," which Friedman mentions only after he has passed the topographical dichotomy off as fact.[160] Of no concern, evidently, is that Shia Islam, and specifically Tehran, which Friedman casts as America's primary regional adversary, does not factor into either Egyptian-Turkish-Moroccan-Syrian or Saudi centers of gravity.

A glance at Ridgeway's "Letters from Arabia" reveals possible reasons he has won the sympathy of Friedman, such as a shared conviction that Arabs can be referred to generally as "Ahmed" as well as a propensity for ethno-technological generalizations. (Consider two consecutive sentences from Ridgeway's first "letter" in 2004: "Ahmed is a whiz. Arabians have rapidly evolved into CyberArabs, and they love it."[161]) As for the thoughtful and provocative contents of the particular letter that is referenced by Friedman—the title of which he does not share: "Those Drunken, Whoring Saudis: Desert Islam's Problem with Women"—these include the assertion that the Saudis were "previously an insignificant mob of goat-herders and woman-beaters" before acquiring "delusions of grandeur" from the combined hosting of oil reserves and Mecca, which enabled them to set their sights on becoming "the most important women-beating goat-herders in the world."[162]

Friedman quotes selectively from the article, such that the women-beating goat-herders are lost in the ellipsis he inserts to take the place of approximately eleven paragraphs of Ridgeway's report.[163] The ellipsis, which also encompasses Ridgeway's complaint about the lack of an "Arab version of [British actress] Barbara Windsor, who should be recognised and celebrated as an icon of women's progress,"[164] ends just prior to the observation that "Desert Islam has taken the spice and color out of Arab life."[165] Friedman reproduces Ridgeway's claim that "perhaps the best symbol of all that has been lost is the coquettish, slightly tipsy Arab woman so beloved of old Arab comedies [whom Ridgeway has explained during the ellipsis was scantily clad, sometimes 'sexy and even lewd']. Then she was laughed at. Now she would be stoned to death."[166]

Friedman sees no need to question the suggestion that a comically flirtatious, sometimes lewd, one-dimensional female caricature is the best indication of a modernized, liberal Middle Eastern state. In fact, starting on the very same page of *Hot, Flat, and Crowded* that features Ridgeway's coquettish Arab woman, Friedman provides the full text of a 2008 *Newsweek* article that also implies a connection between modernity and displays of female sexuality. The piece is said to make "clear" the Egyptian inability to counteract the influence of the wealthy financiers of de-modernizing Desert Islam, and discusses how "Abir Sabri, celebrated for her alabaster skin, ebony hair, pouting lips and full figure, used to star in racy Egyptian TV shows and movies" but is now "performing on Saudi-owned religious TV channels, with her face covered, chanting verses from the Qur'an."[167]

Of course, the point of taking issue with Friedman's reproduction of such characterizations is not to argue that women must indeed be told what they can and cannot do with their bodies. Rather, it is to demonstrate that, beneath a veil of egalitarian discourse and calls for Arab/Muslim female empowerment, Friedman manages in such cases to perpetuate a view of women as objects to be celebrated, as opposed to thinking subjects.[168] As for Friedman's representation of non-Oriental females in the U.S. military—specifically those implicated in the aforementioned door-to-door delivery of the "Suck. On. This" message from Basra to Baghdad, as well as the female F-15 bombardier and the blond guard at Bagram Air Base discussed in the previous section[169]—this is one component of Friedman's Orientalist policy of discrediting the Arab/Muslim world via humiliation.

With the dedication of someone who is endeavoring to forge reality through repetition, Friedman regularly declares Arabs and Muslims humiliated. Evidence abounds, such as the aforementioned existential neurosis plaguing God 3.0[170] and the fact that an "American diplomat in Saudi Arabia" has explained to Friedman that "there are many Arabs ... who are 'frustrated and feeling inferior.' They 'have a lot of pent-up emotions.'"[171] During a discussion with Joseph Stiglitz in 2006, Friedman contends that Arab/Muslim frustration, which is a "big part" of why "we" have problems with them, is a result of the fact that "when the world is flat you get your humiliation fiber optically. You get your humiliation at 100 megabytes per second ... [and] you can see just where the caravan is and just how far behind you are really clearly."[172] Given that mediator Ted Koppel then interrupts Friedman mid-sentence with a reminder about the "paucity of inventions" in the Arab world, we never find out who exactly the "they" is in Friedman's following thought: "The word they use most often is humiliation—"[173]

One possibility, however, turns up in *The World Is Flat*, when Friedman invites readers to "talk to young Arabs and Muslims anywhere, and this cognitive dissonance and the word 'humiliation' always come up very quickly in conversation."[174] I, for one, cannot recall having the word "humiliation" come up in the past decade of conversations with young Arabs and Muslims, but perhaps I haven't been in the right "anywhere." It meanwhile appears from Friedman's failure to provide any conversational examples that the "they" might actually consist of former Malaysian Prime Minister Mahathir Mohammed, who Friedman reports used the term "humiliated" five times in reference to Islamic civilization during his farewell speech in 2003.[175]

A perusal of Mahathir's speech reveals that the word "humiliated" only occurs in tandem with the word "oppressed," which indicates that he views humiliation as something inflicted rather than as an essentially intrinsic Muslim quality.[176] Given that Friedman's concern for the contents of the speech does not extend beyond the authentic confirmation of Muslim humiliation it provides, Mahathir's remarks on the causes of humiliation are ignored, among them: "None of our countries are truly independent. We are under pressure to conform to our oppressors' wishes about how we should behave, how we should govern our lands, how we should think even."[177] Instead, Friedman declares the American Civil War a relevant model for the region and concludes that only the following scenario will resolve Arab/Muslim feelings of disempowerment: "The best thing outsiders can do for the Arab-Muslim world today is try to collaborate with its progressive forces in every way possible ... so as to foster a similar war of ideas within their civilization."[178]

That this fairly blatant authorization of imperial warmongering in the name of dispelling humiliation occurs in a book first published two years into the Iraq war is somewhat difficult to reconcile with Friedman's own assertion that "one of the first things I realized when visiting Iraq after the U.S. invasion was that the very fact that Iraqis did not liberate themselves, but had to be liberated by Americans, was a source of humiliation to them."[179] Even more confounding is that, in a 2004 series on the *Slate* website entitled "Liberal Hawks Reconsider the Iraq War," Friedman claims, despite having already visited post-invasion Iraq, that "the right reason for this war was to partner with Arab moderates in a long-term strategy of dehumiliation and redignification."[180] The focus of the strategy, we are reminded, was to be the implementation of the Arab Human Development Report of 2002, which "said the Arab world is falling off the globe because of a lack of freedom, women's empowerment, and modern education."[181]

Published by the U.N. Development Program, the Arab Human Development Report has been enthusiastically promoted by Friedman based on his perception that its authentic Arab authors expose "the reasons for Arabs' backwardness and humiliation"[182] and the details of "the increasingly dysfunctional Arab-Muslim world—which produces way too many terrorists."[183] Again, if one glances at the report itself, one finds a more discerning use of vocabulary, as in the criticism of "deeply rooted shortcomings in Arab institutional structures"; in fact, the only time in 168 pages that the term "humiliation" appears is in Palestinian politician Hanan Ashrawi's statement on how Israeli military checkpoints are "the most brutal expression of a discriminatory and pervasive system of willful humiliation and subjugation."[184]

That Friedman is quite forthcoming at times about the United States' role in maintaining Middle Eastern dictators and monarchs—and thus in effectively sanctioning regional political inertia and popular disenfranchisement—is clear from his warning with regard to the report:

> There is a message in this bottle for America: For too many years we've treated the Arab world as just a big dumb gas station, and as long as the top leader kept the oil flowing, or was nice to Israel, we didn't really care what was happening to the women and children out back.[185]

Given Friedman's institutionalized habit of self-contradiction, however, the United States is spared permanent and irreversible culpability, and Friedman issues the following decree in 2005 in honor of the Asian tsunami: "It is not an exaggeration to say that, if you throw in the Oslo peace process, U.S. foreign policy for the last 15 years has been dominated by an effort to save Muslims—not from tsunamis, but from tyrannies, mostly their own theocratic or autocratic regimes."[186] Obviously, the new theme of a decade and a half of Muslim-saving—accompanied by Friedman's indignant assertions that Americans should not "hold your breath waiting for a thank-you card" in response to tsunami aid and that "the tensions between us and the Muslim world stem primarily from the conditions under which many Muslims live, not what we do"[187]—fails to jibe with Friedman's assessment in 2002 that the anger of Arabs and Muslims is partly due to "U.S. support for anything Israel does"[188] and partly to the fact that "most of them live under antidemocratic regimes backed by America."[189] For additional evidence of the occasionally self-righteous attitude of the U.S. savior, meanwhile, see Friedman's recounting in *Longitudes* of his experience at the Islamabad Marriott in 2001, when a female Lebanese TV journalist criticizes him for "unfair" treatment of Arabs and Muslims and asks if he knows "how much the world hates you"—i.e., America: "At that point I nearly lost it. I snapped back: 'Do you know how much we hate *your* lack of democracy, do you know how much we hate *your* lack of transparency, *your* lack of economic development, the way you treat your women?'"[190] This may be a good time to juxtapose Friedman's reliance on the lack of Arab/Muslim female freedom and empowerment as an indication of backwardness with the findings of a 2011 global survey by the Thomson Reuters Foundation, according to which the incidence of female infanticide and sex trafficking in India have propelled Friedman's vaunted democracy into the top five most dangerous countries for women, alongside Afghanistan, the Democratic Republic of the Congo, Pakistan, and Somalia.[191]

The U.S.-as-savior theme is resurrected in 2009, when U.S. army "Maj. Nidal Malik Hasan, who apparently killed 13 innocent people at Fort Hood" is described as being "just another angry jihadist spurred to action by 'The Narrative'"—Friedman's latest reductionist imposition on the Arab/Muslim world, which posits that "America is dedicated to keeping Muslims down" and ignores the past "two decades in which U.S. foreign policy has been largely dedicated to rescuing Muslims or trying to help free them from tyranny."[192] Of course, no "narrative" is ever deemed necessary to explain such phenomena as the torturers of Abu Ghraib, U.S. army "kill teams" in Afghanistan who slaughter civilians and then pose with the corpses[193], U.S. newspaper columnists who endorse the Israeli mass targeting of civilians in Gaza and Lebanon for pedagogical purposes,[194] or Columbine-style massacres of young Americans by other young Americans, as Friedman prefers to cast Muslim massacres of other Muslims as uniquely horrifying and indicative of civilizational decay. He additionally tempers what criticism he does muster of U.S. atrocities by way of a hypocrisy-displacement technique: "I … know the sort of abuse that went on in Abu Ghraib prison goes on in prisons all over the Arab world every day, as it did under Saddam—without the Arab League or Al Jazeera ever saying a word about it. I know they are shameful hypocrites."[195] In 2011, meanwhile, Friedman resumes peddling his former argument about U.S. contributions to the stifling of democracy: "For the last 50 years, America (and Europe and Asia) have treated the Middle East as if it were just a collection of big gas stations."[196]

Returning to the issue of the Arab Human Development Report, Friedman specifies in 2003 that its "courageous" authors, who have ignited the "war of ideas" demanded by Friedman, "do not believe in the Iraq-war model of political change."[197] This does not stop him from concluding in the very same article that the U.S. "should stop talking about 'terrorism' and W.M.D. and make clear that we're in Iraq for one reason: to help Iraqis implement the Arab Human Development Reports, so the war of ideas can be fought from within."[198] The tendency to override Arab/Muslim opinion and agency is incidentally addressed by Friedman himself in later years when he affirms: "Arab and Muslims are not just objects.

They are subjects. They aspire to, are able to and must be challenged to take responsibility for their world."[199] Again, however, Arab/Muslim subjectivity is called into question in this case by Friedman's condescendingly authoritative tone and his accompanying recap of the "ferocity" of the American Civil War, which ends with the edict: "Islam needs the same civil war."[200]

In an article written in 2005, Friedman applauds the release of the latest Arab Human Development Report "focus[ing] on 'the acute deficit of freedom and good governance' in the Arab world," and explains that the question of why "the modern Arab world [has been] largely immune to the winds of democracy that have blown everywhere else" was for years avoided in the West, in part "because a toxic political correctness infected the academic field of Middle Eastern studies—to such a degree that anyone focusing on the absence of freedom in the Arab world ran the risk of being labeled an 'Orientalist' or an 'essentialist.'"[201] That Western discussion of the Arab world has been hampered in such a way by political correctness is blatantly false, as Friedman undoubtedly knows, given that *From Beirut* features citations of the work of Orientalist icon Bernard Lewis, Princeton University's acclaimed promoter of the notion that Islamic culture is inherently defective.[202] Furthermore, if Friedman would simply rely on the same tactic he uses in 2004 to discern that the Palestinians have no concrete plans to educate their youth—a Google search of the terms "Yasir Arafat" and "Palestine" and "education," in different orders[203]—he would quickly discover that Edward Said himself criticizes the lack of democracy in the Arab world. The difference between Said and Friedman, of course, is that the former does not offer his criticism as a reason for U.S. military attack.[204]

A few months prior to Friedman's warning about stifling political correctness, he announces that Arab states "are all what others have called 'tribes with flags'—not real countries in the Western sense," and that the purpose of the Bush team's "unleash[ing of] the latent civil war" in Iraq is to see whether the various Iraqi tribes can "voluntarily organize themselves[205] around a social contract for democratic life," an experiment Friedman says "was always a shot in the dark—but one that I would argue was morally and strategically worth trying."[206] Because the Iraqi civil war is currently one "in which the murderous insurgents appear to be on the side of ending the U.S. 'occupation of Iraq,'" however, Friedman determines that "we have to have a proper election in Iraq so we can have a proper civil war there"—i.e., one that does not implicate the entity that unleashed it: "The civil war we want is a democratically elected Iraqi government against the Baathist and Islamist militants."[207] Flash forward to 2011 and Friedman displaces the blame for civil war–mongering: "For all of the murderous efforts by Al Qaeda to trigger a full-scale civil war in Iraq, it never happened."[208]

The role of Friedman's Orientalist posture in justifying shots in the dark that produce Iraqi body counts of well over a million cannot be emphasized enough. The staggering human loss inflicted by the United States in Iraq—as well as in Afghanistan and Pakistan and less directly in Lebanon and Palestine—is clearly mitigated by Friedman's consistent dehumanization of the "Other," with Arabs and Muslims variously portrayed as angry,[209] uncivilized,[210] and sexually repressed[211] supporters of bin Laden[212] (despite the existence of encouraging pockets of, for example, "emphatically pro-Western Saudis, who have studied in America, visit regularly, and still root for their favorite American football teams"[213]). Depictions of the Middle East as inherently and inevitably violent meanwhile cause additional contributions of violence to be perceived as nothing out of the ordinary.

Visiting Jordan in the wake of 9/11, Friedman draws the following conclusion after contemplating King Abdullah's decorative handgun collection on the wall of his private study: "All those guns … explained another reason why Jordanians and Arabs were not as shocked by September 11 as Americans: They do not live in Mr. Rogers' neighborhood. They live in Mr. Hobbes's neighborhood."[214] In one of the more striking examples of Friedman's dehumanizing methods, he proceeds to compile a list of "outrageous and terrifying ... things that go on around [neighbor-hood residents] every day," which includes "the '48, '56, '67, '73, and '82 wars" and "Black September (when a Palestinian gunman assassinated a Jordanian prime minister outside the Cairo Sheraton and then knelt down to try to sip his blood)."[215] That this bit of trivia about the behavior of a single Palestinian occurs as the only outrageous and terrifying detail in such a sequence of events—the very catalyst for which lies in what Friedman has reduced to the number "48": the destruction of over 530 Palestinian villages, the killing of approximately 10,000 Palestinians, and the expulsion from Palestine of approximately 750,000 more[216]—underscores the biased nature of Friedman's narrative.

Especially in the post-9/11 world, Friedman has exhibited enormous displeasure about the failure of Muslims to adequately condemn terrorism. In his post-9/11 dispatch entitled "World War III," Friedman posits: "Surely Islam, a grand religion that never perpetrated the sort of Holocaust against the Jews in its midst that Europe did, is being distorted when it is treated as a guidebook for suicide bombing" and asks: "How is it that not a single Muslim leader will say that?"[217] The alleged silence of Muslim leaders is of course called into question by such things as the condemnation of the 9/11 attacks as "barbaric and criminal" by the Organisation of the Islamic Conference, representing fifty-seven countries, the condemnation of the attacks by Iran's Ayatollah Ali Khamenei, and Bush's announcement to Congress that "the terrorists prac-tice a fringe form of Islamic extremism that has been rejected by Muslim scholars and the vast majority of Muslim clerics."[218]

Unconvinced, Friedman continues to demand that Muslims recognize that "the suicidal rage of their fanatics is dragging down their whole civilization,"[219] which is "itself committing suicide."[220] He suggests the Sunni world in particular is lacking a "moral center"[221] and determines that "the Sunni silent majority isn't all that upset when suicide bombers blow up Jews, Christians or Shiite civilians."[222] One can imagine the reaction if a *New York Times* columnist were to imply, for example, that the majority of the world's Jewish population delights in blowing up Arab civilians. Friedman, on the other hand, is permitted to serenely and uninterruptedly peddle his recklessly unfounded interpretations of the thoughts and aspirations of legions of Orientals.

In 2005 Friedman decrees: "Terrorists willing to blow themselves up at funerals and weddings of their own faith are individuals who have become completely disconnected from humanity."[223] Connection to humanity is somehow not threatened when members of the U.S. air force blow up the very same events,[224] nor are Americans ever required to collectively denounce trends exemplified by the 2005 execution of twenty-four unarmed Iraqi civilians, including young children and a seventy-six-year-old wheelchair-bound amputee, by U.S. Marines in the city of Haditha.[225] Friedman's explanation for the executions is that "occupations that drag on inevitably lead to Hadithas,"[226] which does not stop him, two years later during a visit to an American field hospital in Iraq, from issuing the following pompously shallow warning with regard to the "melting pot" that is the U.S. military: "We don't deserve such good people—neither do Iraqis if they continue to hate each other more than they love their own kids."[227]

Meriting further discussion is Friedman's approach to democracy promotion in the Arab/Muslim world, the ostensible goal of the U.S. invasion and occupation of Iraq. Friedman writes in *Longitudes*:

> I would much prefer democratically elected Arab and Muslim leaders we can live with, even if they don't particularly like us, than dictators, autocrats, and kings who profess to like us, but whose people detest us because they view us as sustaining their unjust regimes.[228]

The extent of Friedman's concern for popular discontent is called into question by the fact that, the year of the book's publication, he promotes Pakistani dictator Pervez Musharraf as a regional example and the author of a potential "mind-set-shattering breakthrough for the Muslim world … because for the first time since Sept. 11, a Muslim leader has dared to acknowledge publicly the real problem: that Muslim extremism has been rooted in the educational systems and ruling arrangements of many of their societies, and it has left much of the Muslim world in a backward state."[229] Thus does the Friedman formula for regional progress come to rest in this case on dictators who confirm Muslim backwardness and criticize ruling arrangements of their societies but nonetheless remain dictators.

Musharraf is not the only unelected leader to win the sympathies of Friedman. As previously mentioned, Friedman confesses in 2003 to having "a soft spot for the de facto Saudi ruler" in the same article in which he curiously determines that "the problem with Saudi Arabia is not that it has too little democracy. It's that it has too much."[230] Honors are also bestowed on Jordan's "savvy"[231] and "visionary young King Abdullah,"[232] enabler of the U.S.–Jordan Free Trade Agreement,[233] whose "progressive agenda" and "innovative modernization program" are occasionally thwarted by Arab satellite TV channels conspiring to distract the population from progress by bombarding them with images of Israeli brutality against Palestinians, who themselves "have been experts at seducing the Arab world into postponing its future until all the emotive issues of Palestine are resolved."[234]

Explains Friedman in 2002: "This is the real Arab street story: Progressive Arab states, like Jordan, Morocco and Bahrain, which want to build their legitimacy not on how they confront Israel but on how well they prepare their people for the future, are being impeded."[235] Given that Friedman himself states on more than one occasion that the lack of Arab democracy is due in part to U.S. support for despots and monarchs on the condition that they be "nice to Israel,"[236] it is not clear why he intermittently suggests that democratic modernization will be facilitated if despots and monarchs are *nicer* to Israel. It is also not clear how the victims of Israeli policies of ethnic cleansing and occupation are to blame for the lack of Arab democracy when they are not the ones lauding the "progressive king" of Bahrain[237] and its "innovative Crown Prince" Sheik Salman bin Hamad bin Isa al-Khalifa.[238]

Friedman has "known and liked for many years" the latter al-Khalifa, whose progressive qualifications are verified by his appearance in *Hot, Flat, and Crowded* eating pizza at a Bahraini bistro with Friedman while the daughter of a woman in a headscarf at the table next to them is "dressed like an American teenager and had what looked like a tattoo on her left shoulder."[239] The pizza excursion is said to have taken place in 2007, which is incidentally the year after the publication of a certain news item in the *Financial Times*, reported by Friedman in *The World Is Flat*, according to which the recent blocking of Google Earth by the Bahraini government has only made some Bahraini citizens—themselves faced with a housing shortage—all the more intent on utilizing the Internet tool to explore the vast properties of the ruling regime.[240]

The article quotes Bahraini political blogger Mahmood al-Yousif as explaining that some of Bahrain's royal palaces occupy "more space than three or four villages" and "block access to the sea for fishermen. People knew this already. But they never saw it. All they saw were the surrounding walls."[241] Friedman is perhaps so consumed with celebrating Google's contributions to the flattening of the world that he fails to recall his previous warning to "never trust a country with high walls and tinted windows."[242] None of the details he provides concerning Internet censorship and oppression of Bahrain's Shia majority meanwhile prompt Friedman to retract the progressive and innovative résumé he has awarded the Sunni family that has presided over the country for over two centuries, although he does concede during the 2011 Bahraini uprising that there are "hard-liners in the ruling al-Khalifa family" who view life "as a zero-sum sectarian war," which "is why the guns came out there very early."[243]

As for the "progressive emir" of Qatar[244] who launches Al Jazeera, Friedman rejoices in 1999:

It was al-Jazeera that broadcast Saddam Hussein's recent call for the elimination of all the Arab leaders—particularly the Saudis—at a time when no state-owned Arab television would broadcast such a threat. Little Qatar's satellite station is now driving the rest of the Arab world crazy, in between reruns from the Discovery Channel.[245]

Little Qatar soon begins to drive other people crazy, however, and in 2003 Al Jazeera transforms from an icon of freedom into an enemy combatant and peddler of "Saddamism," which Friedman defines as "an entrenched Arab mind-set, born of years of colonialism and humiliation, that insists that upholding Arab dignity and nationalism by defying the West is more important than freedom, democracy and modernization."[246] Evidence of the channel's newfound anti-democracy includes its insistence on referring to the U.S. occupation of Iraq as an occupation, a term Friedman nonetheless begins to employ himself sans quotation marks;[247] Al Jazeera meanwhile briefly redeems itself in 2006 by hosting a "stunning interview" with an Arab American psychiatrist who confirms that the current relationship between the West and the Arab/Muslim world constitutes "a clash between civilization and backwardness, between the civilized and the primitive, between barbarity and rationality."[248]

This same year, Friedman vouches for the rationality of Western civilization in the context of the Israeli war on Lebanon: "Yes, yes, I know. I am a too-rational Westerner. I don't understand the Eastern mind and the emotional victory [Hezbollah leader Hassan] Nasrallah will reap from all this pain."[249] That Friedman has not really relinquished his Orientalist interpretive powers is clear from his immediate addition: "It isn't whether you win or lose; it's whether you kill Jews,"[250] the rational Western basis of which fails to account for Israel's subsequent admission that it planned the war in advance and for the fact that Hezbollah is not the one presently flattening civilian apartment complexes.[251] It is also worth keeping in mind when speaking of rationality that

Friedman's third Pulitzer Prize, awarded for "clarity of vision ... in commenting on the worldwide impact of the terrorist threat,"[252] occurs the same year as his analysis: "No, the axis-of-evil idea isn't thought through—but that's what I like about it."[253]

Let us meanwhile apply the concept of rationality to Friedman's fondness for certain Arab kingdoms and emirates, which expands in 2006 with the following proclamations:

1. "Dubai is precisely the sort of decent, modernizing model we should be trying to nurture in the Arab-Muslim world."
2. "Dubai is about nurturing Arab dignity through success not suicide."
3. "So whatever happens with the Iraq experiment—but especially if it fails—we need Dubai to succeed."[254]

Viewing these statements from a rational perspective, one might ask why Friedman has devoted so much time to urging the Iraq war when its outcome appears to be less critical than what happens in non-war-requiring Dubai, or why the United States must "collaborat[e] with Iraqis to try to build one decent, progressive, democratizing society in the heart of the Arab East"[255] when the Bahraini monarchy is already conducting "innovative experiments with democracy"[256] and when Friedman already categorizes Jordan, Morocco, and Bahrain as "progressive Arab states."[257] The need for a new democratic precedent is additionally unclear given Friedman's own classification in 2002 of Lebanon as "the first and only real Arab democracy."[258]

Jump ahead to the 2010–11 revolts in the Middle East, which are allowed to proceed for a month and a half with no comment from the *New York Times* foreign affairs columnist–cum–Middle East expert, who then surfaces on February 1 with the lede: "I'm meeting a retired Israeli general at a Tel Aviv hotel."[259] Friedman eventually moves on to Cairo, where we learn that "up to now, the democracy movement in the Arab world was largely confined to the U.S.-led liberation of Iraq, which, because it was U.S.-led, has not been able to serve as a model for emulation."[260] Other reasons it has been unable to serve as a liberation model might be inferred from Friedman's assessment in 2005: "What the Bush team has done in Iraq, by ousting Saddam, was not to 'liberate' the country—an image and language imported from the West and inappropriate for Iraq—but rather to unleash the latent civil war in that country. Think of shaking a bottle of Champagne and then uncorking it."[261]

Perhaps given that the price of crude oil is approximately $96 a barrel at the start of the Egyptian revolution,[262] Friedman refrains from reminding readers of his signature First Law of Petropolitics, according to which the pace of freedom in "petrolist" states like Egypt increases when the price of oil is low, not high.[263] Friedman does manage to cast other personal convictions as being validated by the regional uprisings, as in his reminder about Arab/Muslim backwardness: "Humiliation is the single most powerful human emotion, and overcoming it is the second most powerful human emotion. That is such a big part of what is playing out here."[264] Sticklers for accuracy might point out that "overcoming humiliation" does not technically qualify as an emotion; Friedman's assertion that "it is no accident that the Mideast democracy rebellions began in three of the real countries [as opposed to "tribes with flags"]—Iran, Egypt and Tunisia—where the populations are modern"[265] does not meanwhile appear to be compatible with, for example, his previous description of a train ride from Cairo to Alexandria: "While all these [cellular] phones were chirping inside the train, outside we were passing along the Nile, where barefoot Egyptian villagers were tilling their fields with the same tools and water buffalo that their ancestors used in Pharaoh's day … Inside the train it was A.D. 2000, outside it was 2000 B.C."[266]

Such inconsistencies are of course trivial when compared with the unveiling in March 2011 of Friedman's "back-of-the-envelope guess list of what I'd call the 'not-so-obvious forces' that fed this mass revolt" across the Arab/Muslim world.[267] The list is, quite simply, a ludicrous grouping of "forces" that Friedman would *like* to have been behind the revolt: the Obama Factor, Google Earth (again based on the 2006 news item concerning Bahrain), Israel, the Beijing Olympics, and the Fayyad Factor.[268]

Despite having recently written about "the nasty job that Qatar's Al Jazeera TV just did in releasing out of context all the Palestinian [Authority] concessions [to Israel]—to embarrass the Palestinian leadership,"[269] and despite his incessant complaints about Arab TV channels beaming images of Israeli brutality against Palestinians into the Arab/Muslim world,[270] Friedman manages to co-opt Al Jazeera in his explanation of why Israel is a not-so-obvious force.[271] According to Friedman, because Al Jazeera has also beamed stories into the Arab world about the rape conviction of former Israeli president Moshe Katsav and the resignation of former Israeli Prime Minister Ehud Olmert following corruption charges, the network has contributed to Arab appreciation for Israel: "When you live right next to a country that is bringing to justice its top leaders for corruption and you live in a country where many of the top leaders are corrupt, well, you notice."[272]

You probably also notice when Olmert is charged for corruption but not for his role in the 2008–9 deaths of 1,400 people, primarily civilians, in another territory you live right next to, or the deaths of 1,200 other neighbors, primarily civilians, in 2006.[273] Living right next to a U.S.-backed police state in the West Bank meanwhile probably means that you include neither Obama nor Palestinian Prime Minister Salam Fayyad in your list of forces inspiring you to rebel against your own U.S.-backed police state.

It would be just as logical for Friedman to attribute the Arab uprisings to Israeli yogurt containers and cornflakes, the subjects of a secondhand anecdote in The Lexus about a Syrian tour guide who is said to be more concerned with the superior appearance of said products on Israeli television—as compared to black-and-white Syrian yogurt containers and wilt-prone cornflakes—than he is about the Israeli occupation of the Golan Heights.[274] Friedman may yet detect the revolt-inspiring role of these items, however, given that there is no limit to the number of times contemporary history can be revised. Less than a month prior to the issuance of the list of "not-so-obvious forces," for example, Friedman detects that the real "engine of change" in the region in fact consists of "China, Twitter and 20-year-olds."[275]

China's contributions include being able to "make Egyptian Ramadan toys more cheaply and appealingly than low-wage Egyptians" and participating in the "whole Asian-led developing world's rising consumption of meat, corn, sugar, wheat and oil" that has precipitated the "rise in food and gasoline prices that slammed into this region in the last six months [and] clearly sharpened discontent with the illegitimate regimes."[276] The latest installment of Friedman's Singapore trivia is thrown in on the side, and we learn that the Singaporean regime is "obsessed with things as small as how to better teach fractions to third graders," while Hosni Mubarak is not.[277]

The progressive accolades of former Friedman allies are meanwhile revised in accordance with the new concept of illegitimate regimes, and we learn that, for example, Jordan's "visionary young King Abdullah" has in fact been presiding over a system of "in-your-face corruption and crony capitalism that everyone in the public knew about."[278] After years of lauding the U.S.–Jordan Free Trade Agreement as an unparalleled economic achievement in the region, Friedman reports while visiting Amman in February that "my ears are ringing today with complaints about corruption, frustration with the king and queen, and disgust at the enormous gaps between rich and poor."[279]

As for Friedman's acknowledgement that the uprisings were largely propelled by the rise in food and gasoline prices, he excises the exacerbating influence of commodity speculation—a defining component of free-market capitalism—from the equation.[280] Although condemning the "stifling economic and political structures"[281] against which Arabs are rebelling, he nonetheless advocates a "transition to democracy" that ends with "Egypt looking like Indonesia or South Africa"[282]—i.e., a reinforced bastion of neoliberalism, in which prospects for less-than-stifling economics and politics may appear to dwindle when one considers the IMF's favorable assessment of Egypt (and Tunisia, Libya, and others) directly prior to the start of the uprisings.[283]

Given Friedman's ever-expanding accumulation of self-contradictions, it is ironic that he relentlessly plugs his friend Dov Seidman's book *How*, according to which the centrality of blogs, Facebook, and YouTube to modern life ensures that "more and more of what you say or do or write will end up as a digital fingerprint that never gets erased."[284] Friedman explains that "'how' you live your life and 'how' you conduct your business matters more than ever," which suggests that contradictions and other maneuvers can be easily tracked.[285]

Of course, Friedman has no way of knowing in 2003 that his digital fingerprint containing the sound bite "Suck. On. This" will be set to John Philip Sousa's "Liberty Bell" march and uploaded to YouTube.[286] In the event that the *New York Times* one day concludes that a surplus of distasteful fingerprints is in fact a liability, Friedman might find an alibi in his analysis from 2006 on the hazards of living in a wired world: "I was much smarter when I could do only one thing at a time."[287]

3 THE SPECIAL RELATIONSHIP

Message to Hamas: You may think these suicide bombers will drive Israelis to leave. But they're just digging in, and clinging to normality. The Jews are getting tattoos.

—Thomas Friedman, 2003

I don't doubt for a second President Bush's gut support for Israel, and I think it comes from his gut.

—Thomas Friedman, 2008

In October 2010, during the latest round of the Israeli–Palestinian peace charade, Friedman is summoned to an interview with Israel's Channel 2 television in order to defend his recent dispatch "Just Knock It Off,"[1] in which he is critical of Israeli Prime Minister Benjamin Netanyahu's resistance to a brief continuation of the partial moratorium on Israeli settlement building in the West Bank.[2]

The anchor comments that Netanyahu appears to have really gotten under Friedman's skin this time. Friedman assures her that it is "not about anyone, uh, personal" and explains, amid an abundance of hand flourishes, that he is not asking Israel to sign a deal with the Palestinians specifying "where do we go, where do we withdraw, where do we leave," but rather to create a "test where you take out all the other extraneous stuff—settlements, settlement building, okay—and you sit across the table, and everybody, now, show me your cards."[3]

The very reason for Friedman's critical article and appearance on Channel 2—the settlement issue—has thus been promptly discarded as "extraneous stuff." No hints are provided as to what non-extraneous stuff might entail; Netanyahu meanwhile evolves into an "interesting," "engaging," and "funny"[4] character for whom Friedman professes sympathy, despite having hoped in 2005 for the same man to become head of Likud so that the party would "be free to be itself—to represent the lunatic right in Israel, become a fringe party and drive over a cliff."[5]

That Friedman is able to advertise himself as a serious critic of Israel while simultaneously reiterating that the nation "had me at hello"[6] naturally works in the favor of the Israeli right wing,[7] shifting the spectrum of permissible discourse such that any substantive criticism can be rejected as extremist. Friedman himself writes about the importance of refraining from "destructive criticism" of Israel, done without first "convey[ing] to Israelis that you understand the world they're living in" by listing atrocities committed by regional Arabs and Muslims, such as the killing of Iraqi Shiites by Iraqi Sunnis.[8] "Destructive critics," we are told, seek to "delegitimize Israel" by "dismiss[ing] Gaza as an Israeli prison, without ever mentioning that had Hamas decided … to turn it into Dubai rather than Tehran, Israel would have behaved differently, too."[9] The problem with this sort of logic is that, even if it could be scientifically argued that Gaza has been turned into Tehran, such transformations are not illegal under international humanitarian law, whereas Israel's blockade of Gaza is.[10] It is furthermore unclear why, if the illegal use of white phosphorus munitions against honorary Tehrans is not a problem,[11] Friedman finds it appalling that the Iranian regime is capable of attacking civilians with more mundane weaponry in the real Tehran.

In keeping with the goal of constructive criticism, Friedman begins his "Just Knock It Off" lecture with the following disclaimer: "Say what you want about Israel's obstinacy at times, it remains the only country in the United Nations that another U.N. member, Iran, has openly expressed the hope that it be wiped off the map.[12] And that same country, Iran, is trying to build a nuclear weapon."[13] Without bothering to comment on Israel's existing nuclear arsenal or to explain the relevance of the country's U.N. membership given its history of flouting the organization's resolutions,[14] Friedman proceeds to the gist of the article: Netanyahu should take advantage of the opportunity to test whether the current leaders of the Palestinian Authority are perhaps valid partners for peace.

The 2010 peace test is not the first to be administered to Palestinians. As with the Iraq war, Friedman regularly detects critical junctures in the Arab–Israeli conflict and issues ultimatums to relevant parties, which generally prove untenable and have to be reissued with some variation down the line. The onus is always ultimately on the Arab half of the conflict, however, to prove itself in one way or another, and Arab leaders are variously instructed to stage a "psychological breakthrough" to the Israeli public,[15] conduct an "emotional appeal,"[16] and forge a "bond of trust" in order to assure Israelis of their "legitimate right … not to be randomly blown up at the grocery store."[17] It is unclear how Arabs, who do not understand their own psychology and have to have Palestinian "collective madness"[18] and "narcissistic rage"[19] explained to them by Friedman and his coterie of pro-Israel pundits, are nonetheless expected to understand Israeli psychology and how to appeal to it. Israeli leaders are meanwhile not required to recognize legitimate rights of Palestinians, such as to not to be bulldozed in their homes.[20]

The potential effectiveness of Arab emotional overtures to the Israeli public is additionally called into question by Friedman's scattered assessments of the maneuverings of the Israeli regime. In 1997, during Netanyahu's first stint as prime minister, we are informed that he "talks about the peace process as though it were the diplomatic equivalent of taking out the garbage, and signals to Palestinians that his concept of peace may be just a new form of occupation."[21] The following year Friedman declares: "Mr.

Netanyahu's whole approach to the Palestinians is based on the notion that there is no Palestinian people, with its own interests and politics. That's why he negotiates with America and gives the Palestinians a choice of accepting what he is willing to offer America or taking nothing."[22]

Netanyahu nevertheless ascends anew to the post of omniscient peace adjudicator in 2010, tasked by Friedman with determining whether the current leaders of the non-people can be dealt with, shortly after the release of a video in which the prime minister boasts of having derailed the Oslo Accords.[23] What Netanyahu is currently willing to offer America has incidentally been hinted at earlier this same year when U.S. Vice President Joe Biden's visit to Israel overlaps with the announcement of new illegal settlement construction in Arab East Jerusalem.[24] According to Friedman, the proper response is for Biden to snap his notebook shut and return from whence he came, leaving the following note for the Israeli government: "Friends don't let friends drive drunk."[25] Seven months later, drunk drivers become "interesting" and "funny" administrators of peace tests, and settlements become "extraneous." (Seven months after that, Palestinians are saddled with Friedman's latest surefire formula for achieving nothing, and he swears that, if thousands of them simply march to Jerusalem every Friday carrying an olive branch in one hand and a bilingual sign in the other specifying a desire for two states based on the 1967 borders "with mutually agreed adjustments," it will rapidly "become a global news event" and will result in the uploading to YouTube of original peace maps designed by the marchers in collaboration with invited delegations of other Arab and Israeli marchers.[26])

More remarkable than Friedman's intermittent sympathy for Netanyahu, meanwhile, is his rehabilitation of Ariel Sharon, found by Israel's Kahan Commission to bear "personal responsibility" as Israeli Minister of Defense for the 1982 massacre at the Sabra and Shatila refugee camps in Beirut.[27] This particular event, during which approximately two thousand Palestinian refugees are exterminated by Israel's Lebanese allies,[28] takes place during Friedman's service as *New York Times* bureau chief in Beirut and, as he recounts in *From Beirut to Jerusalem*, constitutes "something of a personal crisis" for him.[29]

The Israel Friedman encounters during the war in Lebanon is "not the heroic Israel I had been taught to identify with."[30] This is not surprising, given obvious aesthetic differences between, on the one hand, scenes of an Israeli invasion that kills 17,500 people, primarily civilians,[31] and scenes from high school summers spent at a kibbutz south of Haifa on the other. The latter hand merits recollections like: "Everything and everyone in the country seemed larger than life. Every soldier was a hero, every politician a statesman, every girl a knockout."[32]

Friedman's description in *From Beirut* of the role of the Six-Day War in igniting the "romance" between Israel and American Jews, who "could not embrace Israel enough; they could not fuse their own identities with Israel enough" comes with the accompanying affidavit: "I know. I was the epitome of this transformation."[33] Friedman elaborates:

> It was Israel's victory in the 1967 war which prompted me to assert my own Jewishness—not five years of Hebrew school as a young boy, not five summers at Herzl Camp in Wisconsin, and not my bar mitzvah. Hebrew school only embarrassed me, because I had to get on the Hebrew bus in front of the Gentile kids at my elementary school, and my bar mitzvah bored me, except for opening the envelopes stuffed with money. But Israel as a badge of pride actually saved me as a Jew at a time when I easily could have drifted away, not only from religious practice, but from Jewish communal identification altogether.[34]

Someone who openly adopts a state founded on a policy of ethnic cleansing as a personal "badge of pride" does not, of course, qualify as an unbiased commentator on the Middle East. Consider Friedman's celebrated treatment of the Sabra and Shatila massacre, which he professes to initially take "seriously as a blot on Israel and the Jewish people," and which causes him to "boil … with anger—anger which I worked out by reporting with all the skill I could muster on exactly what happened in those camps."[35] Laboring "day and night" on a four-page spread for the *New York Times*, Friedman acknowledges being driven by "conflicting impulses" to both "nail [Israeli Prime Minister Menachem] Begin and [Ariel] Sharon … in the hope that this would help get rid of them" and to "prove Begin and Sharon innocent."[36] Surmises the impending Pulitzer recipient: "Although an 'objective' journalist is not supposed to have such emotions, the truth is they made me a better reporter."[37]

Actually, the truth is that Friedman's emotions enable him to cast *himself*, and not the two thousand slaughtered Palestinians, as the real victim of Sabra and Shatila, an arrangement spelled out quite clearly in his recounting of his exclusive interview with Israeli commander in Lebanon, Major General Amir Drori:

> I must admit I was not professionally detached in this interview. I banged the table with my fist and shouted at Drori, "How could you do this? How could you not see [what was happening in the camps]? How could you not know?" But what I was really saying, in a very selfish way, was "How could you do this to me, you bastards? I always thought you were different. I always thought we were different."[38]

Friedman's questions remain rhetorical, and "so the next morning I buried Amir Drori on the front page of the *New York Times*, and along with him every illusion I ever held about the Jewish state."[39] The burial is hardly as dramatic as Friedman implies, though it does contain many more details of Arab suffering than he is inclined to report in later years. Acknowledging that the Israelis equipped the Lebanese militia assassins "with at least some of their arms and provisions and assisted them with flares during nighttime operations," and that the southern end of Shatila camp "can be seen very clearly with the naked eye from the Kuwaiti Embassy traffic circle—the site of the telescope and binocular-equipped Israeli observation post," Friedman nonetheless finds it necessary to temper the incriminating truth with the following bizarre disclaimer: "Whether the Israelis actually looked down and saw what was happening is unknown."[40]

Compare this assessment with that provided by veteran British journalist Robert Fisk, who does not possess a badge of pride called Israel and has never harbored any illusions as to Israeli "purity of arms." Entering Sabra and Shatila immediately after the massacre, Fisk reports, regarding its perpetrators, that "their handiwork had clearly been watched—closely observed—by the Israelis, by those same Israelis who were still watching us through their field-glasses."[41] It is safe to assume that, had the positions of the Israelis and Palestinians been somehow reversed in the camps, Friedman would have wasted no time in reasoning that persons inside observation posts *observe*.

The conclusion of Friedman's revolutionary, Pulitzer-inducing exposé consists merely of a toned-downed version of the Israeli fabrication that there were two thousand Palestine Liberation Organization (P.L.O.) guerrillas inside Sabra and Shatila: "Clearly there were some, but the weight of the evidence suggests that the number was in the low hundreds at most."[42] As for the permanence of the burial of illusions about the Jewish state, Friedman writes in *From Beirut* in 1989: "I'll always want [Israel] to be the country I imagined in my youth. But what the hell, she's mine, and for a forty-year-old, she ain't too shabby."[43]

Despite detecting Israeli hypocrisy in the failure to adequately punish the government official deemed to bear personal responsibility for the Sabra and Shatila massacre,[44] meanwhile, Friedman produces the following column on the occasion of now–Prime Minister Ariel Sharon's incapacitating stroke in 2006: "Wanted: An Arab Sharon." According to Friedman, "Israel's most ruthless Arab fighter and unrestrained settlement builder" has now developed a "positive side [to] his legacy"[45] by uprooting Jewish settlements in

Gaza—the purpose of which project is bluntly outlined in a 2004 *Haaretz* interview with Dov Weisglass, senior adviser to Sharon, who explains that disengagement from Gaza will freeze the peace process:

> And when you freeze that process, you prevent the establishment of a Palestinian state, and you prevent a discussion on the refugees, the borders and Jerusalem. Effectively, this whole package called the Palestinian state, with all that it entails, has been removed indefinitely from our agenda… All with a [U.S.] presidential blessing and the ratification of both houses of Congress.[46]

Friedman himself reports in 2004 that Sharon's "aides have made clear that he is getting out of Gaza in order to entrench Israel even more deeply in the West Bank and the Jewish settlements there,"[47] a detail that mutates in his very next article into "Sharon's hugely important effort to withdraw Israel from Gaza."[48] As for P.L.O. Chairman Yasser Arafat's failure to realize that the Israeli offer at Camp David in 2000—approximately 16 percent of historic Palestine[49] divvied up between noncontiguous enclaves under de facto Israeli control—"would have satisfied the vast majority of [Palestinian] aspirations for statehood,"[50] Friedman's convenient powers as arbiter of justice and interpreter of Palestinian souls allow him to ignore things like the admission by former Israeli Foreign Minister and Camp David participant Shlomo Ben-Ami that "if I were a Palestinian, I would have rejected Camp David as well."[51] In a hypothetical memo from Bill Clinton to "The Arab Street," Friedman sneers: "If you want to continue fighting it out and avoiding a deal that gives you 95 percent of what you want, well, there's nothing more I can do."[52]

Friedman's unique access to Palestinian aspirations for Jerusalem meanwhile results in a range of suggestions regarding the city's final status, from the need for a "Palestinian toehold around Jerusalem,"[53] to the need for at least "one square block" in East Jerusalem over which the Palestinians "have full control and can fly their flag,"[54] to the option of renaming the village of Abu Dis, now separated from Jerusalem by Israel's cement wall, "Al Quds."[55] After asserting in 1997 that "Israel's hold over [Jerusalem] is unchallenged, and I'm glad it is,"[56] Friedman chides House Speaker Newt Gingrich the following year for declaring the city "'the united and eternal capital of Israel'—in contravention of U.S. policy that Jerusalem's final status should be negotiated by the parties. I hope Jerusalem stays Israel's eternal capital too, but to rub this in the face of Palestinians when the U.S. is trying to persuade them to accept other compromises is stupid."[57]

Following the rejection of Camp David, the Palestinians' next blunder is to react to Sharon's "silly provocation" in September 2000, when he and a thousand Israeli riot police descend upon the Haram al-Sharif/Temple Mount in Arab East Jerusalem to assert Jewish claims to the area.[58] According to Friedman's subsequent lecture, the Palestinians are to intuit that "Sharon thrives politically when you all behave like a mob,"[59] and that he should thus be welcomed "with open arms"[60] during provocative visits, even when they occur several years prior to his alleged about-face from "most ruthless Arab fighter and unrestrained settlement-builder."

It then turns out that the lack of an open-armed welcome is part of the alleged Palestinian effort to thwart peace by "turn[ing]" current Israeli Prime Minister Ehud Barak "into Sharon," a goal that is swiftly achieved with Sharon's triumph in the 2001 Israeli prime ministerial elections.[61] "Of course," Friedman explains, "the Palestinians couldn't explain it in those terms, so instead they unfurled all the old complaints about the brutality of the continued Israeli occupation and settlement-building."[62] Why complaints about brutality and occupation should be considered outdated just because the crimes have continued for various decades becomes even more of a puzzle when Friedman himself unfurls such statements as that "the Israeli propaganda that the Palestinians mostly rule themselves in the West Bank is fatuous nonsense" and that "Israeli confiscation of Palestinian land for more settlements is going on to this day—seven years into Oslo."[63]

Other possible synonyms for Sharon aside from "ruthless Arab fighter" are suggested during Friedman's visit to the Jidda office of the Saudi *Okaz* newspaper in 2002, where he converses with a group of journalists, academics, and businesspeople. The following exchange is recorded in *Longitudes and Attitudes*:

> Okaz reporter: "Why don't you call Ariel Sharon a terrorist? By your definition of terrorism, he is murdering innocent civilians."
>
> "OK," I said. "Let's make a deal." I then took out a blank piece of white paper. "Let's have a contract. I promise that in the future I will always call Ariel Sharon a terrorist in my columns—on the condition that in the future you will always call Palestinians who blow up Israeli kids in pizza parlors terrorists. Do we have a deal?"
>
> I got no takers.[64]

What this sort of bargaining implies, of course, is that whether or not Friedman reports the truth may at times depend on what other journalists are reporting. Not long after the exchange in Jidda, meanwhile, Friedman directly encourages the murder of innocent civilians by announcing in March 2002: "Israel needs to deliver a military blow that clearly shows terror will not pay."[65] Otherwise, we are told, the Palestinian suicide-bombing strategy "will eventually lead to a bomber strapped with a nuclear device threatening entire nations,"[66] although it is not explained why this scenario has been averted in the case of suicide bombing strategies by other nationalities, such as Lebanese, Tamil, and Japanese. As Robert Fisk notes: "The Israelis certainly followed Friedman's advice."[67] A month and a half later, following the devastation of Jenin and other West Bank locales, Friedman adds as an afterthought: "Israeli rightists and settlers deliberately label any Palestinian resistance to the Israeli occupation of the West Bank as 'terrorism' in order to rope the U.S. into supporting Israel's continued hold on the occupied territories as part of America's global war on terrorism."[68]

Friedman informs us that his job description as foreign affairs columnist is "tourist with an attitude,"[69] which somehow intermittently evolves into a license to prescribe military onslaughts by governments with dismal records of distinguishing between civilians and combatants. That Friedman's touristic "attitude" so often manifests itself as haughty and dehumanizing contempt for Palestinians meanwhile provides additional, indirect encouragement of Israeli repression, as the Israel Defense Forces (I.D.F.) may be forgiven for not realizing that there are civilians among populations "gripped by a collective madness"[70] and "so blinded by their narcissistic rage that they have lost sight of the basic truth civilization is built on: the sacredness of every human life, starting with your own."[71]

As for behavior of the I.D.F. itself that might also qualify as defying the "sacredness of every human life," Friedman waits approximately twenty-seven days following the 1996 Israeli massacre of 106 civilian refugees sheltered at the U.N. compound in the south Lebanese village of Qana to acknowledge the details of the event, at which point he quotes *Haaretz* journalist Ari Shavit as confirming: "We didn't kill them with prior intent. We killed them because the yawning gap between the unlimited sacrosanct importance which we attribute to our own lives and the very limited sacred character we attribute to the lives of others allowed us to kill them."[72] As Edward Said notes, Friedman demonstrates a clear understanding in *From Beirut* "of how a self-serving myth of victimization still controls the Israeli self-image."[73] This does not prevent him, however, from assisting in mythical propagation by proclaiming suicide bombing "something no modern society, any society has ever really encountered,"[74] which he does approximately one year after acknowledging that it was the Tamil Tigers and not the Palestinians who "perfected suicide as a weapon of war."[75]

The 2006 Israeli war on Lebanon that extinguished 1,200 lives, mainly civilian, might meanwhile also qualify as a phenomenon not normally encountered by modern societies. Friedman defines himself as one of the few observers of this conflict to detect an Israeli victory, and goes as far as to then invoke the war as an optimistic precedent in 2009 when Israel is ravaging Gaza.[76] The key to victory in 2006, we are told, was "the education of Hezbollah," which Israel achieved by determining that "the only long-term source of deterrence was to exact enough pain on the civilians—the families and employers of the militants—to restrain Hezbollah in the future." Declaring that this strategy was "not pretty, but it was logical," Friedman proposes "the education of Hamas" as the goal of the current operation in Gaza.[77]

There are manifold problems with this line of reasoning. One, to cite the killing of 1,200 people as an instructive example is indisputably obscene. Two, it is not up to Israel or to Friedman to decide that the Fourth Geneva Convention prohibiting collective punishment and targeting of civilians in wartime is illogical. Three, the suggestion that Israel can curb Lebanese approval of resistance operations by slaughtering civilians is debunked in Friedman's own newspaper, which reports "mushrooming public support for Hezbollah" during the war and regional "public anger focused on Israel for the civilian deaths and widespread destruction in Lebanon."[78] Four, the "families/employers of the militants" scheme hardly accounts for the scope of Israeli targets, which include Christian joggers north of Beirut and children in pickup trucks fleeing Sunni villages in south Lebanon in accordance with Israeli orders.[79] Five, what the hell is a militant employer?

More questions are raised by Friedman's interpretation of the border skirmish that leads to the war: "Israeli soldiers were napping when this war started—that's why they got ambushed— for the very best reasons: They have so much more to do with their lives, and they live in a society that empowers and enables them to do it."[80] Evidence of the empowering and enabling nature of Israeli society is that American investor Warren Buffett has recently purchased a company in northern Israel, which still does not explain how napping or participating in a universal military draft indicates having "so much more to do" with one's life, or why soldiers whose government had planned a war in advance[81] would be napping on a hostile border. Also perplexing is how Friedman is able to maintain his exuberance over Israel's empowerment of individuals when he himself reports in 2007: "Israel's poverty rate is still the highest in the West, by far: 24.4 percent of the entire population and 35.2 percent of all children are described as poor, living under the official 'poverty line.' In the Arab and the ultra-Orthodox Jewish sectors, child poverty is especially high: more than 50 percent."[82]

Regarding the hoped-for "education of Hamas"[83] via Israel's twenty-two-day pummeling of Gaza in 2008–9, during which Palestinian civilians are killed at a rate of 400:1 vis-à-vis their Israeli counterparts,[84] Friedman offers an initial take on the carnage:

> The fighting, death and destruction in Gaza is painful to watch. But it's all too familiar. It's the latest version of the longest-running play in the modern Middle East, which, if I were to give it a title, would be called: "Who owns this hotel? Can the Jews have a room? And shouldn't we blow up the bar and replace it with a mosque?"[85]

Israel's present existence on the vast majority of former Palestinian land, not to mention Friedman's own reportage on rampant Jewish settlement construction in the region, suggests that there is no dearth of rooms for Jews in the area. Friedman's theatrics also fail to account for the fact that the ceasefire agreement between those allegedly seeking a room and those allegedly plotting to blow up the bar is broken by the former party as a prelude to the latest version of the play.[86] As for Friedman's warning regarding Hamas's "call to replace Israel with an Islamic state,"[87] such a project has been denied by the likes of former Mossad head Ephraim Halevy, who acknowledges that the organization is "ready and willing to see the establishment of a Palestinian state in the temporary borders of 1967" and that "Israel, for reasons of its own, did not want to turn the [Gaza] ceasefire into the start of a diplomatic process with Hamas."[88]

Undeterred, Friedman informs readers in favor of a two-state solution that "you have to hope for the weakening of Hamas" because it has rejected the recognition of Israel by the Fatah-led Palestinian Authority in the West Bank, and because "nothing has damaged Palestinians more than the Hamas death-cult strategy of turning Palestinian youths into suicide bombers."[89] The "death-cult strategy" has thus suddenly become the sole dominion of Hamas, despite Friedman's proclamation on the occasion of the death of Fatah leader and P.A. President Yasser Arafat in 2004 that he was "a bad man," due in part to the fact that Friedman's Google search of the terms "Yasir Arafat" and "martyrdom" and "jihad" has produced more relevant results than has his search of the terms "Yasir Arafat" and "Palestine" and "education."[90] It is also worth mentioning that Friedman himself acknowledges that not a single suicide bombing has occurred in Israel since 2006,[91] i.e., three years prior to the current non-suicidal killing and maiming of hundreds of Palestinian youths in Gaza.

As for the monopoly on Palestinian rejection of Israel now assigned to Hamas, it is worth recalling that Noam Chomsky singles out Friedman and the *New York Times* in the 1980s for refusing to mention Arafat's offers, from 1984 to 1988, to enter into direct negotiations with the Israelis aimed at mutual recognition, and for preferring instead to insist on the lack of a negotiating partner for Israel and on Arab rejectionism.[92] A full twelve years after Arafat's formal recognition of Israel's right to exist in 1988, Friedman continues to advertise the Palestinian "notion that they can get back land while holding on to their rejection of Israel," which he compares to Israel's "notion that it can have peace while holding on to settlements."[93] The latter illusion does not prevent Friedman from finding it anything but logical that 80 percent of settlers be permitted to remain where they are in any peace agreement.[94]

Prior to joining the ranks of "extraneous stuff" in the afore-mentioned Channel 2 interview in 2010, Israeli settlements are variously referred to as "idiotic,"[95] "insane,"[96] "rapacious,"[97] "greedy,"[98] "an abomination,"[99] and part of a "traditional colonial occupation."[100] Friedman's fundamental concern is not that the

West Bank settlements infringe on the freedoms of non-settlers, banned from Jewish-only thoroughfares and cut off from their own backyards by Israeli fences, but rather that the un-free non-settlers might then demand a single democratic state:

> As Palestinians find themselves isolated in pockets next to Jewish settlers—who have the rule of law, the right to vote, welfare, jobs, etc.—and as hope for a contiguous Palestinian state fades, it's inevitable that many of them will throw in the towel and ask for the right to vote in Israel.[101]

Such a scenario must be averted at all costs, because "if American Jews think it's hard to defend Israel today on college campuses, imagine what it will be like when their kids have to argue against the principle of one man, one vote."[102] That Friedman openly favors ethnocracy over democracy in Israel does not speak highly of his qualifications for chaperoning the installation of the second system in Iraq. As for non-Jewish citizens[103] of the current Jewish democracy, Friedman recognizes their plight on occasion, such as in a 1986 article about a Jewish journalist who disguises himself as an Arab and suffers pervasive discrimination accordingly.[104]

It remains to be seen how long Friedman can argue the imminent threat of apartheid without classifying the current system as such.[105] He meanwhile stresses that Israel must withdraw from occupied territories "not because Israel is wrong, but because Zionism is a just cause that the occupation is undermining,"[106] a calculation that skips over the very foundation of the cause in expansionism and Palestinian dispossession, as well as the fact that Israel *is* wrong inasmuch as the settlements are illegal under international law, as Friedman himself admits that they are not being occupied in self-defense (and that they are "idiotic," "an abomination," etc.).

The onus is never on Israel, however, to definitively cease its "traditional colonial occupation" as a jumping-off point for peace negotiations, and Friedman goes as far as to caution in 2001 that the unilateral uprooting of "some" of the settlements will "trigger a Jewish-Jewish civil war" and thus "provide a huge victory for Palestinian radicals—who will have gotten land for war."[107] It is impossible to determine under what legal or moral system the unilateral halting of an illegal occupation should be advised against on account of its potential effects on the harmony of the citizens of the occupying power.[108] With regard to Friedman's Googling of Arafat, meanwhile, it should be noted that, whatever Arafat's faults, illegally occupied peoples are not required by international law to upload education plans in English to the Internet as a prerequisite to occupation reversal, and Google searches of other terms related to Palestinian education—"Israel bombs Gaza university,"[109] for example—also produce results.

Friedman condemns Arafat for unleashing the second Intifada in 2000 in accordance with his preference "to play the victim rather than the statesman"[110] but later determines that "when this intifada started it was directed partly at [Arafat's] corrupt leadership,"[111] despite his alleged launching of it. At the 2001 Davos World Economic Forum, Friedman accuses Arafat of "torch[ing]" the "olive branch" extended to him by Israeli Foreign Minister Shimon Peres "in the wake of an 11th-hour Barak bid to conclude a final deal with the Palestinians in Taba," Egypt, site of the post–Camp David negotiations.[112] In reality, the 11th-hour bid and "far-reaching offer" consists of Barak canceling a meeting with Arafat, after which the talks do not resume.[113] As for Arafat's alleged "torching," this consists of "denounc[ing] Israel for its 'fascist military aggression' and 'colonialist armed expansionism,' and its policies of 'murder, persecution, assassination, destruction and devastation.'"[114]

Keep in mind that Friedman himself accuses Israel of colonialist expansionism, and that he used to report instances of murder and persecution with greater frequency prior to assuming the role of "tourist with an attitude."[115] By currently refusing to integrate these details into an overall picture of systematic repression and brutality by the state of Israel against Palestinians, however, he deprives the victims of a context legitimizing their complaints. Friedman meanwhile concocts this analogy for Arafat's behavior at Davos: "It would be as though [French President Charles] de Gaulle had offered to withdraw from Algeria and the Algerians said: 'Thank you. You're a fascist. Of course we'll take all of Algeria, but we won't stop this conflict until we get Bordeaux, Marseilles and Nice as well.'"[116]

In the event that one wants to take Friedman's analogical recklessness seriously, one might infer the following from his comparison:

1. In exchange for granting independence to Algeria, which it did while simultaneously inundating the country with more colonists, France was able to maintain its eternal and undivided capital at Algiers as well as to annex the ever-expanding portions of Algeria with a high concentration of *pied-noirs*. Algerians are currently permitted to collect garbage in certain parts of Algiers and to maintain their own capital in an irrelevant village outside the city.
2. Accusing Israel of crimes of which it is guilty, such as colonialism, is equivalent to demanding possession of various Israeli metropolises.
3. Since Friedman also accuses Israel of colonialism, this indicates that he too is harboring territorial designs.

It is easy to see why Friedman's immunity from editing should occasionally be challenged. It is more difficult to see the logic behind his prediction that Israeli settlement "expansion is a shameful act of colonial coercion that will meet the fate of all other colonial enterprises in history" when all other colonial enterprises do not commence with the very founding of the colonizer state on the land to be colonized.[117]

Friedman portrays the idea that Arafat is "negotiating [for peace] with one hand and building hate against Israelis in Palestinian mosques and textbooks with the other" as a transgression equivalent to Israel's "negotiating with one hand and still building settlements with the other."[118] This is additionally deceptive, given that hatred is neither illegal nor quantifiable, and that it is determined to be at the "core" of the Israeli occupation, as well, which is "driven ... by dangerous religious and nationalist fanatics, seething with contempt for Arabs."[119] Friedman might ask himself whether Palestinian hate-building is not facilitated by continued confiscation of Palestinian land by such a demographic. (He might also ask himself whether letting the word "textbooks" slip does not call into question the lack of Palestinian education plans.) The suppression of hatred is meanwhile not deemed a necessary prerequisite for peace in the former Yugoslavia, and in 2000 Friedman advises NATO to tacitly partition Kosovo because "it's obvious that the Kosovar Serbs and Albanians hate each other."[120]

Friedman's predilection for double standards favoring Israel is visible time and again, as is his predilection for calling attention to double standards *not* favoring Israel. When Turkey and Brazil broker a fuel swap deal with Iran in 2010 with the aim of peacefully defusing the Iranian nuclear issue, Friedman declares the maneuver to be "as ugly as it gets" and asks how two alleged democracies can embrace a "Holocaust-denying" president who "uses his army and police to crush and kill Iranian democrats."[121] He never questions how the United States can embrace a nation that crushes American peace activists with bulldozers,[122] and his own recommendation for dealing with Iran's alleged[123] nuclear ambitions appears to be for the United States "to stop saying ... publicly" that Israel will not strike Iran, and to instead follow the example of former Vice President Dick Cheney in order to "keep alive the prospect that Israel could do something crazy"[124]—an obvious prescription for regional stability. In the same article in which he accuses Turkey and Brazil of supreme ugliness and teetering democracy for ignoring human rights violations and "violently repressed labor leaders" in Iran, meanwhile, Friedman parrots the assessment by his friend Moisés Naím, editor of *Foreign Policy*, that Colombia is "one of the great democratic success stories" of Latin America.[125] This is the same Colombia, of course, that presently enjoys the worst human rights record on the continent, and where more trade unionists have been assassinated in the past two decades than in the rest of the world combined.[126]

As for other bouts of hypocrisy, consider Friedman's reaction to the revelation in the late 1990s that Swiss banks are withholding the assets of Holocaust victims after having tolerated Nazi use of their services during World War II. Friedman declares that "some of the Swiss people's most cherished national self-images [are] myths," that it is necessary for the Swiss to "have an accounting with themselves—one in which they acknowledge that just because they host the Red Cross and the U.N. doesn't absolve them of moral responsibilities in the world,"[127] and that it is up to the current generation of Swiss to counteract this "moral bankruptcy" by using "some of their money ... to build a Holocaust memorial in Switzerland that would teach the Swiss about their own unspeakable, and unspoken, chapter of history."[128]

Now consider Friedman's analysis of the moral responsibility of the nation that, in addition to regularly targeting Red Cross and U.N. installations and vehicles in Arab areas,[129] continues to this day to pursue the ethnic cleansing project it began in 1948[130]: "Israel doesn't have to assume explicit responsibility, but it should be generous in saying to Palestinians that they have suffered a historical injustice and have a moral right to return to their original homes," because "for Palestinians to limit themselves they need to feel that their narrative as a dispossessed people struggling to recover their homeland is also affirmed."[131] Thus the Swiss, who did not perpetrate the Holocaust, are morally accountable to its victims and urged to erect a memorial, while the Israelis are merely encouraged to charitably allow the Palestinians the amount of gratification required for them to abandon their demand for a literal rather than moral right of return for refugees.

The idea that justice can be sufficiently approximated via symbolic concessions from Israel is advanced in less politically correct terms in Friedman's 1988 interview with the Israeli newspaper *Yediot Ahronot*, in which he announces: "I believe that as soon as Ahmed has a seat in the bus, he will limit his demands."[132] Chomsky has questioned whether journalists can also achieve promotion to the post of *New York Times* chief diplomatic correspondent by suggesting Sambo or Hymie be given a seat in the bus.[133]

Ahmed's promotion to a bus seat meanwhile appears to be a more complicated matter, seeing as he resurfaces—this time with a friend—in the section of *Longitudes* in which Friedman is gleaning post-9/11 insights from the Israeli army on how to deal with suicide terrorism: "There is no way [the Israelis] will ever know Ahmed from Mohammed the way Ahmed and Mohammed do."[134] It is possible that Friedman has already understood the importance of co-opting members of the terrorist-producing population during Ahmed's original apparition in 1988, when Chomsky notes that Friedman also "proposed the brutal Israeli-run regime of south Lebanon as a model for the occupied [Palestinian] territories" —clearly not the bus seat envisioned by Ahmed.[135]

During the second Intifada in 2002, Friedman declares that "the Palestinians have long had a tactical alternative to suicide: nonviolent resistance, à la Gandhi," which "would have delivered a Palestinian state 30 years ago."[136] Given that Friedman resided in Jerusalem at the start of the first Intifada in 1987, he is well aware that the Palestinians have long *employed* tactical alternatives to suicide, something he confirms with his suggestion in *From Beirut* that stone-throwing is compatible with "the teachings of Mahatma Gandhi."[137] Friedman elaborates on the Palestinians' "operational" adoption of stones, "encouraged and exploited by Yasir Arafat and the PLO leaders":

> What the Palestinians under occupation were saying by using primarily stones instead of firearms was that the most powerful weapon against the Israelis was not terrorism or guerrilla warfare … The most powerful weapon, they proclaimed, was massive non-lethal civil disobedience. That is what the stones symbolized.[138]

The sudden possibility in 2002 of a thirty-year-old Palestinian state is also called into question by the fact that 2002 minus thirty years is 1972, which is sixteen years before Friedman advises giving Ahmed a seat in the bus. Moreover, Friedman goes to great lengths in *From Beirut* to explain that the Jew who "got a seat" on the "subway of life" in 1948 has now "gotten used to the whole seat" and thus "keeps *The New York Times* locked in front of his face," while the little old shopping bag–laden lady (played by Arafat) shouts in reference to the seat: "I am ready to share. I am ready to share."[139] In 2004 Friedman nonetheless claims that, had Arafat informed Palestinians that "Palestine will have to be divided with the Jews forever," and "had he ever adopted the nonviolence of Gandhi, Arafat would have had three Palestinian states by now—Israel's reckless settlements notwithstanding."[140] Although this is presumably not what Friedman intends, the statement is accurate insofar as reckless settlement patterns ensure the foundation of any Palestinian "state" on multiple, noncontiguous plots of land.

Additional doubts are cast on the feasibility of a thirty-year-old state in 2002 when Friedman pens the following passage around the time of the hypothetical state's twenty-sixth birthday in 1998:

> In May, Secretary of State Madeleine Albright met with the Israeli Prime Minister, Benjamin Netanyahu, and the Palestinian leader Yasir Arafat in London, presented them with a carefully balanced U.S. peace plan and told them each they had until the next week to say yes. If they did, the President himself would oversee the opening of final-status talks between them. If they said no, reporters were told, the U.S. would make clear publicly its plan and who was blocking it. Mr. Arafat said yes, Mr. Netanyahu said no. Ms. Albright has barely been heard from on this issue since.[141]

Friedman's historical revisions also excise from the record his own previous reports on Israeli brutality, mass arrests, and other forms of popular suffocation such as the fact that, "by simply pressing a few buttons on a computer, an Israeli officer could restore or revoke all the documents a Palestinian needed to survive under the Israeli occupation."[142] Despite reporting that "there was a real attempt [during the first Intifada] by Palestinians to set up their own schools and food-sharing and communal-support programs" but that the "Israeli system was too powerful for the Palestinians to elude its grasp easily,"[143] Friedman blissfully decrees in 2002 that Palestinians "would have had a quality state a long time ago" had they announced: "We are going to build a Palestinian society, schools and economy, as if we had no occupation."[144] According to this newfound logic, nothing in the world is really impossible, and cities can be built in the middle of the ocean simply by pretending the water is not there.

Regarding the facility with which an independent Palestinian economy can be forged while under the thumb of an Israeli economy that is intertwined with a U.S. economy, Friedman addresses some of the complications that arise during the first Intifada given Palestinian existence as a captive labor pool and captive market. After explaining that many Palestinians are eventually forced to return to work in Israel for purposes of survival, he notes:

> Palestinian children, often eleven- and twelve-year-olds, continued rioting, throwing stones, and getting shot. Their deaths seemed to become the warrant which allowed their parents to go on working in Israel and not engage in truly significant civil disobedience. Palestinians would point to the number of people being killed each day and say, "See, we are suffering. Now let us have our state."[145]

It is no less than preposterous, of course, to insinuate that Palestinian parents might view the killing of their children as an excuse not to abandon their jobs. It meanwhile appears that the failure of the alleged "See, we are suffering" strategy to achieve its intended effect may have something to do with certain economic realities mentioned in *The Lexus and the Olive Tree* in 1999: "By exporting software, chips and other high-tech innovations Israel is exporting the power sources of today's information economy, and every country wants that power, no matter what Israel is doing to

the Palestinians."[146] Friedman notes that "everyone comes courting Israel, no matter what the state of the peace process," and that
"every major American high-tech company has a branch in Israel
... or owns part of an Israeli computer company,"[147] which makes
it all the more difficult to understand how the Palestinians, with
such a coalition of corporate interests pitted against them, are also
supposed to ignore what Israel is doing and to go about erecting
their economy as if there were no occupation fueled by economic
and military aid from the global superpower.[148]

The Lexus/olive tree dichotomy is itself conceived in reference
to the Israeli-Palestinian conflict. In May of 1992, Friedman is
"eating a sushi box dinner and traveling at 180 miles per hour"
on the bullet train to Tokyo, having visited the Lexus car factory
south of the city where he remained "fascinated watching the
robot that applied the rubber seal that held in place the front
windshield of each Lexus."[149] Catching sight of a newspaper article
about uproar in the Middle East over the U.S. State Department
spokeswoman's "controversial interpretation of a 1948 United
Nations resolution" concerning the Palestinian right of return,[150]
Friedman realizes that the Japanese "were building the greatest
luxury car in the world with robots" while the Arabs and Israelis
"were still fighting over who owned which olive tree."[151] Thus does
the Japanese car come to symbolize the human "drive for suste-
nance, improvement, prosperity and modernization" in parts of
the world "dedicated to modernizing, streamlining and privatizing
their economies in order to thrive in the system of globalization,"
while Mediterranean vegetation represents "everything that roots
us, anchors us, identifies us and locates us in this world."[152]

To illustrate the struggle between the Lexus and the olive tree
in the post–Cold War system, Friedman recounts his experience
in the lobby of NATO headquarters in Brussels in 1999, which
hosts the following scene: "A Russian journalist, circling the Coke
machine, under the CNN screen, speaking Russian into a cell
phone, in NATO headquarters, while Kosovo burned—my mind
couldn't contain all the contradictions."[153] As for his "favorite 'Lexus

trumps olive tree in the era of globalization' story,"[154] this concerns the son of assassinated P.L.O. leader Abu Jihad, whose business card in 1995 reads: "Jihad al-Wazir, Managing Director, World Trade Center, Gaza, Palestine."[155] The encouraging turnaround in a single generation does not, however, prevent Gaza from eventually endeavoring to resemble Mogadishu[156] and then Tehran[157] instead of Dubai, which Friedman alleges without pointing out that the United States has not in recent history contributed to the instigation of civil war in said emirate.[158] It would meanwhile seem that there has already been a definitive trumping of the olive tree by the Lexus in the case of Israel, whose confiscation of Palestinian trees has not interrupted its high-tech functions, and Friedman writes in *The Lexus* itself: "In the mid-1980s ... Japan, Inc., would only sell its really good cars to the Arabs. Not anymore. You can get any Lexus you want in Israel today, because in economic terms, Israel today is a bigger energy exporter than Saudi Arabia."[159]

Sectors of Israeli society most attached to metaphorical olive trees include religious Jews, who reportedly oppose globalization partly out of a concern that former Israeli Prime Minister Shimon Peres's professed notion that his grandchildren and Arafat's grandchildren "would all make microchips together" constitutes a threat to the Jewish character of the state.[160] In the end, of course, the Israelis make microchips by themselves while Friedman lectures the "Arab Street" in 2001: "In an age when others are making microchips, you are making potato chips."[161] That the point of microchip-making and globalization itself is not to benefit the general "street" is clear from Friedman's remark in *The Lexus* that "suddenly, Israeli textile workers, who are not ready for the Intel factory that is also being built in Israel, find their jobs going to Jordan" as a result of the Israeli–Jordanian peace agreement.[162] The backlash against globalization in Jordan is meanwhile being waged by such groups as the "anti-Israeli-made banana cream pie fundamentalists," who call for a boycott of the Internet café that has prompted the following enthusiastic endorsement from Friedman to its proprietor: "'Let me get this straight,' I said, 'the banana cream pie at the Internet cafe in Amman is made by the wife of the Israeli deputy ambassador! That's great. I love it."'[163]

The reason the fundamentalists do not share Friedman's enthusiasm, we are told, is that they are among "all those millions of people who detest the way globalization homogenizes people … [and] erases the distinctiveness of cultures."[164] Friedman is presumably aware that banana cream pie is not a distinctly Israeli cultural phenomenon, just as he is presumably aware on some level that it is absurd to portray boycotts of Israeli products for well-known political reasons as resistance to cultural homogenization. As for academic boycotts, Friedman refrains from detecting a simple olive-tree obsession in the 2007 proposal from Britain's University and College Union for a boycott of Israeli universities complicit in the occupation of Palestinian land,[165] and instead classifies the move as "rank anti-Semitism," given "all the other madness in the Middle East."[166] The other madness includes that Syria is a suspect in the 2005 assassination of Lebanese Prime Minister Rafik Hariri and that Sudan is engaging in genocide.

Thus is a measure that unmistakably complies with Friedman's demand for nonviolent resistance—and that aims to punish the same occupation that Friedman himself consistently claims to oppose—branded with the anti-Semitic label on the pages of the *New York Times*.[167] That Britain may not be as heavily invested in Syrian and Sudanese academic institutions and representatives as in Israeli ones does not appear to concern Friedman, nor does he attempt to explain how it is, for example, that the Syrian university system directly contributed to the Hariri assassination—an event he continues to portray as Syrian handiwork despite the fact that the Special Tribunal for Lebanon has moved on to other targets (with the conspicuous exclusion of Israel[168]). Recognizing the "ugly and brutal manner" in which the West Bank has been carved up, and noting the current function of the I.D.F. as "an army of occupation to protect the settlers and their roads," Friedman nonetheless stresses that the continuing occupation is "hardly Israel's fault alone," because "the Palestinians are in turmoil."[169]

Once again, it is not clear why Friedman, who cannot tolerate having his meals interrupted by other people's cell phone conversations,[170] is under the impression that the Palestinians should grin and bear a situation he personally characterizes as consisting of "trigger-happy soldiers and roadblocks."[171] The prohibition on criticizing Israel without first condemning some group or grouping of Arabs and/or Muslims is meanwhile also applicable in the case of the 2008–9 Gaza bloodbath, when the prerequisite for permission to critique Israel's "slicing through" the territory is a denunciation of Islamist suicide bombings in Iraq,[172] despite the fact that Iraqi suicide bombers are not currently the primary recipients of U.S. military aid.

Friedman appears to have forgotten that he has answered the question of why Israel is consistently singled out for criticism in *From Beirut*, where he quotes Israeli statesman Abba Eban as explaining that "the world is only comparing us to the standard we set for ourselves. You can't go out and declare that we are the descendants of kings and prophets and then come and say, 'Why does the world demand that we behave differently from Syria?'"[173] Friedman furthermore appears to be undecided as to whether the Palestinians are over-portrayed or under-portrayed in the media, and he goes from arguing a media bias against Israel and excessive coverage of Israeli violence against Palestinians[174] to declaring that "It might seem, and does seem to many Palestinians, terribly unjust that the Israelis have tremendous visibility while they do not. In order to explain this, they often resort to the conspiracy theories about Jews dominating the news media."[175]

The alleged conspiracy does not stop Friedman from providing a list detailing the "extraordinary lengths" Israel goes to "to project and protect its image," such as disseminating pro-Israel material to U.S. media outlets and monitoring U.S. newspapers for "hostile" content, which—if detected—is said to be promptly combated via letter-writing campaigns and visits to editors by Israeli embassy or consulate staff.[176] The declared lack of Palestinian visibility is in turn difficult to reconcile with Friedman's claim that Palestinians are "mistak[ing] public attention for sympathy and headlines for heartstrings"; he meanwhile reasons that the Palestinians are powerless to reform their relative lack of importance because they are not part of the biblical "super story" and are not the "carriers of the biblical-moral tradition that has helped to shape Western civilization and all that falls under the title of Judeo-Christian ethics."[177]

During the second Intifada the Palestinians become "as responsible for those horrific TV images [of Israelis brutalizing them] as Israelis" are.[178] The victims of Israeli occupation and devastating military campaigns are not the only ones to blame for forcing the Israelis to appear as victimizers on television, however. Culpability is also assigned to former victimizers of the Jews, and Friedman informs us that international uproar over the devastation of the West Bank town of Jenin in 2002 is merely a result of the European desire "to describe what [Sharon] did in Jenin as a massacre, so that the Europeans can finally get the guilt of the Holocaust off their backs and be able to shout: 'Look at these Jews, they're worse than we were!'"[179] (According to Robert Fisk, it is the Israeli army itself that "first gave the impression that there had been a massacre of civilians inside the city."[180]) On top of all of this, Friedman now has to contend with the rise of the Internet and Arab satellite television, which does not portray the West Bank invasion and the bulldozing of houses on top of civilians as something "any other nation would have done."[181]

New media capabilities are especially dangerous given high birth rates among disproportionately angry sectors of the global population, and Friedman accuses the "Arab media explosion" of bias and of "taking images of the Israeli–Palestinian conflict and beaming them to [the Arab] population explosion, nurturing rage against Israel, America and Jews in a whole new Arab generation."[182] The result of this intersection of explosions, according to Friedman, is that ten members of the new generation will end up convincing their respective fathers to write checks for $100,000 for Pakistani door-to-door salesmen toting suitcase nuclear bombs.[183]

In 2010, meanwhile, further disproportionate criticism is leveled against Israel when an Israeli commando attack on the Turkish-flagged Freedom Flotilla endeavoring to break the Gaza siege kills nine Turkish humanitarian activists, including a teenager with U.S. citizenship.[184] Friedman immediately assigns quotation marks to the word "humanitarian" and mimics Israeli government propaganda according to which the activists were seeking to accrue violent headlines for their cause: "Israel's intelligence failed to fully appreciate who was on board, and Israel's leaders certainly failed to think more creatively about how to avoid the very violent confrontation that the blockade-busters wanted."[185] The Israeli Foreign Ministry, however, provides creative proof of said violent intentions by adding the category "Weapons found on Mavi Marmara" to its Flickr photostream and uploading images of marbles, keffiyehs, binoculars, and a metal pail. A featured photograph of slingshots decoratively labeled "Hizbullah" is specified as having been taken on Feb 7, 2006, i.e., over four years prior to the flotilla attack.[186]

In the wake of the 2008–9 onslaught on Gaza and the 2010 flotilla incident, Friedman warns that "there is something foul in the air. It is a trend, both deliberate and inadvertent, to delegitimize Israel"—terminology that has presumably been appropriated from Netanyahu.[187] According to Friedman, the trend has led to the following situation: "If you just landed from Mars, you might think that Israel is the only country that has killed civilians in war."[188] Leaving aside details such as that Israel was not at war with the Turkish humanitarian aid vessel, Friedman announces: "I'm not here to defend Israel's bad behavior. Just the opposite. I've long argued that Israel's colonial settlements in the West Bank are suicidal for Israel as a Jewish democracy."[189] Thus is Friedman's personal formula for proper criticism of Israel effectively reduced to two easy steps:

1. Israel kills civilians.
2. Friedman criticizes Israeli settlements for jeopardizing the continued Israeli ability to deny Palestinians rights in a single, multiethnic democracy.[190]

Criticism of Israeli/Jewish influence over U.S. foreign policy requires a more complex approach, as is clear from the "Diary" section of *Longitudes*, in which Friedman recounts his post-9/11 jaunt to Saudi Arabia. Five pages after describing his calm and conscientious response to a senior Saudi minister who asks whether it is true that "the Jews in America control all the banks and media,"[191] Friedman reports walking out of a meeting with editors and columnists at Al-Medina newspaper because a certain Abdul Mohsen Musalam "launched in on me that the whole problem in the Middle East was that America was 'controlled by the Jews,' and he knew this to be true, he said, because a few years ago some American congressman came through Saudi Arabia and told them that."[192]

Friedman wonders how Musalam would feel if he "visited *The New York Times* editorial board and someone there piped up that the whole problem in the world was that Muslims and Arab oil money controlled everything—and we knew this to be true because a Lebanese parliamentarian once came through and told us that it was so?"[193] First of all, this is not far from the sort of reductionism that regularly appears in Friedman's own columns (though he generally refrains from citing Lebanese parliamentarians as backup—who, it bears adding, are slightly less relevant to the Saudi parliament than is a U.S. congressman to the U.S. Congress). It is thus not clear why Friedman finds Musalam's generalization "insulting"[194] but does not see anything wrong with, for example, assigning Palestinians to the anti-civilization side of World War III along with the (non-Palestinian) 9/11 hijackers.[195] Even more importantly, Friedman himself asserts in retrospect that the Israelis "had the run of the White House" under the Bush administration.[196]

Despite informing Saudi crown prince Abdullah in 2002 that "the Jews of the Clinton administration are gone" and that their replacement "WASPs" of the Bush administration "couldn't care less about the Israeli–Palestinian conflict. It is not an issue that resonates with them at all,"[197] Friedman announces the following year that the Bush team "has fallen so deep into the pocket of Ariel Sharon you can't even find it any more"[198] and that Bush may "be remembered as the president who got so wrapped around the finger of Ariel Sharon that he indulged Israel into thinking it really could have it all—settlements, prosperity, peace and democracy."[199] The year after that, Friedman proclaims that one of the reasons for the "steadily rising perception across the Arab-Muslim world that the great enemy of Islam is JIA—'Jews, Israel and America'" is that the Bush team is "embracing Ariel Sharon so tightly that it's impossible to know anymore where U.S. policy stops and Mr. Sharon's begins."[200] Proof of Friedman's awareness that there is no lack of influential Jews in the current administration can meanwhile be found in an article by Friedman's *Haaretz* companion Ari Shavit, published shortly after the start of the Iraq war and featuring an informal interview with Friedman at the *New York Times* offices in D.C., where Friedman reads him "witty lines" from his latest article.[201]

In his own article, Shavit describes the Iraq war as being promoted in Washington "by a small group of 25 or 30 neoconservatives, almost all of them Jewish," among them Deputy Secretary of Defense Paul Wolfowitz and Chairman of the Defense Policy Board Advisory Committee Richard Perle.[202] Friedman's response to Shavit's question about whether the Iraq war is "the great neoconservative war" is transcribed as follows:

It's the war the neoconservatives wanted, Friedman says. It's the war the neoconservatives marketed. Those people had an idea to sell when September 11 came, and they sold it. Oh boy, did they sell it. So this is not a war that the masses demanded. This is a war of an elite. Friedman laughs: I could give you the names of 25 people (all of whom are at this moment within a five-block radius of this office) who, if you had exiled them to a desert island a year and a half ago, the Iraq war would not have happened.[203]

Friedman's shameless amusement at the infliction of untold human tragedy on Iraq in accordance with elite—corporate and Zionist[204]—interests, which he openly admits do not intersect with those of the majority of Americans, highlights the transparency of his manipulation of the pro-democracy argument for war. It also renders his pro-war slogan that "Some things are true even if George Bush believes them,"[205] repeated to Shavit "with a smile,"[206] all the more repugnant. As for his amended specification to Shavit that the Iraq war is in fact not entirely a neocon project and that "what led us to the outskirts of Baghdad is a very American combination of anxiety and hubris,"[207] the necessity of distinguishing between neoconservatism and hubris is not clear, nor is the relevance of anxiety to the "Suck. On. This." formula.

Friedman's detection of "unquestioning [U.S.] Congressional support for Israel"[208] the very same year that he walks out on the Saudi Musalam for his story about the U.S. Congress member does not meanwhile prompt Friedman to reconsider the encounter, nor does his previous analysis of the power wielded in Congress by the Israel lobby: "When the Israel lobby calls senators, like Connie Mack and Joe Lieberman, and tells them to jump, the only question they ask is: How high?"[209] Additional observations that should have perhaps caused Friedman to walk out on himself include the following take on Israeli settlements:

For years, the Conference of Presidents of Major American Jewish Organizations and the pro-Israel lobby, rather than urging Israel to halt this corrosive process, used their influence to mindlessly protect Israel from U.S. pressure on this issue and to dissuade American officials and diplomats from speaking out against settlements. Everyone in Washington knows this, and a lot of people—people who care about Israel—are sick of it.[210]

History may yet produce a term along the lines of "schizofriednia" to signify self-contradiction, selective memory, and failure to integrate one's thoughts. In the meantime, it is worth noting that Musalam does stage a follow-up appearance in a Friedman column, but only because he has been thrown in jail for writing a poem about the corruption of Saudi judges. Friedman allows that "the only thing to do" in this case for his would-be ally in Middle Eastern democratizing endeavors is to call for his release—"not for his sake"—by the Saudis, who have apparently not internalized the correct lesson regarding freedom of speech from Friedman's walk-out stunt. [211]

Another outcome of Friedman's Saudi sojourn is that he is able to insinuate that he is the muse behind the Saudi peace plan of 2002. Not only does Friedman convince Abdullah to allow him to publish an off-the-record conversation in which the crown prince expresses the desire for a normalization of relations with Israel in exchange for an Israeli withdrawal from the occupied territories, Friedman also considers it a distinct possibility that Abdullah has extracted the very idea to "help transform Saudi Arabia from terrorist factory to peacemaker" from one of his columns.[212] The relevance of any such transformation is unclear given Friedman's acknowledgement that the Saudi offer will in any case be rejected by Sharon.[213]

On the last day of Friedman's visit to "the Magic Kingdom," he returns to his hotel room "deeply depressed" after informing some members of the Saudi royal family, who insist on blaming Israel for the Arab anger that produced 9/11, of his "fear that the cultural, political, and religious gulf between us may just be unbridgeable."[214] Apparently unaware that he himself will announce later this year: "Look, no one should doubt that the rage boiling among Arab youth today—which exploded on 9/11—is due in part to anger at U.S. support for anything Israel does. That anger is real,"[215] Friedman phones a friend to ask: "Do you know where I can get a drink—moonshine, firewater, bootleg, anything?"[216] Fortuitously, an incoming call from another Saudi who confirms that "until we get over this tribal outlook, we will never develop" restores Friedman's optimism: "I told this person that he had really salvaged my trip. He left me feeling that there are more than just a handful of people in Saudi Arabia who can be America's partners."[217]

As for appropriate Palestinian partners, the arrival of unelected Prime Minister Salam Fayyad to the scene in 2007 eliminates the need for Friedman's oft-repeated suggestion that Israel and the United States "invite NATO to occupy the West Bank and Gaza and set up a NATO-run Palestinian state."[218] A U.S.-educated economist who shares Friedman's conviction that the Palestinians require only a perfunctory validation of the right to return,[219] Fayyad appears to be the antidote to the Palestinian failure to develop, which according to Friedman's "new Mideast paradigm" of 2001 partially fuels the Arab–Israeli conflict by producing "tension between a developed society that is succeeding at modernization and an underdeveloped one that is failing at it and looking for others to blame."[220] As usual, Friedman issues this paradigm with no regard for his own recognition of such facts as that the Israelis "got many of their benefits from Oslo up front," such as trade opportunities with a host of nations, including China and India, which "contribut[ed] to a soaring of Israeli living standards," while the Palestinians had to contend with "the U.S. and American Jews turning a blind eye" and permitting Israel "to keep on seizing Palestinian land to expand settlements."[221]

Prior to hailing Fayyad as one of the "not-so-obvious forces" behind the Middle East uprisings of 2010–11,[222] Friedman credits him with "unleash[ing] a real Palestinian 'revolution'"[223] and "testing out the most exciting new idea in Arab governance ever," which Friedman dubs "Fayyadism":

Fayyadism is based on the simple but all-too-rare notion that an Arab leader's legitimacy should be based not on slogans or rejectionism or personality cults or security services, but on delivering transparent, accountable administration and services.[224]

The legitimacy component of the exciting new concept is presumably why Friedman never mentions that Fayyad is not elected and was instead illegally appointed to his post by P.A. President Mahmoud Abbas—whose own official mandate ended in 2009—without the required approval of the Palestinian Legislative Council.[225] Exciting new administrational and security changes meanwhile include the conversion of the West Bank into a police state with one of the highest security-to-population ratios in the world, in which Palestinian forces function in collaboration with the Israelis and the CIA.[226]

Given that such an arrangement in Palestine is compatible with not only Zionist but also neoliberal designs, it is not difficult to see why Friedman welcomes the Fayyadist "revolution." As Conflicts Forum's Aisling Byrne writes in *Foreign Policy*:

> The classic components of a counter-insurgency strategy are clearly being worked out for Palestine: the establishment of a Palestinian élite committed to working to [an] American-(Israeli) plan, the establishment of security services whose only allegiance is to this pro-American élite, full-spectrum control over the economy, destruction of all opposition to the project, employment provision and foreign aid directed at the delivery of economic benefits to the population ("improved quality of life") sufficient to suggest at least a semblance of popular support in order to offset the odium of authoritarianism, and the financial dependency of the people on the élite.[227]

As Byrne notes, 2009 sees a 72 percent increase in coordinated activities between Israeli security forces and the Palestinian National Security Forces (N.S.F.), "the so-called 'Dayton Battalions,' a paramilitary force … trained and funded by the Americans and some Europeans under the former guidance of Gen. Keith Dayton," U.S. Security Coordinator for Israel and the P.A.[228] This same year, Friedman visits Jenin in the company of Dayton "and his little team," where he watches with Orientalist approval a "company of newly trained, proud and professional-looking" N.S.F. troops "listening with obvious respect to the American general telling them: 'What you've done has done more to advance the Palestinian national project than anything else … You took care of your people at a difficult time. That is how the security forces of a country behave.'"[229] Lest readers doubt native gratitude for lessons in civilization from foreign masters, Friedman quotes an N.S.F. colonel who affirms that "General Dayton is our friend" and who provides the following example of newfound professionalism in Palestinian security operations: "We told the people during the Gaza demonstrations, 'You can protest, but you must do it in a modern way.'"[230]

The demonstrations in question are those that have recently taken place in the West Bank during Israel's massacre—in a modern way—of over 1,400 of the colonel's fellow Palestinians in Gaza. Friedman confirms that the N.S.F. troops "have been warmly received by the locals"[231] and that "what really got Israel's attention was that during the [war], the West Bank never blew up."[232] A less optimistic take on the forced modernization of wartime protests appears in *The New York Review of Books*:

> The most damage to the reputation of the Palestinian security forces occurred during the Israeli war in Gaza … In plainclothes and uniform, PA officers in the West Bank surrounded mosques, kept young men from approaching Israeli checkpoints, arrested protesters chanting Hamas slogans, and dispersed demonstrators with batons, pepper spray, and tear gas.[233]

Other details contained within the *New York Review of Books* report are that Fayyad "has repeatedly been found in polls to have less legitimacy than the Hamas prime minister in Gaza, Ismail Haniyeh" and that "Freedom House now gives the PA the same rating for political rights that it does for civil liberties—'not free.'"[234] It bears reiterating that Freedom House ratings constitute the foundation of Friedman's First Law of Petropolitics.

In the meantime, Friedman declares that "for the first time since

Oslo, there is an economic-security dynamic emerging on the ground in the West Bank," such that a "Palestinian peace partner for Israel may be taking shape again," and pinpoints "the recruitment, training and deployment of four battalions" of the N.S.F. as "the key to this rebirth."[235] The United States is encouraged to provide "more money" for training, while Friedman determines in reference to the impending new Palestinian state that "Hamas and Gaza can join later. Don't wait for them. If we build it, they will come."[236]

It is not clear why "they will come" when "they" are currently being tortured[237] by a key to Palestinian rebirth that is intent on eradicating them, and when, for example, the IMF cites greater economic growth in Gaza than the West Bank in the first half of 2010,[238] despite Netanyahu's hyping of an alleged West Bank economic boom.[239] Friedman meanwhile loyally reports the inauguration of a "Cinema City" multiplex and a "multistory furniture mart designed to cater to Israelis" in the West Bank city of Nablus.[240]

According to Friedman's rebirthing calculations, the honor of firstborn Palestinian peace partner thus belongs to Yasser Arafat, whose eventual downgrade by Friedman to "bad man"[241] is presumably what has necessitated the repetition of the reproductive cycle. Friedman's assessment in 1997 that only Arafat's ability to "guarantee real security … will constantly have [Prime Minister] Netanyahu under pressure to take Oslo to its logical conclusion" comes with the illustrative example of "real security" as the recent "swift cooperation between Israeli and Palestinian security services to prevent a blowup in Hebron after the shooting rampage by an Israeli fanatic."[242] Given contemporary praise for the N.S.F.'s prevention of a blowup in the West Bank during Israel's rampage in Gaza, it would appear that Israeli–Palestinian "peace" is largely contingent upon the successful containment of Palestinian reactions to fanatical Israeli behavior.

The initial security assessment occurs in a column entitled "Half-Pregnant in Hebron," in which Netanyahu "is half-pregnant all right, and it's Israel's silent majority that got him there."[243] The half-fetus is said to be a result of Netanyahu's strategic thought process, which Friedman interprets as follows: "I'll withdraw from Hebron to satisfy the [Israeli] majority that wants the peace process to continue, but I won't commit to all the further redeployments in the West Bank after Hebron that might lead to a Palestinian state, to satisfy my ideology."[244] How infant Palestinians factor into a half-pregnancy among Israelis is further clarified with Friedman's decree that "If Mr. Arafat were smart, he'd let Mr. Netanyahu be half-pregnant and sign the Hebron deal now."[245] That the N.S.F. might meanwhile be not only the key to the rebirth of a potential Palestinian peace partner but itself a factory of ready-made Palestinians is suggested by General Dayton's May 2009 brown-nosing at the Washington Institute for Near East Policy (WINEP), the think tank of the Israel lobby, during which he reports that "senior IDF commanders ask me frequently, 'How many more of these new Palestinians can you generate, and how quickly.'"[246]

Obstetrics-related ambiguities increase when Salam Fayyad, who has ostensibly only recently emerged from the womb of the N.S.F., himself announces in 2010 the impending arrival of "this baby"—i.e., a Palestinian state—"around 2011."[247] In his response to the birth announcement, entitled "An immaculate conception?," Columbia University professor Joseph Massad casts Fayyad as "both mother and midwife" and speculates that a paternity test would point to Barack Obama. Reviewing the reduction in birth weight that accompanies successive Palestinian birthing attempts, Massad writes in *The Electronic Intifada*:

> Obama's baby can only be born if a new Palestinian leader accepts the terms of Camp David, now even further reduced than when Ehud Barak offered them to Arafat in 2000. With tens of thousands more settlers, more Palestinian lands taken by the apartheid wall, and more confiscations of land across the West Bank and East Jerusalem, the 65 percent of the West Bank (marketed by US and Israeli propaganda as more than 95 percent of the West Bank) rejected by Arafat will be reduced further and re-offered to the Palestinian people by Fayyad himself.[248]

The United States is meanwhile cast in the role of obstetrician rather than father in *From Beirut*, tasked with figuring out whether the Arabs and Israelis are really trying to get pregnant with each other or whether they are just claiming to and then sleeping in separate bedrooms. According to Friedman, the United States is supposed to "measure how serious the parties are … the same way an obstetrician would do it—by observing what they say to each other, not what they say to us."[249] It is not clear what methods obstetricians generally employ to monitor their patients' private discourse, or whether the couple's sex life is not adversely affected by annual $3 billion influxes[250] from the obstetrician to one of the partners. Undeterred, Friedman instructs the United States to say to the couple: "I don't expect you to love each other. The sooner you live apart, the better off you will both be."[251]

Perhaps it is to avoid a situation in which the United States is seen to be advocating procreation immediately followed by divorce that Friedman subsequently assigns sole jurisdiction over the birthing process to the Israelis.[252] In 2008, following "a little drive" through "an ugly quilt" of walls, Israeli checkpoints, and settler-only roads in the West Bank, Friedman divulges his fear that "Israel will remain permanently pregnant with a stillborn Palestinian state in its belly."[253] A more credible analysis of gestational complications is provided by *Haaretz* journalist Gideon Levy, who determines in 2010 that the "Israeli peace camp is still an unborn baby," due primarily to "the [Israeli] left's impossible adherence to Zionism in its historical sense" and refusal to "understand [that] the Palestinian problem … was created in 1948, not 1967."[254] Friedman's first Intifada-era instruction to the Palestinians to "make themselves so indigestible to Israelis that they want to disgorge them into their own state"[255] meanwhile highlights the possibility of a Palestinian entrance into the world via other Israeli orifices, not only vaginal, and of a potential new bestseller along the lines of *The Lexus and the Laxative*.

The U.S. role as obstetrician endures various revisions, and Friedman goes from categorizing U.S. participation in resolving the Arab–Israeli conflict as merely "an act of kindness" and a "huge, morally responsible favor" in the post–Cold War era[256] to a necessity in the post-9/11 era, when U.S. troops are "literally walking the Arab street" and the country must endeavor to accrue "Muslim good will to protect themselves."[257] It is not clear why Friedman issues the latter assessment four months after advising the Obama administration to "take down our 'Peace-Processing-Is-Us' sign and just go home" because "right now we want it more than the parties,"[258] an attitude that is itself in defiance of his previous declaration on Middle East peacemaking: "For there to be any progress, America must want peace more than the parties themselves."[259]

It is imperative to note that, even in the wake of the global economic recession, Friedman comes close to suggesting a curtailment of exorbitant amounts of U.S. aid to Israel approximately two times.[260] In November 2009 he states in reference to both the Israelis and the Palestinians: "If the status quo is this tolerable for the parties, then I say, let them enjoy it. I just don't want to subsidize it or anesthetize it anymore. We need to fix America."[261] His decision in October 2010 that "it is time for all the outsiders who spoil [said parties] to find another hobby"[262] meanwhile functions as the conclusion to the "Just Knock It Off" dispatch that prompts Friedman's summoning onto Israel's Channel 2 to explain his blasphemy, for which he atones by confessing affection for Netanyahu.[263]

In December 2010, meanwhile, Friedman's speculation that financially stricken American schools and fire departments would happily receive $3 billion from the U.S. government occurs in an article with the following lede:

The failed attempt by the U.S. to bribe Israel with a $3 billion security assistance package, diplomatic cover and advanced F-35 fighter aircraft—if Prime Minister Bibi Netanyahu would simply agree to a 90-day settlements freeze to resume talks with the Palestinians—has been enormously clarifying. It demonstrates just how disconnected from reality both the Israeli and the Palestinian leaderships have become.[264]

Only in the sixth paragraph of the article do we learn how it is that the Palestinians are equally to blame for Israel's rejection of multibillion-dollar goodies in order to continue confiscation of Palestinian land (Abbas let "a great two-state deal" from former Israeli Prime Minister Ehud Olmert "fritter away"[265]), which is three paragraphs after he has instructed negotiators from both sides to Google the terms "budget cuts and fire departments" and "schools and budget cuts."[266]

Of course, the Palestinians are not the only group authorized to share the guilt for Israeli transgressions. The Gaza offensive of 2008–9, for example, is advertised by Friedman as a platform for Hamas, Hezbollah, and Iran to "turn Obama into Bush. They know Barack Hussein Obama must be (am)Bushed."[267] The necessity of the (am)Bushing, the aim of which is to prolong the favorable "wave of anti-U.S. anger,"[268] is unclear given Obama's silence regarding the bloodbath. Israeli Reut Institute president Gidi Grinstein meanwhile informs Friedman that the continued Israeli occupation of the West Bank is itself a scheme by "Iran & Co." to cause Israel to implode by sucking it into "imperial overstretch."[269] In 2011 Friedman himself declares that apartheid may be "inevitable" due to the alleged fact that "the main goal of the rejectionists today [Iran, Syria, Hezbollah, and Hamas] is to lock Israel into the West Bank—so the world would denounce it as some kind of Jewish apartheid state."[270] The lock-in project is presumably facilitated by Israel's willingness to erect hundreds of miles of concrete barrier in accordance with rejectionist goals.

The Iranian ringleader figures into Friedman's recommendations to Channel 2 regarding other Israeli options aside from implosion, and Friedman emphasizes that, in the event that Israel "find[s] itself in a situation where it has to take on Iran in some military way," the world might take more kindly to the maneuver if the peace process with the Palestinians is perceived to be continuing.[271]

The idea that Ahmed's seat in the bus can serve as a carte blanche of sorts does not indicate Friedman's support for an attack on Iran, which he claims to oppose.[272] He may simply be trying to market Jewish democracy preservation in terms that appeal to the Israeli regime.

Friedman would nonetheless do well, prior to dispensing advice in fields including but not limited to war, to review his own words of caution during the prelude to the invasion of Iraq: "It's O.K. to throw out your steering wheel as long as you remember you're driving without one."[273]

CONCLUDING NOTE

When widely followed public figures feel free to say anything, without any fact-checking, we have a problem.

—Thomas Friedman, 2010

We arrive at the question of where to turn for information in an age dominated by media pundits without steering wheels.

As is clear from a passage that occurs midway through *The World Is Flat*, Friedman is under the impression that the absence of editorial restraining mechanisms is a defect belonging to specific domains within the realm of information proliferation:

> Yes, the reader in me loves to surf the Net and read the bloggers, but the citizen in me also wishes that some of those bloggers had an editor, a middleman, to tell them to check some of their facts one more time before they pressed the Send button and told the whole world that something was wrong or unfair.[1]

Of course, any middleman assigned to Friedman would be faced with the dilemma of how to check such "facts" as that Palestinians are collectively mad,[2] that terrorism bubbles speak,[3] or that "the Caribbean nation of Honduras had developed a green consciousness over the years [that] was being undermined by a shortage of condoms."[4] In order to illustrate some of the challenges to

Friedman's discourse that arise from the flat world of unedited bloggers, let us introduce as a foil Dr. Adrienne Pine, anthropologist at American University in Washington, D.C., who blogs at quotha.net on matters primarily relating to the Central American nation where environmentalism has allegedly been stymied by a condom deficit.

Pine deals variously and simultaneously with issues of free trade, the *maquiladora* industry, biofuels, mining, poverty, violence, alcoholism, the drug war, militarization, paramilitarization, indigenous groups, national identity, gender relations, elite political domination, and, most recently, the resistance to the U.S.-validated coup d'état against President Manuel Zelaya in 2009. Zelaya was overthrown after committing such infractions as raising the minimum wage in certain sectors and suggesting a popular consultation on the possibility of rewriting the Honduran constitution, composed during the epoch in which the nation was affectionately referred to as the "U.S.S. Honduras."

Given that her analysis occurs within a solid historical context highlighting the corrosive influences of colonialism, U.S. imperialism, and neoliberalism, Pine's observations on the—perhaps seemingly limited—subject of Honduras are conducive to comprehending the forces at work not only in Latin America but globally as well. Friedman, as we have seen, prefers to amputate the effects of such forces from the milieu in which people and countries operate and to propagate an ahistorical and counterfactual reality according to which, for example, corporate globalization constitutes the panacea for the very ills it creates.

To start off with a simple comparison, consider Pine's straightforward assessment of the Central American Free Trade Agreement (CAFTA) in her book *Working Hard, Drinking Hard: On Violence and Survival in Honduras*:

> As its counterpart, the North American Free Trade Agreement (NAFTA), has done in Mexico, CAFTA will result in a flood of cheap U.S. products disastrous for the Honduran market. It

deregulates corporations, removing consumer protection so that—to take a controversial example—drug companies can price-gouge as they do in the United States. It also further lowers corporate taxes, perpetuating and deepening a public-sector crisis in which already struggling Honduran workers shoulder a disproportionate tax burden.[5]

Now recall Friedman's own approach to CAFTA, which consists of:

1. Writing a column insisting that the agreement is critical for Central American development and accusing U.S. Congress members opposed to the accord of behavior worthy of the French, otherwise known as the "antiglobalist Gaullist Luddites."[6]
2. Getting the agreement's name wrong in a subsequent interview while admitting to not having perused its contents—beyond the two words "free trade"—prior to composing his adulatory column.[7]

Pine discusses the international relevance of themes of inequality and human rights abuse in Honduras in a 2008 interview about her book, in which she conveys her aim to "help people to tie that inequality and its deadly consequences to a much larger international system of inequalities currently being exacerbated by the neoliberal economic model."[8] The incisiveness of Pine's evaluations, excerpted below, is particularly blatant when juxtaposed with the racist smokescreens Friedman has been known to erect in his explanations of international phenomena, such as the idea that too many black males in U.S. inner cities are failing[9] or that Arabs and Muslims are disproportionately backward and angry.[10]

Argues Pine in the interview:

Human rights abuses [in Honduras], whether they are carried out by private security guards working for companies owned by the leaders of the 1980s [C.I.A.-trained] death squad "Battalion 316," by the underpaid and poorly-trained police force, or by *maquiladora* owners, are inseparable from structural adjustment programs being imposed by the IMF and World Bank, with no democratic involvement on the part of the Honduran people. Such programs have dramatically decreased the security of the Honduran people by denying them access to public education, public healthcare, and public oversight of their government, while providing massive profits to private corporations who are not required to return the favor in the form of taxes. At the same time, people have been distracted by the extremely high levels of violent crime, often carried out by agents of the state and private industry. Thus, many call for a different kind of security than that offered by education and healthcare. This arrived in Ricardo Maduro's presidency [2002–6] in the form of "Zero Tolerance," a draconian crime control policy imported [from] former New York City Mayor Rudolph Giuliani, and resulted in what I call an "invisible genocide" and what Hondurans refer to as "street cleaning"—the murder of thousands of youths, primarily unemployed young men who were marked as criminals by a society that had no room for them.

So, although I am referring [in the book] to the particular case of Honduran human rights abuse, the various structures that facilitate them are international in scope. While Giuliani's policy did not result in large-scale killings in New York, many accused it of criminalizing poverty and cleaning the streets to aid economic investment that never trickled down to the poor. Zero tolerance was implemented in New York and then Honduras to stop a violent yet vague threat, "delinquency," just as the Patriot Act, which reconfigured the U.S. constitution toward creating a security state, was implemented in the name of stopping the vague enemy, "terrorism." Similarly, the privatization of schools and healthcare in the United States, part of the Washington consensus model followed by the IMF and World Bank, has significantly increased the structural vulnerability of a large part of the population, a fact which is reflected in the poor educational outcomes, and high mortality and morbidity rates among people in that country.[11]

Pine relentlessly exposes the oppressive conditions in which various sectors of Honduran society exist—factory workers, farmers, teenage gang members, the anti-coup resistance front, the LGBT community. Of course, Pine actually speaks to and spends time in the company of the impoverished and maligned subjects about whom she writes, asserting their humanity in defiance of the system that denies it. This modus operandi stands in stark contrast to that of Friedman, who, for example, blissfully declares after chatting with the owner of a Victoria's Secret factory in Sri Lanka in 1999 that it is "stupid" to oppose globalization: "The [anti-WTO] Seattle protesters need to understand that. The people of Sri Lanka already do"[12] Lest anyone remain skeptical as to the shared identity between the Victoria's Secret factory owner and all Sri Lankans, Friedman later testifies that "in terms of conditions, I would let my own daughters work in [said factory]."[13] Readers of *The World Is Flat*, a treatise written under the supervision of corporate CEOs, are meanwhile invited to "just ask any Indian villager" in order to confirm the need for the antiglobalization movement to "grow up."[14]

In Friedman's view, the idea that the 0.2 percent of the Indian population employed in the high-tech sector[15] can now obtain credit cards with which to purchase American goods constitutes a sign of national advancement.[16] In Pine's view, the "perfection of consumerism" among Honduran *maquiladora* employees is not indicative of progress but rather of "corporate and government control of worker time and fertility, and the creation of a new class of consumers without the kind of economic power to effect any real large-scale changes in standard-of-living."[17] This assessment would appear to be confirmed by such facts as that Honduras continues to be the third poorest country in the western hemisphere,[18] despite Friedman's encouraging report in 2000 that "Honduras, little Honduras, already exports seven times more textiles and apparel to the U.S. than all 48 nations of sub-Saharan Africa combined."[19] It also suggests that opponents of free trade are perhaps not the primary component, as Friedman argues, of "The Coalition to Keep Poor People Poor."[20]

Pine's reference to fertility control conveniently brings us back to the theory—presented in *The Lexus and the Olive Tree*—that a shortage of condoms among Honduran villagers is affecting the green outlook that the country is alleged to have developed. The theory is not Friedman's personal invention and has instead been appropriated from a 1998 *World Watch* magazine article by Howard Youth, who lists a number of obstacles to conservationism aside from population growth, such as the palm oil plant mentioned in the very first paragraph.[21] By zeroing in on the condom detail that occurs mid-article, Friedman apparently fails to consider the possibility that the existential hazards posed to the environment by rampant human reproduction might be more effectively seared into the reader's consciousness were he to offer as an example a country with a population larger than that of New York City.

Given the Honduran government's history of obsequiousness to international mining and other environmentally destructive industries, it is not difficult to determine who benefits from placing the blame on the poor Honduran masses for disrupting national ecosystems with their existence. Pine herself incidentally draws attention to government propaganda, issued in the aftermath of Hurricane Mitch's devastation of Honduras in 1998, according to which the flooding that occurred was a result of the citizenry's ecological recklessness and the accumulation of trash in street drains. As Pine points out, such claims "ignore … the lack of garbage collection services [offered in certain areas by the state] and the fact that by far the worst polluters are *maquiladoras* and other industries which enjoy tax-free status in Honduras and are not required to clean up their messes, placing the moral onus for Mitch's destruction on unmodern, unsanitary individuals."[22] She additionally argues that the death toll from the disaster could have been mitigated had even minimal taxes been levied upon the *maquiladora* industry, "which has benefited more from IMF and World Bank liberalization policies tied to debt relief than any other industry," in order to improve the country's infrastructure.[23]

As for potential solutions to the Honduran birth control short-age, Pine expounds on the role of the *maquiladora* in curbing reproduction in the interest of "developmental progress":

> For demographers, if women are having fewer children and working for money, they are assumed to have better control over their fertility options than in the inverse scenario. However, most women working in maquiladoras are subject to tight and direct control of their fertility. Many are obligated to take birth control at the factory, and if they do become pregnant are faced with the choice between keeping their baby or keeping their job. In some extreme cases, as informants have recounted and one doctor who has worked in these maquiladoras himself informed me, abor-tions are performed in clinics inside the factories. Other abuses of maternity rights afforded to women under Honduran law are pervasive throughout the industry. Both factory owners and gov-ernment officials are complicit in this exercise, the former directly and the latter for refusing to enforce labor laws. Rather than exer-cise increasing control over their fertility it seems that women have traded one set of lacking options for another.[24]

As previously mentioned, simpler methods of population control in Honduras meanwhile include extrajudicial executions of what Pine refers to as an "excess demographic":

> Young men, especially poor young men who are undisciplined by the factory workplace or by institutions like Alcoholics Anonymous or Evangelical Christianity, are a threat that must be removed. This is necessary to achieve "security," itself a means to creating an "Investment-Friendly Infrastructure" to attract "Foreign-Direct Investment."[25]

Indeed, former chief of internal affairs for the Honduran police force María Luisa Borjas herself confirmed to me in 2009 that President Ricardo Maduro's Zero Tolerance policy of 2002–6 had resulted in a criminalization of youth and the extermination of three thousand young people via a liberal application of the term "gang member."

That Friedman may also view the world in terms of excess demographics is implied by his conviction that the Israeli slaughter of 1,200 people in Lebanon constitutes "the education of Hezbollah," his hope for a similar "education of Hamas" in Gaza,[26] and his infinite justifications for the mutilation of Iraq, such as this post-invasion pronouncement: "America sliced right through Iraq. It did so because we are a free-market democracy that is capable of amassing huge amounts of technical power."[27] While the sliced-through population continues to dwindle in number as a result of U.S. technical power, our point man for free-market democracy tries his best to remain optimistic about the possible emergence of a proper Iraqi demographic: "As much as I believe we did good and right in toppling Saddam, I will whoop it up only when the Iraqi people are really free—not free just to loot or to protest against us, but free to praise us out loud, free to speak their minds in any direction."[28]

As Friedman regularly reminds audiences, his friend Uzi Dayan, a general in the Israel Defense Forces, once told him: "Tom, I know why you're an optimist. It's because you're short and you can only see that part of the glass that's half full."[29] Given that the positive connotations of optimism are questionable in situations characterized by military-inflicted punishment, persons genuinely concerned with the roots of injustice might find more reason for hope in the work of those legions of scholars, journalists, bloggers, and activists who, like Pine, expose the corporate media glass as decidedly empty and refrain from using the expression "whoop it up" in the context of massive civilian casualties.

Other individuals whose failure to whitewash human suffering would undoubtedly exclude them from the optimist category include Al Jazeera's Sherine Tadros and Ayman Mohyeldin, who report the devastation of Operation Cast Lead from inside Gaza while Friedman pontificates from afar on the need for Palestinian civilian casualties. Journalists Amira Hass and Gideon Levy of *Haaretz* have consistently ensured the visibility in Israel's mainstream press of the Israeli occupation's ruinous effects on Palestinian society, thus establishing a robust counter-narrative to Friedman's loftily scattered assertions, such as that the Palestinians can erect a state simply by ignoring the fact that they are occupied. Joseph Dana and Lia Tarachansky document Israeli settlement proliferation and regular nonviolent Palestinian protests against the West Bank separation wall, the conspicuous lack of international media coverage of which permits Friedman at the late date of 2011 to unironically advocate for weekly nonviolent Palestinian marches in order to attract media attention.[30] Ali Abunimah and Ramzy Baroud regularly debunk the propaganda surrounding alleged Israeli peace overtures and the application of the rejectionist label to the Palestinians. Max Ajl explores the intersections of Zionism, capitalism, and the oil and arms industries and eloquently pulverizes the logic behind the demand for a Palestinian Gandhi—an entity Friedman is able to advertise as the answer to Palestinian statelessness only by ignoring the fact that he himself characterized Palestinian mass civil disobedience in the 1980s as compatible with Gandhian principles.[31]

The ease with which thoughts from this particular decade might slip one's mind is highlighted in a rare Friedman appearance in 2006 on *Democracy Now!*, the TV/radio news program hosted by independent media pioneer Amy Goodman, who relentlessly pursues news stories that have been dishonestly or inadequately dealt with in the corporate media. Goodman's superior attention to detail is once again underscored with her reminder to Friedman of his 1980s reference to Palestinians as "Ahmed," which he claims not to remember on account of having said "100,000 words since then."[32] Australian journalist and documentary filmmaker John Pilger has meanwhile, for the past several decades, investigated subjects ranging from Israel/Palestine to Vietnam and Cambodia to Afghanistan and Iraq to globalization, and has produced evidence in all areas to contradict Friedman's assessment that "Many big bad things happen in the world without America, but not a lot of big good things."[33]

In Iraq, American journalist Dahr Jamail has provided an unadulterated portrait of the occupation by refusing to embed with the U.S. military and thus experiencing the war zone at a human level. Jamail shows the killing and displacement of millions of Iraqis to be a direct consequence of the U.S. invasion, whereas Friedman prefers to trot out theories such as that Sunni Muslims are prone to blowing themselves up[34] or that the resistance to U.S. occupation is being waged by the "Iraqi Khmer Rouge."[35] In addition to humanizing the victims of U.S. military excess, Jamail also documents the traumatic effects of combat on U.S. soldiers and the phenomenon of rape in the military, areas Friedman wholly eschews in order to portray the armed forces as a bastion of multi-ethnic teamwork.[36]

Nir Rosen, who has reported extensively from Iraq and Afghanistan, writes about the "little Abu Ghraibs" that accompany any military occupation:

> The big scandals like Abu Ghraib, or the "Kill Team" in Afghanistan, eventually make their way into the media where they can be dismissed as bad apples and exceptions, and the general oppression of the occupations can be ignored. But an occupation is a systematic and constant imposition of violence on an entire country. It's 24 hours of arresting, beating, killing, humiliating and terrorising.[37]

That Friedman precisely follows the bad-apple-dismissal formula outlined by Rosen is suggested by his 2009 analysis of the U.S. performance in Iraq: "We left some shameful legacies here of torture and Abu Ghraib, but we also left a million acts of kindness and a profound example of how much people of different backgrounds can accomplish when they work together."[38] Friedman's warmongering apologetics on behalf of empire and capital meanwhile attest to his representative role in Western mainstream media, defined by Rosen as being largely composed of journalists who "perpetuate the dominant ideology" and act as "the functional tools for a bourgeois ruling class."[39] Noting the American journalistic tendency to propagate racist perceptions of the "other" while engaging only on the most superficial level with society in Iraq and elsewhere, Rosen warns:

> American reporting is problematic throughout the third world, but because the American military/industrial/financial/academic/ media complex is so directly implicated in the Middle East, the consequences of such bad reporting are more significant. Journalists end up serving as propagandists [who] justify the killing of innocent people instead of [as] a voice for those innocent people.[40]

There is no dearth of truthful information in contemporary circulation, accessible through the din of the establishment media. Rosen defines the duty of conscientious journalists as "speaking truth to the people, to those not in power, in order to empower them."[41] Part of speaking the truth is exposing those journalists who do not.

ACKNOWLEDGEMENTS

Unending thanks to Tariq Ali and Andy Hsiao at Verso, to Muhammad Idrees Ahmad, Ann el Khoury, Jasmin Ramsey, and Robin Yassin-Kassab at PULSE Media, and to Jeanette and Joe Fernández, Linda and Kurt Fernández, and Joey and Lauren Fernández.

Thanks also to Dahr Jamail at *Al Jazeera*, Ramzy Baroud at *The Palestine Chronicle*, Hamid Dabashi at Columbia, Alex Cockburn at *CounterPunch*, Norman Finkelstein, Robert Fisk, Chase Madar, Roxanne Dunbar-Ortiz, Ali Mendos, Adriana and Gianluca Mazza, Abdellah Erraoui, Andrés *el cuñado* Tejeda, Hassan al Mohamed, Ken Kelley, Mariette Henke, Suha Afyouni, Diego Osorno, Cyril Mychalejko, Kristin Bricker, Jesse Freeston, Neil Brandvold, Arturo Viscarra, Jeremías López, Alex Palencia, Tom Chartier, Bill Manville, Michelle Witte, and Mustafa Habib—who sacrificed suitcase space to transport the Friedman canon to me in Beirut.

Thank you to Amelia Opalińska, my longtime hitchhiking companion and beloved friend, and to Carlos Calderón and Flaco García (*chingaos*).

And thank you to everyone from Colombia to Syria who has ever picked Amelia and me up on the side of the road, hosted us at their home, or through any other form of kindness made life worth living and reaffirmed the magnanimity of the human spirit.

NOTES

INTRODUCTION

1 Thomas Friedman, *The World Is Flat*, p. 4. Subsequent footnote entries refer to works by Thomas Friedman unless a different author is cited.

2 *Ibid.*, p. 3.

3 *Ibid.*, p. 7.

4 *Ibid.*

5 *Ibid.*, p. 5.

6 *Ibid.*, p. 32.

7 *Ibid.*, p. 150.

8 "The Sand Wall," *New York Times*, April 13, 2003.

9 *Ibid.*

10 "Iraq, Upside Down," *New York Times*, September 18, 2002.

11 "Winning the Real War," *New York Times*, July 16, 2003.

12 "Thinking About Iraq (I)," *New York Times*, January 22, 2003.

13 "Head Shot," *New York Times*, November 6, 1997. Other Friedman advice from the 1990s on how the U.S. should deal with Saddam: "Blow up a different power station in Iraq every week, so no one knows when the lights will go off [and] use every provocation by Saddam to blow up another Iraqi general's home." This advice occurs in the same article in which Friedman recounts the rumor that Nigerian dictator Sani Abacha's demise was caused by Indian prostitutes armed with poisoned Viagra; Friedman notes: "It's worth thinking about Nigeria as we reflect on where to go next with Iraq" ("Rattling the Rattler," January 19, 1999).

14　"Fire, Ready, Aim," *New York Times*, March 9, 2003.

15　"The Case for Illegal Mingling," *New York Times*, November 25, 2007.

16　See Luke Baker, "Iraq Conflict Has Killed a Million Iraqis: Survey," *Reuters*, January 30, 2008.

17　"My Favorite Teacher," *New York Times*, January 9, 2001.

18　The dates listed refer to the original publication; revised and expanded editions have since been issued. The versions I refer to in this book are as follows: *From Beirut to Jerusalem*, New York: Farrar, Straus and Giroux, 1991 (first revised edition); *The Lexus and the Olive Tree: Understanding Globalization*, New York: Anchor Books, 2000 (first Anchor Books edition, newly updated and expanded); *Longitudes and Attitudes: The World in the Age of Terrorism* (updated subtitle), New York: Anchor Books, 2003 (first Anchor Books edition, newly updated and expanded); *The World Is Flat: A Brief History of the Twenty-first Century*, New York: Picador, 2007 (release 3.0, further updated and expanded); and *Hot, Flat and Crowded: Why We Need a Green Revolution—And How It Can Renew America*, New York: Farrar, Straus and Giroux, 2008.

19　See Section I.

20　"A Theory of Everything," *New York Times*, June 1, 2003.

21　"War of Ideas, Part 4," *New York Times*, January 18, 2004.

22　See Section III.

23　"Show Me the Money," *New York Times*, November 9, 2008.

24　"Shoulda, Woulda, Can," *New York Times*, May 27, 2004.

25　*The Lexus and the Olive Tree*, p. 348.

26　"Beware of Icebergs," *New York Times*, November 9, 2001.

27　*From Beirut to Jerusalem*, p. 313.

28　*The Lexus and the Olive Tree*, p. 4.

29　*Longitudes and Attitudes*, p. xiv.

30　"Shoe Leather and Tears," *New York Times*, May 12, 2006.

31　"A Deadly Embrace," *New York Times*, October 6, 1999.

32　"The Land of 'No Service,'" *New York Times*, August 15, 2009.

33　*Longitudes and Attitudes*, p. xii.

34　*Ibid.*, p. xiv.

35　"Shoe Leather and Tears," *New York Times*, May 12, 2006. The article is written on the occasion of Rosenthal's death. Friedman claims the reason Rosenthal "exploded at my insubordination" in 1982 was that, after using the word "indiscriminate," Friedman wrote a memo accusing the editors who removed it of cowardice. He concludes in 2006: "They don't make 'em like that anymore. God love ya, Abe. May your memory be a blessing."

36   "Chicken à l'Iraq," *New York Times*, October 9, 2002.

37   See *Longitudes and Attitudes*, pp. 346–7.

38   "Beware of Icebergs," *New York Times*, November 9, 2001.

39   This particular allegation occurs in an article entitled "Chile, First and Forever" (June 26, 1997): "Chile, unlike Poland, Hungary or the Czech Republic, actually shares a border with Russia. Check it out. The Russian slice of Antarctica is right next to the southern tip of Chile." Kaliningrad, the Russian territory that borders Poland, is thus booted out of existence.

40   Compare *The World Is Flat*, p. 9, with *The World Is Flat*, p. 201.

41   See Section II.

42   "It's No Vietnam," *New York Times*, October 30, 2003.

43   "The Chant Not Heard," *New York Times*, November 30, 2003.

44   *Ibid.*

45   Robert Fisk, *The Great War for Civilisation: The Conquest of the Middle East*, New York: Alfred A. Knopf, 2005, p. 500. See Section III for more details on the West Bank invasion.

46   For Obama's courting of Friedman, see Mark Landler, "Obama Seeks Reset in Arab World," *New York Times*, May 11, 2011. According to Friedman's analysis of the uprisings, the president's middle name (Hussein) is one detail in the "mix of forces" that has suddenly prompted the Arab masses to reflect on their own lack of empowerment. Friedman quotes the hypothetical reaction of the masses to Obama's 2009 Cairo speech: "Hmmm, let's see. He's young. I'm young. He's dark-skinned. I'm dark-skinned. His middle name is Hussein. My name is Hussein. His grandfather is a Muslim. My grandfather is a Muslim. He is president of the United States. And I'm an unemployed young Arab with no vote and no voice in my future."

47   See James Rainey, "Thomas L. Friedman and the High Cost of Speaking," *Los Angeles Times*, May 13, 2009. According to the article, Friedman is forced on one occasion to return his speaking fee to the San Francisco Bay Area Air Quality Management District after the payment is publicized because "*[New York] Times* ethics guidelines

allow staffers to take speaking fees only from 'educational and other nonprofit groups for which lobbying and political activity are not a major focus.'"

48 See Section I.

49 "No Mullah Left Behind," *New York Times*, February 13, 2005.

50 *The World Is Flat*, p. 565.

51 Garrett M. Graff, "Thomas Friedman Is on Top of the World," *Washingtonian*, July 1, 2006. The article's many intriguing tidbits include that Friedman was permitted to do "two big projects" for his high school paper during his senior year: "a three-part series on the John F. Kennedy assassination, written after he became obsessed with the conspiracy theories, and 'Love In the Halls,' an exposé on an 'epidemic' of students kissing in the school hallways."

52 "Thomas Friedman wins the inaugural FT and Goldman Sachs Business Book of the Year Award," ft.com, August 22, 2005.

53 Matt Taibbi, "The People vs. Goldman Sachs," *Rolling Stone*, May 26, 2011.

54 "Why How Matters," *New York Times*, October 15, 2008.

55 See, for example, "Anxious in America," *New York Times*, June 29, 2008.

56 "Adults Only, Please," *New York Times*, January 27, 2010.

57 "A Gift for Grads: Start-Ups," *New York Times*, June 8, 2010.

58 See Garrett M. Graff, "Thomas Friedman Is On Top of the World," *Washingtonian*, July 1, 2006.

59 *The World Is Flat*, p. 437.

60 *The Lexus and the Olive Tree*, p. 104. As for the fate of the "other systems," the end of Soviet communism is credited with enabling Russians to "dress in a rainbow of colors, instead of different shades of cement" ("Happy Nation," *New York Times*, April 30, 1995).

61 "Transcript: A TimesSelect/TimesTalks Event on Globalization," *New York Times*, April 25, 2006.

62 "The Old Ball Game," *New York Times*, February 21, 1998.

63 *Ibid.*

64 *Longitudes and Attitudes*, p. 398.

65 *The World Is Flat*, p. 639.

66 *The Lexus and the Olive Tree*, p. 469.

67 Edward Said, "The Orientalist Express: Thomas Friedman Wraps Up the Middle East," *Village Voice*, October 17, 1989.

68　Ibid.

69　All articles were accessed via the website of the New York Times (nytimes.com). There may be slight differences between the online and print versions of articles. In cases in which the online and print versions were published on different days, the online publication date is used.

70　"Iowa Beef Revolutionized Meat-Packing Industry," New York Times, June 2, 1981.

71　"Thomas Friedman: Americans 'Fed Up' With Israel," uploaded to youtube.com on October 25, 2010, by israelnews (Israeli Channel 2 News).

72　New York Times, April 18, 2007; see pulitzer.org/citation/2002-commetary.

73　"Who's Crazy Here?," New York Times, May 15, 2001.

1 AMERICA

1　"When Friends Fall Out," New York Times, June 1, 2010.

2　Ibid.

3　Ibid.

4　For the attack cited by Friedman, Hamas's condemnation of which was reported in mainstream venues such as Reuters, see "Gunmen Attack UN Gaza Summer Camp," Ynetnews, May 23, 2010. For an example of Israeli anti-U.N. operations that Friedman neglects to report during the 2008–9 war on Gaza, see Chris McGreal and Hazem Balousha, "Gaza's Day of Carnage—40 Dead as Israelis Bomb Two U.N. Schools," Guardian, January 7, 2009. For the Israeli slaughter of 106 refugees sheltered at the U.N. compound in Qana, Lebanon, in 1996, see Robert Fisk, Pity the Nation: The Abduction of Lebanon, New York: Thunder's Mouth Press/Nation Books, 2002, p. 669.

5　The video of the presentation can be accessed via the Özyeğin website, ozyegin.edu.tr: "The Launch of Research@Özyeğin With the Participation of Thomas Friedman," June 15, 2010.

6　"When Friends Fall Out," New York Times, June 1, 2010.

7　"The Launch of Research@Özyeğin With the Participation of Thomas Friedman," June 15, 2010.

8　Ibid. The only vocabulary term Friedman checks to make sure his audience has understood is "gerrymandering," as "stick-to-it-iveness" is apparently deemed readily translatable.

9   *Ibid.*

10 The book is co-authored by Friedman's "intellectual soul mate" Michael Mandelbaum. See Friedman's interview with Don Imus, "Tom Friedman on Book Leave," Fox Business, January 4, 2011, video.foxbusiness.com.

11 "Follow The Money," *New York Times*, October 13, 1996.

12 "Talk Later," *New York Times*, September 28, 2001.

13 *The Lexus and the Olive Tree*, p. 248.

14 *Ibid.*, p. 253.

15 *Ibid.*, p. 252.

16 "Stop the Music," *New York Times*, April 23, 1999.

17 "This Is a Test," *New York Times*, March 21. 2000.

18 "More Sticks," *New York Times*, April 6, 1999.

19 *Ibid.*

20 "Stop the Music," *New York Times*. Such wartime diversions are not deemed reprehensible when it comes to Israeli cleansing of ethnic populations, and Friedman assures readers of *From Beirut to Jerusalem* that "while the [first] *intifada* was raging on American television, thousands of Israelis were going to the Tel Aviv fairgrounds every evening to ride Ferris wheels, eat cotton candy, and visit all the booths at the exposition marking Israel's fortieth anniversary of independence" (pp. 442–3).

21 "Steady as She Goes," *New York Times*, May 11, 1999.

22 "Stop the Music," *New York Times*.

23 "Expanding Club NATO," *New York Times*, October 26, 2003. Friedman's opposition to NATO expansion, based on his desire to engage rather than irk Russia, is abandoned in favor of absorbing Israel, Iraq, and Egypt into the organization. For more on the reasons for NATO's war, see "Global Balkans Interviews Tariq Ali: Neo-Liberalism and Protectorate States in the Post-Yugoslav Balkans," *Global Balkans Network*, February 26, 2008, and "On the NATO Bombing of Yugoslavia: Noam Chomsky Interviewed by Danilo Mandic," April 25, 2006, accessible via chomsky.info. Chomsky summarizes the admission by Clinton administration official Strobe Talbott that the war was undertaken "because Serbia was not carrying out the required social and economic reforms, meaning it was the last corner of Europe which had not subordinated itself to the U.S.-run neoliberal programs, so therefore it had to be eliminated."

24   "Good News, Bad News," *New York Times*, June 4, 1999.

25   "Kosovo's Three Wars," *New York Times*, August 6, 1999.

26   "Tilting the Playing Field," *New York Times*, May 30, 2004.

27   *The World Is Flat*, p. 587.

28   *Hot, Flat, and Crowded*, p. 96. Excluded from the FLOP are "countries that have a lot of crude oil but were well-established states, with solid democratic institutions and diversified economies, before their oil was discovered—Norway, the United States, Denmark, Great Britain."

29   *Ibid.*, p. 93.

30   *Ibid.*

31   *Ibid.*, pp. 94–5.

32   "Russia's Last Line," *New York Times*, December 23, 2001.

33   *The World Is Flat*, p. 55.

34   *Hot, Flat, and Crowded*, p. 95.

35   *Ibid.*, pp. 96–7.

36   *Ibid.*, p. 101.

37   *Ibid.*, p. 95. For a scathingly entertaining critique of *Hot, Flat, and Crowded*, see Matt Taibbi, "Flat N All That," *New York Press*, January 14, 2009. In response to Friedman's napkin, Taibbi plots a series of graphs such as "Number of One-Eyed Retarded Flies in the State of North Carolina vs. Likelihood of Nuclear Combat on Indian Subcontinent," reasoning that "if you're going to draw a line that measures the level of 'freedom' across the entire world and on that line plot just four randomly-selected points in time over the course of 30 years—and one of your top four 'freedom points' in a 30-year period of human history is the privatization of a Nigerian oil field—well, what the fuck? What can't you argue, if that's how you're going to make your point?"

38   One of the graphs is also from the Freedom House "Nations in Transit" report, which Friedman fails to specify he consulted.

39   Freedom House rates the "Freedom Status" of countries as "Free," "Partially Free," or "Not Free." Data is accessible via the organization's website, freedomhouse.org, under "Freedom in the World Comparative and Historical Data." This is not to suggest that any serious theorist should rely on the U.S. State Department–funded organization but rather that those who do should check their work.

40   "The Real Patriot Act," *New York Times*, October 5, 2003.

41   "Drowning Freedom in Oil," *New York Times*, August 25, 2002.

42 "Iraq, Upside Down," *New York Times*, September 18, 2002. In a subsequent article ("You Gotta Have Friends," September 29, 2002) the advised sequence of events is amended such that the debating occurs prior to the doing.

43 See Geoffrey Lean, "Iraq War May Have Increased Energy Costs Worldwide by a Staggering $6 Trillion," *AlterNet*, May 27, 2008.

44 "Seeds for a Geo-Green Party," *New York Times*, June 16, 2006.

45 *Ibid.*

46 See, for example, "More Poetry, Please," *New York Times*, October 31, 2009.

47 "C.E.O.'s, M.I.A.," *New York Times*, May 25, 2005.

48 "Time to Reboot America," *New York Times*, December 24, 2008.

49 "A Biblical Seven Years," *New York Times*, August 27, 2008.

50 "Hunting the Tiger," *New York Times*, October 21, 2004.

51 See Dave Lindorff, "Your Tax Dollars at War: More Than 53% of Your Tax Payment Goes to the Military," *CommonDreams.org*, April 13, 2010.

52 *The Lexus and the Olive Tree*, p. 464.

53 Kari Lydersen, "War Costing $720 Million Each Day, Group Says," *The Washington Post*, September 22, 2007. The estimate was based on the work of Nobel Prize–winning economist Joseph Stiglitz and Harvard's Linda Bilmes. Friedman's swimming observation is inspired by Warren Buffett's comment regarding financial crises that "only when the tide goes out do you find out who is not wearing a bathing suit" ("Swimming Without a Suit," April 21, 2009).

54 "What's Our Sputnik?," *New York Times*, January 17, 2010.

55 "Their Moon Shot and Ours," *New York Times*, September 25, 2010.

56 *Hot, Flat, and Crowded*, p. 318.

57 *Ibid.*, p. 322.

58 *Ibid.*, p. 321.

59 *Ibid.*, p. 322.

60 *Ibid.*

61 See Project Censored, "U.S. Department of Defense is the Worst Polluter on the Planet," *Project Censored: Top 25 of 2011*, projectcensored.org.

62 "Time for Plan B," *New York Times*, August 4, 2006.

63 "The U.S.S. Prius," *New York Times*, December 18, 2010.

64 *The Lexus and the Olive Tree*, p. 467. As for Friedman's 1995

observation that "unfortunately, the Vietnam syndrome has been replaced among politicians with the gulf war syndrome," he is apparently unaware that the latter term has already been assigned to an actual illness and instead defines it as reluctance to engage in long-term or high-casualty military operations abroad ("Global Mandate," *New York Times*, March 5, 1995).

65   "Dear Dr. Greenspan," *New York Times*, February 9, 1997.

66   For the UNICEF estimate, see John Pilger, "Iraq: Yet Again, They Are Lying to Us," johnpilger.com, March 20, 2000.

67   *The Lexus and the Olive Tree*, p. 318

68   *Ibid.*

69   *Ibid.*, pp. xxi–xxii.

70   *Ibid.*, p. xxii.

71   *Ibid.*, p. 468.

72   *Hot, Flat, and Crowded*, p. 147.

73   Joseph Massad, "Under the Cover of Democracy," *Al Jazeera*, June 8, 2011.

74   "Don't Mess With Moody's," *New York Times*, February 22, 1995.

75   *The World Is Flat*, p. 434.

76   *Ibid.*, p. 433.

77   *Ibid.*, p. 23.

78   *Ibid.*

79   *The Lexus and the Olive Tree*, p. 52.

80   "30 Little Turtles," *New York Times*, February 29, 2004.

81   *Ibid.*

82   *Ibid.*

83   *Ibid.*

84   *The World Is Flat*, p. 632.

85   "30 Little Turtles," *New York Times*.

86   Naomi Klein, "Outsourcing the Friedman," *The Nation*, March 22, 2004.

87   *The Lexus and the Olive Tree*, p. 147.

88   "Where Freedom Reigns," *New York Times*, August 14, 2002. Friedman cites a fatality tally of "600 Muslims, and dozens of Hindus." For an account of the massacres that does not focus on the superiority of Indian democracy, see Siddharth Varadarajan, ed., *Gujarat: The Making of a Tragedy*, New Delhi: Penguin Books, 2002.

89   *Ibid.*

90 "The Secret of Our Sauce," *New York Times*, March 7, 2004.

91 Defined as "the phenomenon that is enabling, empowering, and enjoining individuals and small groups to go global so easily and so seamlessly" (*The World Is Flat*, p. 10). According to Friedman, it is the result of a "triple convergence," the first converging component of which involves ten "flatteners," among them technologies known as "steroids because they are amplifying and turbocharging all the other flatteners" (p. 187).

92 "Letting India in the Club?," *New York Times*, March 8, 2006.

93 See "Arundhati Roy on India, Iraq, U.S. Empire and Dissent," *Democracy Now!*, May 23, 2006, in which Roy also discusses results of fifteen years of economic liberalization in India, such as the country's possession of more than half of the world's malnourished children and the displacement of rural Indians by the hundreds of thousands due to the corporatization of agriculture. Friedman, of course, prefers to focus on other sections of the population: "Indeed, there is a huge famine breaking out all over India today, an incredible hunger. But it is not for food. It is a hunger for opportunity that has been pent up like volcanic lava under four decades of socialism" ("A Race to the Top," June 3, 2005). For Kashmir, see "Acclaimed Indian Author Arundhati Roy Faces Arrest for Questioning India's Claim on Kashmir," *Democracy Now!*, October 27, 2010.

94 "The $110 Billion Question," *New York Times*, March 6, 2011.

95 See, for example, Andy Worthington, "UK Sought Rendition of British Nationals to Guantánamo; Tony Blair Directly Involved," andyworthington.co.uk, July 15, 2010, and Nigel Brew et al., "Australians in Guantanamo Bay: A Chronology of the Detention of Mamdouh Habib and David Hicks," Parliament of Australia: Parliamentary Library (Chronologies Online), May 29, 2007.

96 *The World Is Flat*, pp. 541–2.

97 "The Launch of Research@Özyeğin with the Participation of Thomas Friedman," June 15, 2010.

98 "The Want Ads," *New York Times*, November 10, 1996.

99 *Hot, Flat, and Crowded*, p. 180. Friedman decrees: "When do we feel best about ourselves as Americans? *It's when we are doing things for others with others*."

100 *Ibid.*, p. 205.

101 "The Price Is Not Right," *New York Times*, April 1, 2009.

102 "Green the Bailout," *New York Times*, September 28, 2008.

103 *Hot, Flat, and Crowded*, p. 372.

104 "Can I Clean Your Clock?," *New York Times*, July 5, 2009.

105 "Who's Sleeping Now?," *New York Times*, January 10, 2010.

106 In a November 2010 interview on Fox's *Imus in the Morning*, Friedman however claims to respond as follows to Chinese friends who accuse him of exaggerating Chinese strengths: "I say, 'You know what, baby? You bet I do. 'Cause you're my Sputnik.'" Video accessible via Jeff Poor, "Friedman Admits He Deliberately Exaggerates China Threat," *Media Research Center Network*, November 12, 2010.

107 "Peking Duct Tape," *New York Times*, February 16, 2003. For other instances of hubris directed at the Chinese, see Friedman's 1999 suggestion that the U.S. administration should be saying the following to China's leaders: "I have heard enough about the bombing of your embassy in Belgrade. We both know it was an accident, and if you keep it up, I'm going to close the visa window at our embassy in China ... Let's see how many of your young people want to go to Moscow University for an M.B.A. By the way, there's no Disney World in Vladivostok" ("In Your Faces," *New York Times*, May 28, 1999). He is similarly peeved in 2001 when China demands an apology for the collision between a U.S. spy plane and Chinese fighter jet off the Chinese coast, and advises apologizing for a host of other things, like providing a market for China's exports and paving the way for Chinese entry into the WTO: "Yes, we should apologize for all these things and promise to stop all of them immediately" ("Sorry About That," *New York Times*, April 6, 2001). By 2009 he has decided that China is an autocracy "led by a reasonably enlightened group of people" ("Our One-Party Democracy," *New York Times*, September 9, 2009).

108 "The Lexus and the Shamrock," *New York Times*, August 3, 2001.

109 "Follow the Leapin' Leprechaun," *New York Times*, July 1, 2005.

110 "Our War With France," *New York Times*, September 18, 2003.

111 "A Race to the Top," *New York Times*, June 3, 2005.

112 "30 Little Turtles," *New York Times*, February 29, 2004.

113 "Cyber-Serfdom," *New York Times*, January 30, 2001.

114 "We Are All French Now?," *New York Times*, June 24, 2005.

115 See "The FP Top 100 Global Thinkers," *Foreign Policy*, December 2010.

116 "Cyber-Serfdom," *New York Times.*

117 Friedman's commencement address at Williams is accessible via humanity.org: "Listen to Your Heart," June 5, 2005.

118 "The Fast Eat the Slow," *New York Times* , February 2, 2001.

119 "Time to Reboot America," *New York Times*, December 24, 2008.

120 "Calling All Luddites," *New York Times*, August 3, 2005.

121 *The Lexus and the Olive Tree*, p. 421.

122 Las Vegas, however, continues to fulfill the pre- and post-technological need to rub up against people: "Walking through the casino in Las Vegas I was struck by all the shouting around the craps tables—strangers high-fiving each other in victory and consoling each other in defeat. You can't do that gambling online alone in your basement. Las Vegas is thriving today precisely because it is such a tactile place, so full of people rubbing against people—at shows, in casinos, in fantasy hotels and in giant swimming pools. Las Vegas is the future because it's the past" ("Surfing Alone," May 30, 2000).

123 "52 to 48," *New York Times*, September 3, 2003.

124 For Monsanto's malevolent machinations, see Donald L. Barlett and James B. Steele, "Monsanto's Harvest of Fear," *Vanity Fair*, May 2008. For Goldcorp's behavior in Latin America, see Steven Schnoor's documentary *All That Glitters Isn't Gold: A Story of Exploitation and Resistance*, accessible at *PULSE Media*, October 28, 2010.

125 "China's Sunshine Boys," *New York Times*, December 6, 2006.

126 "Bibi and Barack," *New York Times*, May 17, 2011.

127 "Ah, Those Principled Europeans," *New York Times*, February 2, 2003.

128 *Ibid.*

129 *Ibid.*

130 *Ibid.*

131 "I Love the E.U.," *New York Times*, June 22, 2001.

132 *Ibid.*

133 "Learning From Lance," *New York Times*, July 27, 2005.

134 "Follow the Leapin' Leprechaun," *New York Times*, July 1, 2005.

135 "An American in Paris," *New York Times*, August 20, 1999.

136 "Follow the Leapin' Leprechaun," *New York Times*. Regarding his own job security, Friedman writes in *The World Is Flat* (p. 17): "Thank goodness I'm a journalist and not an accountant or a radiologist. There will be no outsourcing for me—even if some of my

readers wish my column could be shipped off to North Korea. At least that's what I thought. Then I heard about the Reuters operation in India"—which of course does not specialize in cheap imitations of iconic American columnists. The significance of North Korea is meanwhile unclear.

137   "The End of the Rainbow," *New York Times*, June 29, 2005.

138   Sean Kay, "Just How Wrong Can NYT's Friedman Be? Let's Review His Take on Ireland," posted in *Foreign Policy*'s "The Best Defense" blog, ricks.foreignpolicy.com, December 6, 2010. The article appears shortly after the publication of *Foreign Policy*'s Friedman-inclusive "Top 100 Global Thinkers."

139   *Ibid.*

140   *Ibid.*

141   "The French Ostrich," *New York Times*, October 4, 1995.

142   "Where's The Crisis?," *New York Times*, May 23, 1998.

143   For the role of the IMF, World Bank, and WTO in the Asian economic collapse, see Walden Bello, *Deglobalization: Ideas for a New World Economy* (Philippine edition), Ateneo de Manila University Press, 2002, pp. 3–6.

144   "Berlin Wall, Part 2," *New York Times*, December 22, 1997.

145   *New York Times*, March 19, 1999.

146   "The Hot Zones," *New York Times*, February 12, 1997.

147   "Where's The Crisis?," *New York Times*, May 23, 1998.

148   *Ibid.* He elsewhere quotes an Indonesian "reformer" as saying, "My son and I get our revenge on Suharto every day by eating at McDonald's," but does not hazard a guess as to why eating at a U.S. fast food chain qualifies as getting revenge on a U.S. ally ("The Globalutionaries," July 24, 1997). Other musings on Indonesia include Friedman's proposal in *Hot, Flat, and Crowded* of a direct correlation between Indonesian housecleaning industry exports and deforestation: "So, if you go to Indonesia in ten years and see planeloads of young women being shipped out to be maids, you can be sure that the trees will be gone too" (p. 312).

149   "Living Dangerously," *New York Times*, July 10, 1997.

150   "Root Canal Politics," *New York Times*, May 9, 2010.

151   *Ibid.*

152   "Fire, Ready, Aim," *New York Times*, March 9, 2003.

153   Joshua Holland, "Uh-Oh, Tom Friedman Has a 'Meta-Story'

About Tea-Partiers, Greek Riots and the UK Vote," *AlterNet*, May 11, 2010.

154   "Root Canal Politics," *New York Times*.

155   *Ibid.*

156   For a discussion of the reasons behind the Greek economic crisis by persons not fixated on the idea that hairdressers regularly exposed to chemicals are permitted early retirement, see "'The People of Greece Are Fighting for the Whole of Europe': Tariq Ali and Mark Weisbrot Discuss Greece's Economic Crisis and Popular Uprising," *Democracy Now!*, May 11, 2010.

157   "Root Canal Politics," *New York Times*.

158   "The New American Politics," *New York Times*, November 13, 1997.

159   *Ibid.*

160   *The Lexus and the Olive Tree*, p. 449.

161   *Ibid.*, p. 439.

162   "The Price Is Not Right," *New York Times*, April 1, 2009.

163   *The Lexus and the Olive Tree*, p. 462.

164   "Sizzle, Yes, but Beef, Too," *New York Times*, April 22, 2005.

165   "Repairing the World," *New York Times*, March 16, 2003.

166   "Sizzle, Yes, but Beef, Too," *New York Times*.

167   *Ibid.*

168   "No Way, No How, Not Here," *New York Times*, February 18, 2009.

169   *Ibid.*

170   "9/11 Is Over," *New York Times*, September 30, 2007.

171   "A Tweezer Defense Shield?," *New York Times*, October 19, 2001.

172   For Friedman's qualified admission of overreaction to 9/11, see "Daily Show: Thomas Friedman," *The Daily Show with Jon Stewart*, December 1, 2009.

173   "9/11 Is Over," *New York Times*.

174   "The Third Bubble," *New York Times*, April 20, 2003.

175   "War of Ideas, Part 1," *New York Times*, January 8, 2004.

176   "World War III," *New York Times*, September 13, 2001.

177   "Talk Later," *New York Times*, September 28, 2001.

178   For the 2-by-4 comment, made on NPR's "Talk of the Nation," see Eli Clifton, "Thomas Friedman Wields His Trusty 2×4," lobelog. com, December 16, 2009.

179   "Ask Not What ...," *New York Times*, December 9, 2001.

180   *Ibid.* I can testify to the effectiveness of such methods of propaganda, as I still feel an enormous gratitude to Taiwan for manufacturing the pencils I used in elementary school.

181   "Let's Roll," *New York Times*, January 2, 2002.

182   "A Theory of Everything," *New York Times*, June 1, 2003.

183   *The World Is Flat*, p. 618.

184   "Read My Ears," *New York Times*, January 27, 2005.

185   *Ibid.*

186   "A Well of Smiths and Xias," *New York Times*, June 7, 2006.

187   *Ibid.*

188   "Laughing and Crying," *New York Times*, May 23, 2007.

189   "Read My Ears," *New York Times*.

190   For an outline of this dichotomy, see "The Launch of Research@ Özyeğin With the Participation of Thomas Friedman," June 15, 2010.

191   "Losing Our Edge?," *New York Times*, April 22, 2004.

192   *The Lexus and the Olive Tree*, p. 371.

193   *Ibid.*, p. 474.

194   *Ibid.*, p. 475.

195   *Longitudes and Attitudes*, p. 331.

196   *Ibid.* America's "secret sauce" is meanwhile defined in *The World Is Flat* as "a mix of institutions, laws, and cultural norms that produce a level of trust, innovation, and collaboration that has enabled us to constantly renew our economy and raise our standard of living" (p. 336).

197   *Ibid.*

198   *Ibid.*, pp. 332–3.

199   *Ibid.*, p. 331.

200   *Ibid.*, p. 337.

201   "World War III," *New York Times*, September 13, 2001.

202   *Longitudes and Attitudes*, p. 336.

203   *Ibid.*

204   *Ibid.*

205   *Ibid.*, p. 337.

206   *Ibid.*, p. 331. This is presumably the same fist that is elsewhere referred to as the "hidden" safeguard of the U.S. technology industry and economic interests.

207   *Ibid.*, pp. 349–50.

208 *Ibid.*, p. 349.

209 "The New Club NATO," *New York Times*, November 17, 2002.

210 *Ibid.* Those concerned with details might debate whether 20,000 feet or vaporization is a greater impediment to hearing.

211 "Sinbad vs. the Mermaids," *New York Times*, October 5, 2005.

212 *Ibid.*

213 Nancy Gibbs, "Sexual Assaults on Female Soldiers: Don't Ask, Don't Tell," *Time Magazine*, March 8, 2010.

214 "It's All About Schools," *New York Times*, February 10, 2010.

215 *Ibid.*

216 *Ibid.*

217 "Drowning Freedom in Oil," *New York Times*, August 25, 2002.

218 "Dancing Alone," *New York Times*, May 13, 2004.

219 "9/11 Is Over," *New York Times*.

220 "Help Wanted," *New York Times*, April 18, 2007.

221 *Hot, Flat, and Crowded*, p. 23.

222 See, for example, "Anyone Seen Any Democrats Lately?," *New York Times*, October 6, 2002.

223 "Too Much Pork and Too Little Sugar," *New York Times*, August 5, 2005.

224 "Allies Dressed in Green," *New York Times*, October 27, 2006.

225 "In the Age of Noah," *New York Times*, December 23, 2007.

226 This information appears as a footnote on p. 190 of *Hot, Flat, and Crowded*. As for whether what makes sense in Brazil really makes sense, see Douglas Fischer, "Ethanol's Contrasting Climate Footprints," *Climate Central*, February 12, 2010: "A paper published this week in the Proceedings of the National Academy of Sciences found that Brazil risks incurring a 250-year carbon debt based on the deforestation expected by 2020 as it expands production of sugarcane ethanol and soybean biodiesel."

227 "My Favorite Green Lump," *New York Times*, January 10, 2007.

228 "The Next Really Cool Thing," *New York Times*, March 15, 2009.

229 "Dreaming the Possible Dream," *New York Times*, March 7, 2010.

230 *Hot, Flat, and Crowded*, p. 404.

231 "Tea Party With a Difference," *New York Times*, April 24, 2010.

232 "Better Late Than ...," *New York Times*, March 17, 2002.

233 *Hot, Flat, and Crowded*, p. 198.

234 *Ibid.*

235 *Ibid.* For an example of reductionism at its best, see Friedman's 2007 prediction: "When the Big Apple becomes the Green Apple, and 40 million tourists come through every year and take at least one hybrid cab ride, they'll go back home and ask their leaders, 'Why don't we have hybrid cabs?'" ("Save the Planet: Vote Smart," October 21, 2007). This rivals his previous prediction that the U.S.–Jordanian free trade agreement will prompt Arab journalists to go and demand the same from their own regimes ("The Arabs' Road Map," October 20, 2000).

236 "Latin America's Choice," *New York Times*, June 21, 2006.

237 "Senseless in Seattle," *New York Times*, December 1, 1999.

238 *Ibid.*

239 "Surfing the Wetlands," *New York Times*, August 1, 1998.

240 *Ibid.*

241 The ease of changing the world is also called into question in *Hot, Flat, and Crowded* when Friedman reports: "To be sure, in recent years we've seen many collaborations between conservation groups and global companies like Wal-Mart, Starbucks, and McDonald's, which aim to show these companies how to reduce the impact their supply chains and manufacturing processes have on the natural world. But all their efforts are just fingers in the dike" (p. 148).

242 "Senseless in Seattle II," *New York Times*, December 8, 1999.

243 *Ibid.*

244 "Big Ideas and No Boundaries," *New York Times*, October 6, 2006.

245 "The Energy Harvest," *New York Times*, September 15, 2006.

246 See Russ Finley, "A Waste of Print Space: If Friedman Had a Blog, He'd be Learning Right Now," *Grist*, September 18, 2006. Finley also points out that interviewing persons profiting from the ethanol business is probably not the best way to assess fuel effectiveness.

247 Another reason why ignoring the institution is so handy.

248 "Connect the Dots," *New York Times*, September 25, 2003.

249 "We Are All French Now?," *New York Times*, June 24, 2005.

250 See Norman Solomon, "Announcing the P.U.-litzer Prizes for 2006," *Huffington Post*, December 26, 2006.

251 Edward S. Herman, "Thomas Friedman: The Geraldo Rivera of the *New York Times*," *Z Magazine*, November 2003.

252 "Under the Volcano," *New York Times*, September 29, 2000.

253 *The World Is Flat*, p. 548.

254 Sweatshop generalizations are, however, tempered with disclaimers like: "There are still plenty of sweatshops" ("Y2K Plus 5," November 21, 1999).

255 "The Launch of Research@Özyeğin With the Participation of Thomas Friedman," June 15, 2010.

256 Norman Solomon, "Thomas Friedman and Wealth," *The Huffington Post*, October 30, 2006.

257 Edward S. Herman, "Thomas Friedman: The Geraldo Rivera of the *New York Times*," *Z Magazine*, November 2003.

258 *The Lexus and the Olive Tree*, p. 316.

259 Peter Newcomb, "Thomas Friedman's World Is Flat Broke," *Vanity Fair*, November 12, 2008.

260 *Hot, Flat, and Crowded*, p. 412.

261 "The Real Generation X," *New York Times*, December 7, 2008.

262 "Green the Bailout," *New York Times*, September 28, 2008. Compare this with Joseph Stiglitz's thoughts on what should be done with the undeserving, in Sam Gustin, "Economist Joseph Stiglitz: Put Corporate Criminals in Jail," *Daily Finance*, October 22, 2010. Stiglitz is quoted as remarking on supposed justice in the United States: "Somebody is caught for a minor drug offense, they are sent to prison for a very long time. And yet, these so-called white-collar crimes, which are not victimless; almost none of these guys, almost none of them, go to prison." See also Matt Taibbi's exposé of Goldman Sachs crimes, "The People vs. Goldman Sachs," *Rolling Stone*, May 26, 2011, referenced in the introduction to this book:.

263 "Keep It in Vegas," *New York Times*, September 17, 2008. Friedman additionally laments that the demise of Lehman Brothers is "really sad for a 158-year-old company."

264 *From Beirut to Jerusalem*, pp. 31–2.

265 *The World Is Flat*, p. 548.

266 *The Lexus and the Olive Tree*, p. 437.

267 *The World Is Flat*, p. 553.

268 "Protesting for Whom?," *New York Times*, April 24, 2001.

269 *Longitudes and Attitudes*, p. xiv.

270 "Protesting for Whom?," *New York Times*.

271 "The Land of 'No Service,'" *New York Times*, August 16, 2009.

272 *The Lexus and the Olive Tree*, p. 364.

273 *Ibid.*

274   *Ibid.*, p. 349.

275   "New Mexico," *New York Times*, March 15, 1995.

276   "Protesting for Whom?," *New York Times*.

277   "New Mexico," *New York Times*.

278   "Helping Mexico Help Us," *New York Times*, January 25, 1995. For the bailout, see James Sheehan, "How Nafta Caused the Mexican Bailout," *The Free Market* (the Mises Institute monthly) 13:7, July 1995.

279   "What's That Sound?," *New York Times*, April 1, 2004.

280   *Ibid.*

281   "Narcos, No's and Nafta," *New York Times*, May 2, 2010.

282   *Ibid.*

283   For another critique of Friedman's free trade mantra, see David Sirota, "An Open Letter to Tom Friedman," *The Huffington Post*, February 16, 2006.

284   "Losing Our Edge?," *New York Times*, April 22, 2004.

285   "Tinted Windows," *New York Times*, June 23, 1997.

286   *The Lexus and the Olive Tree*, p. 445.

287   "14 Big Macs Later ...," *New York Times*, December 31, 1995.

288   "Tax Cuts for Teachers," *New York Times*, January 11, 2009.

289   "Too Many Hamburgers?," *New York Times*, September 21, 2010.

290   "Can't Keep a Bad Idea Down," *New York Times*, October 26, 2010.

291   *The Lexus and the Olive Tree*, p. 444.

292   "Transcript: A TimesSelect/TimesTalks Event on Globalization," *New York Times*, April 25, 2006.

293   "Tom Friedman on Book Leave," Fox Business, January 4, 2011, video.foxbusiness.com.

294   *The Lexus and the Olive Tree*, p. 379.

295   *Ibid.*

296   "Read My Lips," *New York Times*, June 11, 2003.

297   "Serious in Singapore," *New York Times*, January 29, 2011.

2 THE ARAB/MUSLIM WORLD

1   "In My Next Life," *New York Times*, November 25, 2004. The simpler version of DeLay's crime is "twist[ing] the arms of House Republicans to repeal a rule that automatically requires party leaders to step down if they are indicted on a felony charge—something a Texas prosecutor is considering doing to DeLay because of corruption allegations."

2   *Ibid.*

3   *Ibid.*

4   The function of the word "gut" here is questionable, but may be compatible with Friedman's repeated claim that Americans "don't listen through their ears. They listen through their stomachs" ("From the Gut," September 10, 2008).

5   "An Hour With Thomas Friedman of 'The New York Times,'" *Charlie Rose*, May 30, 2003, charlierose.com.

6   "Iraq, Upside Down," *New York Times*, September 18, 2002.

7   "Tell The Truth," *New York Times*, February 19, 2003.

8   "An Hour With Thomas Friedman of 'The New York Times,'" *Charlie Rose*. Readers with doubts as to whether the Iraqi population in general is commanded by the "terrorism bubble" are invited to peruse Friedman's conceit-ridden post-invasion assessment, in which the only grain of truth is perhaps the compatibility of free-market democracies with slicing: "America sliced right through Iraq. It did so because we are a free-market democracy that is capable of amassing huge amounts of technical power. And it did so because our soldiers so cherish what they have that they were ready to fight house to house from Basra to Baghdad. That was the real shock and awe for Iraqis—because the terrorism bubble said Nasdaq-obsessed Americans were so caught up with the frivolity of modern life, they had lost the will to fight. Wrong." ("The Third Bubble," *New York Times*, April 20, 2003).

9   "An Hour With Thomas Friedman of 'The New York Times,'" *Charlie Rose*.

10 "Because We Could," *New York Times*, June 4, 2003.

11 *Ibid.*

12 "In My Next Life," *New York Times*, November 25, 2004.

13 *Ibid.*

14 "Iraq: Politics or Policy?," *New York Times*, October 3, 2004.

15 "Hummers Here, Hummers There," *New York Times*, May 25, 2003.

16 "Playing the Hand We've Dealt," *New York Times*, May 20, 2007.

17 "Geo-Greening by Example," *New York Times*, March 27, 2005.

18 "Outsourcing, Schmoutsourcing! Out Is Over," *New York Times*, May 19, 2006. Friedman neglects to alert readers, however, to the fact that none other than George Bush is listed on the website as a reference for the company.

19   "Maids vs. Occupiers," *New York Times*, June 17, 2004.

20   *Ibid.* One area in which proper Muslims might seek knowledge is apparently the cellular phone industry, and Friedman reports in the same article noticing "the number of women selling phone cards for cellphone minutes" during a visit to China, "while Islamist terrorists in Iraq and Saudi Arabia are using cellphone technology and cars to create bombs." Another quick-fix proposal for confronting the Arabs with their backwardness is tacked on to the end of the article: "I would suggest that next year the G-8 invite both India and China to join, and hold the next G-10 summit either at one of the manicured campuses of Indian outsourcing companies or in Shanghai's manufacturing hub. Then invite Arab leaders to attend." Given that Friedman admits that the offspring of the Arabs' maids are also leaving many American children "in the dust," his concerted campaign to highlight the defects of the Arab/Muslim world is all the more confounding.

21   These are the two primary activities Friedman says are sanctioned by the terrorism bubble. (See "An Hour With Thomas Friedman of 'The New York Times,'" *Charlie Rose* .)

22   "Tone It Down a Notch," *New York Times*, October 2, 2002. For more on Rumsfeld's no-nonsense toughness, including his authorization of torture and extrajudicial killings, see Marjorie Cohn, "The War Crimes Case Against Donald Rumsfeld," *AlterNet*, November 13, 2006.

23   "Channeling Dick Cheney," *New York Times*, November 18, 2007. Friedman suggests that Obama consider keeping Cheney on as his vice president for this reason.

24   "Grapes of Wrath," *New York Times*, March 12, 2003.

25   "Tone It Down a Notch," *New York Times*.

26   See, for example, *The World Is Flat*, p. 561.

27   *The Lexus and the Olive Tree*, p. 20.

28   For a detailed overview of the premeditated ethnic cleansing of Palestinians that occurred in 1948, see Ilan Pappé, "The 1948 Ethnic Cleansing of Palestine," *Journal of Palestine Studies* 36:1, Autumn 2006, pp. 6–20.

29   For example, see Nour Odeh, "Olives—A Palestinian family affair," *Al Jazeera* Blogs, October 20, 2010: "In the past 10 years alone, Israel has uprooted approximately 1.2 million fruit-bearing trees, most of

them olives. Israel has also confiscated tens of thousands of hectares of Palestinian land as part of its illegal settlement expansion practice and wall building. This means that thousands of Palestinian farmers have been barred or severely restricted from accessing their olive groves."

30   *From Beirut to Jerusalem*, p. 428.

31   David Hirst, *Beware of Small States: Lebanon, Battleground of the Middle East*, New York: Nation Books, 2010. Writes Hirst: "Emboldened by the Balfour Declaration, leading Zionists became increasingly convinced of the need for the Palestinians' 'forcible removal.'"

32   *The Lexus and the Olive Tree*, p. 21.

33   *Ibid*.

34   *Ibid*.

35   *Ibid*.

36   "African Madness," *New York Times*, January 31, 1996.

37   *Ibid*.

38   *Ibid*. Other Friedman forecasts from the 1996 Africa trip include that the United States may risk an eventual transformation into Rwanda if the "freshmen Republicans" in Congress do not cease budgetary stinginess. Advises Friedman: "They might want to come to Africa and glimpse what happens to countries where there is no sense of community, no sense that people owe their government anything, no sense that anyone is responsible for anyone else and where everyone, rich or poor, is left to the tender mercies of the global marketplace" ("Come To Africa," January 28, 1996).

39   "African Madness," *New York Times*. Friedman does not include such details as the U.S.-backed South African invasion of Angola in the 1970s following the collapse of the Portuguese empire. As Noam Chomsky points out in an interview: "The South African attacks in Angola and Mozambique continued until the late 1980s, with strong US support. And it was no joke. According to the UN estimates they killed a million and a half people." See Keane Bhatt, "Chomsky Post-Earthquake: Aid to Haitian Popular Organizations, not Contractors or NGOs," *Upside Down World*, March 8, 2010.

40   "African Madness," *New York Times*.

41   *The Lexus and the Olive Tree*, p. 467.

42   Writes Friedman: "Come Feb. 8, Washington should make clear that

it will not renew the U.N. peacekeeping mandate for Angola, which expires that day, and that the U.S. will throw its diplomatic and material support into helping the freely elected Angolan Government restore its authority over all its territory"—i.e. by vanquishing the Unita movement of former U.S. ally Jonas Savimbi ("African Madness," *New York Times*).

43 "9/11 Lesson Plan," *New York Times*, September 4, 2002.

44 "The Gridlock Gang," *New York Times*, February 26, 2003.

45 "Power and Peril," *New York Times*, August 13, 2003.

46 See Oliver Burkeman and Julian Borger, "War Critics Astonished as US Hawk Admits Invasion Was Illegal," *Guardian*, November 20, 2003. The hawk in question is neocon Richard Perle, Chairman of the Defense Policy Board Advisory Committee.

47 "It's No Vietnam," *New York Times*, October 30, 2003.

48 *Ibid.*

49 "A War for Oil?," *New York Times*, January 5, 2003.

50 "The Democracy Thing," *New York Times*, October 30, 2002.

51 "The Great (Double) Game," *New York Times*, July 31, 2010.

52 "War of Ideas, Part 4," *New York Times*, January 18, 2004.

53 Edward Said, "The Orientalist Express: Thomas Friedman Wraps Up the Middle East," *Village Voice*, October 17, 1989.

54 *Longitudes and Attitudes*, p. 323.

55 *Ibid.*

56 *Ibid.*

57 *Ibid.*, p. 324.

58 *Ibid.*

59 "A Foul Wind," *New York Times*, March 10, 2002.

60 "Bush's Mideast Sand Trap," *New York Times*, August 21, 2002.

61 "Changing the Channel," *New York Times*, April 21, 2002.

62 "My Survival Kit," *New York Times*, February 23, 2003.

63 *Longitudes and Attitudes*, p. 334.

64 "Anyone Seen Any Democrats Lately?," *New York Times*, October 6, 2002.

65 *The Lexus and the Olive Tree*, p. 474.

66 *Ibid.*, p. 294.

67 Martin Luther King, Jr., "Beyond Vietnam: A Time to Break Silence" (speech), April 4, 1967, accessible at World History Archives by Hartford Web Publishing.

68   "Social Insecurity Crisis," *New York Times*, January 4, 2006.

69   "The Peace (Keepers) Prize," *New York Times*, October 11, 2009.

70   See John Pilger, *Year Zero: The Silent Death of Cambodia* (documentary), 1979, accessible at johnpilger.com. Friedman has, however, previously proposed former U.S. diplomat Henry Kissinger, co-architect of the war on Cambodia and himself a Nobel recipient, as one of "the country's best negotiators," who should be dispatched to Iraq in 2007 to deal with an Iraqi parliament that has adjourned for the month of August. Declaring that he "can't imagine how I'd feel if I were the parent of a soldier in Iraq" hearing this news—as though the Iraqi parliament is to blame for a U.S. occupation cheered on by *New York Times* pundits—Friedman rants, "I've been in Baghdad in the summer and it is really hot. But you know what? It is a lot hotter when you're in a U.S. military uniform, carrying a rifle and a backpack, sweltering under a steel helmet and worrying that a bomb can be thrown at you from any direction. One soldier told me he lost six pounds in one day. I'm sure the Iraqi Parliament is air-conditioned" ("Help Wanted: Peacemaker," July 18, 2007).

71   See Kathy Kelly, "Incalculable: The Human Cost of NATO's War on Afghanistan," *PULSE Media*, March 6, 2011.

72   *Longitudes and Attitudes*, pp. 324–5.

73   See Muhammad Idrees Ahmad, "Obama kills over 700 Pakistanis in 44 drone strikes in 2009," *PULSE Media*, January 3, 2010.

74   "Colin Powell's Eyebrows," *New York Times*, November 10, 2002.

75   See, for example, "Talk Later," *New York Times*, September 28, 2001.

76   "At a Theater Near You," *New York Times*, July 4, 2007. It should be noted that it is only after 9/11 that Arab/Muslim behavior is deemed to be a fundamental threat to civilization; for example, Friedman fairly dispassionately discusses the 1982 massacre in Hama of between ten and twenty-five thousand Syrians by the regime of Hafez al-Assad, attributing it in *From Beirut to Jerusalem* to a result of tribe-like politics, authoritarianism, and the tradition of the modern nation-state imposed by imperial Europe (*From Beirut to Jerusalem*, chap. 4).

77   See Section III.

78   "What Day Is It?," *New York Times*, April 24, 2002.

79   "Rights in The Real World," *New York Times*, December 2, 2001.

80   *Ibid.*

81   "Terrorist Software," *New York Times*, November 23, 2001.

82   Cohen's innumerable contributions to Friedman's work over the years include the following assessment in 2003 of European failure to include calls for a free Iraq in their antiwar demonstrations: "For too many Europeans, Arabs are of no moral interest in and of themselves … They only become of interest if they are fighting Jews or being manhandled by Jews. Then their liberation becomes paramount, because calling for it is a way to stick it to the Jews. Europeans' demonstrations for a free Palestine—and not for a free Iraq or any other Arab country—smell too much like a politically correct form of anti-Semitism, part of a very old story" ("The Gridlock Gang," February 26, 2003). No matter that calling for a free Iraq is at this particular moment equivalent to calling for war and thus obviously irrelevant to an antiwar demonstration, or that no other Arab state is currently occupied by the primary recipient of military aid from the global superpower.

83   "Saudi Royals and Reality," *New York Times*, October 16, 2001.

84   See Brian Whitaker, "Selective Memri," *Guardian*, August 12, 2002.

85   "Terrorist Software," *New York Times*, November 23, 2001.

86   See, for example, "The Green Revolution(s)," *New York Times*, June 24, 2009.

87   "World War III," *New York Times*, September 13, 2001.

88   See "'Iraq Does Not Exist Anymore': Journalist Nir Rosen on How the U.S. Invasion of Iraq Has Led to Ethnic Cleansing, a Worsening Refugee Crisis and the Destabilization of the Middle East" (interview), *Democracy Now!*, August 21, 2007.

89   "The Endgame in Iraq," *New York Times*, September 28, 2005.

90   *Ibid.*

91   See, for example, "Iraq, Upside Down," *New York Times*, September 18, 2002.

92   "Call Your Mother," *New York Times*, May 11, 2008.

93   "Goodbye Iraq, and Good Luck," *New York Times*, July 15, 2009.

94   "It's Up to Iraqis Now. Good Luck," *New York Times*, March 10, 2010.

95   See Jonathan Beale, "Diary: Rice's Mid-East Mission," *BBC News*, July 26, 2006.

96   "Time for Plan B," *New York Times*, August 4, 2006. In 2008 Friedman's indignation over the babysitting role increases, and he writes (in a column of advice to John McCain on what to endorse

in his presidential campaign): "In America, baby sitters get paid" ("No Laughing Matter, September 21, 2008). Obviously, babysitters in America do not slaughter their charges as a means of procuring babysitting jobs.

97 See "Thomas Friedman: Afghanistan a 'Special Needs Baby,'" *Fox Nation*, December 7, 2009.

98 *From Beirut to Jerusalem*, pp. 4–5. It is perhaps fortunate that the Jewish state was not erected in Saudi Arabia, as Friedman is not moved to nostalgia for past lives by the scene in Saudi Crown Prince Abdullah's tent during a visit in 2002: "I had this overwhelming sense of being somewhere I had never been before—not only in this life, but in all previous lives. As an American Jew from Minnesota, and as *The New York Times* columnist who had been most critical of Saudi Arabia, I felt like a total alien as all eyes were on me. There were only men present. They seemed to be just sitting around, schmoozing and smoking water pipes, known in Saudi Arabia as 'hubbly-bubbly'" (*Longitudes and Attitudes*, p. 361). Water pipes are of course *not* officially called "hubbly-bubbly" in any Arabic-speaking country, which our bumbling specialist should technically know given that he has studied Arabic, lived in the Middle East, and speaks English.

99 *Ibid.* p. 5.

100 *Ibid.* p. 6.

101 *Ibid.* p. 131.

102 *Ibid.* p. 57.

103 *Ibid.*

104 "When Camels Fly," *New York Times*, February 20, 2005.

105 "A Shah With a Turban," *New York Times*, December 23, 2005.

106 *From Beirut to Jerusalem*, p. 91.

107 Edward Said, "The Orientalist Express: Thomas Friedman Wraps Up the Middle East," *The Village Voice*, October 17, 1989.

108 An example of Friedman's alternate vision occurs in *The Lexus and the Olive Tree*, when two pages after announcing "O.K., O.K., so the rest of the world thinks Americans are obnoxious bullies" (p. 389), Friedman remarks on his attendance at a 1997 conference in Morocco entitled "Globalization and the Arab World": "To be a French-educated Arab intellectual is the worst combination possible for understanding globalization. It is like being twice handicapped"

(p. 391). He then informs us that he responds with "profanities" to a former Algerian prime minister who categorizes globalization as "another American conspiracy to keep the Arab world down" (p. 392).

109 "Light in the Tunnel," *New York Times*, November 13, 2002.

110 "Let Them Come to Berlin," *New York Times*, November 3, 2002.

111 "Vote France Off the Island," *New York Times*, February 9, 2003. Given that Friedman labels three-fifths of the Security Council members—France, Russia, and China—as "free riders" in the Iraq war and ignorant of "the new world order" ("Peking Duct Tape," February 16, 2003), it would seem that France is playing just fine with the majority of its peers. Undeterred, Friedman reminds the world that "if America didn't exist and Europe had to rely on France, most Europeans today would be speaking either German or Russian" ("Vote France Off the Island," *New York Times*). France appears to redeem itself in later years with the arrival of Nicolas Sarkozy, who informs Friedman that "I will always love America" (*Hot, Flat, and Crowded*, p. 177).

112 "Axis of Appeasement," *New York Times*, March 18, 2004.

113 *The Lexus and the Olive Tree*, p. 398. As tends to happen when Friedman employs superlatives, the Super-Empowered Angry Man is variously superseded in immediacy by threats ranging from "petrolism" to Medicare.

114 "The Hackers' Lessons," *New York Times*, February 15, 2000. After noting that bin Laden is "allegedly responsible for blowing up two U.S. embassies in East Africa," Friedman exults: "And do you know what we did to him? We fired 75 cruise missiles at him. We fired 75 cruise missiles at a person! That was a superpower versus a super-empowered angry man." It is not clear why Friedman stops at JOL and doesn't channel his fascination for things corporate and technological into a suggestion for Amazon.bomb. Meanwhile, technology such as Twitter and Facebook is deemed to be the potential key to revolution when in the hands of proper Orientals such as Iranian anti-government protesters in 2009 ("The Virtual Mosque," June 17, 2009).

115 *The Lexus and the Olive Tree*, pp. 374–5.

116 *The World Is Flat*, p. 59.

117 "1977 vs. 1979," *New York Times*, February 14, 2010.

118 See Jason Burke, "Frankenstein the CIA Created," *Guardian*, January 17, 1999, in which appears the following quote from an American official regarding the mujahedeen: "The point is that we created a whole cadre of trained and motivated people who turned against us. It's a classic Frankenstein's monster situation."

119 See Brendan O'Neill, "How We Trained Al-Qaeda," *The Spectator*, September 6, 2003:

> The Bosnia venture appears to have been very important to the rise of mujahedin forces, to the emergence of today's cross-border Islamic terrorists who think nothing of moving from state to state in the search of outlets for their jihadist mission. In moving to Bosnia, Islamic fighters were transported from the ghettos of Afghanistan and the Middle East into Europe; from an outdated battleground of the Cold War to the major world conflict of the day; from being yesterday's men to fighting alongside the West's favoured side in the clash of the Balkans. If Western intervention in Afghanistan created the mujahedin, Western intervention in Bosnia appears to have globalised it.

120 *Longitudes and Attitudes*, p. 355.

121 *Ibid.*

122 *Ibid.*

123 *Ibid.*, p. 370.

124 "Help Wanted," *New York Times*, April 18, 2007.

125 See Rupert Cornwell, "Bush: God Told Me to Invade Iraq," *Independent*, October 7, 2005.

126 "A Poverty of Dignity and a Wealth of Rage," *New York Times*, July 15, 2005.

127 "The Sand Wall," *New York Times*, April 13, 2003.

128 The debut of God 0.0 as an additional humiliating force and honorary member of Western society occurs three years after Friedman has argued (in "The Core of Muslim Rage," March 6, 2002) that the reason the mass murder of Muslims by Hindus does not generate a Muslim response is that Hindus are not part of the "the Muslim narrative":

> When Hindus kill Muslims it's not a story, because there are a billion Hindus and they aren't part of the Muslim narrative. When Saddam murders his own people it's not a story, because it's in the Arab-Muslim family. But when a small band of Israeli Jews kills Muslims it sparks rage—a rage that must come from Muslims having to confront the gap

between their self-perception as Muslims and the reality of the Muslim world.

As mentioned later in this chapter, Friedman's own view of what constitutes a story tends to gloss over trends such as the mass slaying of American high school students by other American high school students.

129 "A Poverty of Dignity and a Wealth of Rage," *New York Times*, July 15, 2005.

130 "No Mere Terrorist," *New York Times*, March 24, 2002.

131 "Suicidal Lies," *New York Times*, March 31, 2002. For a response to this particular article, see M. Shahid Alam, "Lies of Desperation: Answering Thomas Friedman," *CounterPunch*, April 3, 2002.

132 "Lessons From Sri Lanka," *New York Times*, August 7, 2002.

133 "The Search For P.M.D.'s," *New York Times*, May 23, 2004.

134 "The Bell Tolls for Oslo," *New York Times*, March 31, 1997.

135 Robert Pape, "The Logic of Suicide Terrorism: It's the Occupation, Not the Fundamentalism," *The American Conservative*, July 18, 2005. Pape explains that he has compiled "the first complete database of every suicide-terrorist attack around the world from 1980 to early 2004. This research is conducted not only in English but also in native-language sources—Arabic, Hebrew, Russian, and Tamil, and others."

136 See "Thoughts on Gaza; a Reading List; Unity in Iraq," *New York Times*: Thomas L. Friedman blog ("Talking World Affairs"), October 6, 2005. Unsurprisingly, the first book on the list is Bernard Lewis's Orientalist tour de force *What Went Wrong?*

137 Robert Pape, "The Logic of Suicide Terrorism: It's the Occupation, not the Fundamentalism," *The American Conservative*, July 18, 2005.

138 "Reaping What It Sowed," *New York Times*, May 4, 2005.

139 "The New Cold War," *New York Times*, May 14, 2008.

140 The World Is Flat, p. 561.

141 "Buffett and Hezbollah," *New York Times*, August 9, 2006.

142 "Hold Your Applause," *New York Times*, April 9, 2003.

143 "Are There Any Iraqis In Iraq?," *New York Times*, April 8, 2004. Friedman's characterization of the insurgency as such does in fact have some traction if we consider that recruitment and acceptance of both suicide bombers and genocidal communists has historically been facilitated by U.S. military maneuvers.

144 "Mr. Nasty, Brutish and Short-Tempered," *New York Times*, March 10, 2006.

145 "Iraq's Known Unknowns, Still Unknown," *New York Times*, February 24, 2010.

146 "The Kidnapping of Democracy," *New York Times*, July 14, 2006.

147 "The Country We've Got," *New York Times*, January 6, 2005.

148 "All Hail 'McBama,'" *New York Times*, July 23, 2008. For populations that can choose whether or not they want to be democratic, see Friedman's statement in 2007 concerning China's leaders: "I … don't think they are going to opt for democracy. I am not even sure it is the answer for them right now" ("China in Three Colors," September 23, 2007).

149 "Let's Roll," *New York Times*, January 2, 2002.

150 *Longitudes and Attitudes*, p. 386.

151 "Yes, But What?," *New York Times*, October 5, 2001.

152 "Order vs. Disorder," *New York Times*, July 21, 2006.

153 "Fathers and Sons," *New York Times*, February 12, 1999.

154 As Matt Taibbi has perceptively noted, "Friedman never forgets to name the company or the brand name; if he had written *The Metamorphosis*, Gregor Samsa would have awoken from uneasy dreams in a Sealy Posturepedic." Matt Taibbi, "Flathead: The Peculiar Genius of Thomas L. Friedman," *New York Press*, April 26, 2005.

155 *Longitudes and Attitudes*, pp. 376–7.

156 *Ibid.*, p. 377.

157 *Hot, Flat, and Crowded*, p. 82. As for the most questionable metaphor to emerge from the Energy-Climate Era, possibilities include Friedman's comparison (on p. 48) of human society to

> the proverbial frog in the pail on the stove, where the heat gets turned up very slightly every hour, so the frog never thinks to jump out. It just keeps adjusting until it boils to death. I hope we will write a different ending, but let's not fool ourselves: We are the frog, the pail is getting hot, flat, and crowded, and we need a long-term survival plan—a ladder out of the pail.

Why the frog, which we are told is perfectly capable of jumping out of the pail on its own but simply fails to perceive the need, would benefit from the introduction of a ladder to the milieu is almost as unclear as why Indian villagers are said to require stepstools to board the globalization train (*The World Is Flat*, p. 547). Arabs are meanwhile given the option of building an Islamic bridge, a Maoist bridge, or a Jeffersonian bridge to the same train (*The Lexus and the Olive Tree*, p. 392).

158   *Hot, Flat, and Crowded*, p. 26.

159   *Ibid.*, p. 82.

160   *Ibid.*, p. 83.

161   William G. Ridgeway, "Arabia 1425," *The Social Affairs Unit*, October 11, 2004. This is the first of eight "letters" published in this venue. For Friedman's use of the label "Ahmed," see Section III.

162   William G. Ridgeway, "Those Drunken, Whoring Saudis: Desert Islam's Problem with Women," *The Social Affairs Unit*, August 22, 2005.

163   *Hot, Flat, and Crowded*, p. 83.

164   By this standard, "women's progress" depends on female ability to appear onscreen with little clothing and to interpret roles such as "Daphne Honeybutt," as Windsor did in the *Carry On* series Ridgeway references.

165   William G. Ridgeway, "Those Drunken, Whoring Saudis: Desert Islam's Problem with Women," *The Social Affairs Unit*.

166   Qtd. in *Hot, Flat, and Crowded*, p. 84.

167   Qtd. in *Ibid.* See Rod Nordland, "The Last Egyptian Belly Dancer," *Newsweek*, May 31, 2008.

168   The confusion that can potentially be engendered by simultaneously veiled and dynamic female characters is clear from Friedman's interaction in *The Lexus and the Olive Tree* (pp. 353–4) with Fatima Al-Abdali, owner of a popular Internet café in Kuwait City:

> Educated in America, Al-Abdali wears a veil, as a sign of Islamic piety, but is a total Web-head underneath … I said to her: "Look, I'm a little confused. Do the math for me. You are wearing an Islamic head covering, you are obviously a religious person, but you were educated in an American university and now you are bringing the Internet to Kuwait. I don't quite see how it all adds up."

169   To recap, the bombardier is the source of a five-hundred-pound bomb dropped onto a Taliban truck caravan, after which the male F-15 pilot gloatingly shouts down: "You have just been killed by a girl" ("The New Club NATO," *New York Times*, November 17, 2002). The "woman with blond locks spilling out from under her helmet

and an M16 hanging from her side" is the source of a "mind-bending experience" for Al Qaeda POWs at Bagram who are accustomed to a male-dominated society (*Longitudes and Attitudes*, p. 349).

170 *Longitudes and Attitudes*, p. 355.

171 *Ibid*. This particular insight occurs in response to the question of why some Arabs might have been pleased by the humbling of America on 9/11.

172 "Transcript: A TimesSelect/TimesTalks Event on Globalization," *New York Times*, April 25, 2006.

173 *Ibid*.

174 *The World Is Flat*, p. 563. The cognitive dissonance is caused, we are told, by simultaneous attachment to an archaic religion and desire for power in the modern world.

175 *Ibid*.

176 Friedman also fails to mention other terminology employed in the speech, such as: "But today the Jews rule this world by proxy." Mahathir's speech can be read on the website of the Anti-Defamation League, which has highlighted the anti-Jewish passages in bold. "Speech by Prime Minister Mahathir Mohamad," adl.org, October 16, 2003.

177 *Ibid*.

178 *The World Is Flat*, p. 569.

179 "Taking Ownership of Iraq?," *New York Times*, June 25, 2008.

180 "Four Reasons to Invade Iraq," from the series of exchanges entitled "Liberal Hawks Reconsider the Iraq War," *Slate*, January 12, 2004.

181 *Ibid*.

182 "Under the Arab Street," *New York Times*, October 23, 2002.

183 "Tolerable or Awful: The Roads Left in Iraq," *New York Times*, November 8, 2006.

184 United Nations Development Progamme: Regional Bureau for Arab States, "Arab Human Development Report 2002: Creating Opportunities for Future Generations," pp. vii and 32. Several more reports have since been issued; Friedman's attachment to them is underscored in 2004 when the issuance of the latest report is held up ("Holding Up Arab Reform," December 16, 2004):

> I eagerly awaited the third Arab Human Development Report, due in October. It was going to be pure TNT, because it was going to tackle the issue of governance and misgovernance in the Arab world, and the legal,

institutional and religious impediments to political reform. These are the guts of the issue out here. I waited. And I waited. But nothing.

185 "Arabs at the Crossroads," *New York Times*, July 3, 2002. Friedman additionally writes in *Longitudes and Attitudes*: "For far too long we have been in bed with Arab and Muslim dictators who, we told ourselves, are more liberal than their own people. Therefore, we also told ourselves, better to have pro-American dictators than pro-democratic societies that might be anti-American" (p. 345).

186 "Pop-Tarts or Freedom?," *New York Times*, January 16, 2005. The half million Iraqi children whose lives were extinguished thanks to sanctions may be forgiven for not realizing they were being saved by U.S. Ambassador to the U.N. Madeleine Albright, who, on *60 Minutes* in 1996, was asked: "We have heard that a half million children have died. I mean, that's more children than died in Hiroshima. And, you know, is the price worth it?" Her response: "I think this is a very hard choice, but the price—we think the price is worth it." See Rahul Mahajan, "'We Think the Price Is Worth It': Media Uncurious About Iraq Policy's Effects—There or Here," *FAIR (Extra!)*, November/December 2001. How offering the Palestinians a demilitarized set of Bantustans subservient to Israel constitutes saving them from tyranny is meanwhile unclear, and Friedman's admission in this very same post-tsunami article ("Pop-Tarts or Freedom?") that the Bush team's Iraq "performance has been pathetic" and mismanaged does not speak highly for U.S. saving power.

187 "Pop-Tarts or Freedom?," *New York Times*.

188 "The Democracy Thing," *New York Times*, October 30, 2002.

189 "Better Late Than …", *New York Times*, March 17, 2002.

190 *Longitudes and Attitudes*, p. 341.

191 See Owen Bowcott, "Afghanistan Worst Place in the World for Women, but India in Top Five," *Guardian*, June 15, 2011.

192 "America vs. The Narrative," *New York Times*, November 29, 2009. For indications that Hasan was perhaps not just "another angry jihadist," see "Profile: Major Nidal Hasan" from the hardly subversive *BBC News*, November 12, 2009. According to the profile, Hasan's "commitment to the [U.S.] army may have been broken by his opposition to the wars in Iraq and Afghanistan—and by plans to deploy him to a war zone … He is said to have been affected

by injuries he saw at the Walter Reed Medical Army Center, where he worked until recently as a psychiatrist treating troops returning from combat." The profile also notes that Hasan was harassed in the military for being of Middle Eastern descent.

193   See Matthias Gebauer and Hasnain Kazim, "The 'Kill Team' Images: US Army Apologizes for Horrific Photos from Afghanistan," *Spiegel Online*, March 21, 2011.

194   See Section III for Friedman's encouragement of massive casualties in Lebanon in 2006 and Gaza in 2008–9.

195   "Restoring Our Honor," *New York Times*, May 6, 2004.

196   "If Not Now, When?," *New York Times*, February 22, 2001.

197   "Courageous Arab Thinkers," *New York Times*, October 19, 2003.

198   *Ibid.*

199   "www.jihad.com," *New York Times*, December 16, 2009.

200   *Ibid.*

201   "Arabs Lift Their Voices," *New York Times*, April 7, 2005.

202   See M. Shahid Alam, "Scholarship or Sophistry? A Review of *What Went Wrong?* by Bernard Lewis," *Media Monitors Network*, June 25, 2003. As Alam points out in his piece, "mainstream reviewers describe Bernard Lewis as 'the doyen of Middle Eastern studies,' the 'father' of Islamic studies, 'arguably the West's most distinguished scholar on the Middle East,' and a 'Sage for the Age,'" which naturally indicates the lack of a political correctness infection in said academic field. That a toxic correctness works on behalf of other ethnic groups is however hinted at when Friedman plays the anti-Semitism card in response to the proposed boycott of Israeli academic institutions that fuel the occupation of Palestinian land ("A Boycott Built on Bias," June 17, 2007).

203   "Footprints in the Sand," *New York Times*, November 7, 2004.

204   Friedman's Google search might even turn up Said's own response to the first Arab Human Development Report, in which he confirms that "the report correctly says that there is no Arab democracy" and that Arabs have "long been deprived of a sense of participation and citizenship by their rulers." Edward Said, "Disunity and Factionalism," *Al-Ahram Weekly*, no. 599, August 15–21, 2002.

205   Clearly, organization at gunpoint is not by definition voluntary.

206   "The Country We've Got," *New York Times*, January 6, 2005.

207   *Ibid.*

208   "Hoping for Arab Mandelas," *New York Times*, March 26, 2011.

209   See, for example, "A Poverty of Dignity and a Wealth of Rage," *New York Times*, July 15, 2005. For hints as to possible sources of legitimate anger, see Robert Fisk, "Why Do They Hate the West So Much, We Will Ask," *Independent*, January 7, 2009.

210   Ubiquitous examples include "Let's Roll," *New York Times*, January 2, 2002. Regarding the Middle East, Friedman writes: "Countries in that region haven't had a good century in 700 years—and they're not going to soon."

211   Writing in *Longitudes and Attitudes* (p. 357) on the subject of alienated young Muslim men in Europe, Friedman adds the following parenthetical aside:

> There is also something about the fact that virtually none of these young men were married, or had their religious fervor tempered in any way through a relationship with a woman, that must have contributed to their rage and extremism. It is just not normal, but I would need Dr. Freud to help me sort all that out.

According to this line of logic, the Pope and countless other non-Muslims are similarly not normal. As for other instances of emasculating discourse, Dr. Freud might be able to shed some light on Friedman's repeated tantrums about how U.S. politicians view environmental awareness as a pastime for "girlie-men": "Sorry, but being green, focusing the nation on greater energy efficiency and conservation, is not some girlie-man issue" ("The New Red, White and Blue," January 6, 2006).

212   Friedman wavers on the subject of Arab/Muslim support for bin Laden, from his post-9/11, utterly scientific assessment that "one need only visit some of the most popular Arabic Web sites and chat rooms to see that public opinion in the Arab world is split about 50–50" with regard to the justness of the attacks ("The Big Terrible," *New York Times*, September 18, 2001), to his announcement the following year that "the reason the terrorists unleash huge events like 9/11 is precisely because they have no mass following" ("Going Our Way, *New York Times*, September 15, 2002), to his conclusion resulting from an interaction with an Egyptian on a flight from Jordan that "anyone who thought bin Laden was some crazy outlier … was completely fooling himself" (*Longitudes and Attitudes*, pp. 329–30).

213   *Hot, Flat, and Crowded*, p. 89.

214   *Longitudes and Attitudes*, p. 328.

215   *Ibid.*

216   See Nizar Sakhnini, "Palestine Through History: A Chronology (II),"
      The Palestine Chronicle, August 5, 2008. The other wars Friedman
      rattles off had their outrageous and terrifying aspects as well, such
      as the 1982 Israeli invasion of Lebanon that killed over 17,500 people,
      primarily civilians. As for the assassination of the Jordanian prime
      minister, this was hardly the defining moment of Black September,
      during which thousands of Palestinians were slaughtered by the
      Jordanian regime.

217   "World War III," *New York Times*, September 13, 2001.

218   For the OIC, see "Timeline: Organisation of the Islamic Conference,"
      BBC News, December 26, 2010. For Khamenei, see Jim Muir, "Iran
      Condemns Attacks on US," *BBC News*, September 17, 2001. For Bush,
      see "Text: President Bush Addresses the Nation," *The Washington
      Post*, September 20, 2001.

219   "The Core of Muslim Rage," *New York Times*, March 6. 2002.

220   "Silence and Suicide," *New York Times*, October 12, 2005.

221   "The Endgame in Iraq," *New York Times*, September 28, 2005.

222   "'Why Us?' Sunni Arabs Should Ask, 'Why Anyone?'", *New York
      Times*, November 16, 2005.

223   *Ibid.*

224   See the *Democracy Now!* report, "The U.S. Bombs a Wedding Party
      in Afghanistan; Death Toll Estimates Range Between 40 and 250,"
      July 2, 2002; or the *Independent* report, "US Warplanes 'Bomb
      Afghan Wedding Party,'" November 6, 2008; or Jason Ditz, "Dozens
      of Civilians, No Militant Leaders, Killed in US Drone Strike on
      Pakistan Funeral," Antiwar.com, June 24, 2009; or Rory McCarthy,
      "Wedding Party Massacre: Iraqis Claim More Than 40 Killed in US
      Helicopter Attack," *Guardian*, May 20, 2004.

225   See Marjorie Cohn, "The Haditha Massacre," *Truthout*, May 30,
      2006.

226   "Insurgency Out, Anarchy In," *New York Times*, June 2, 2006.

227   "Letter From Baghdad," *New York Times*, September 5, 2007. Those
      wishing to take issue with this sort of rhetoric might inquire about
      the amount of love that Friedman feels for the American kids that he
      enthusiastically ships off to perpetrate the "war of choice" in Iraq.

228   *Longitudes and Attitudes*, p. 345.

229   "Pakistan's Constitution Avenue," *New York Times*, January 20, 2002.

230   "Hummers Here, Hummers There," *New York Times*, May 25, 2003. The reason that there is too much democracy is that "the ruling family is so insecure, it feels it has to consult every faction, tribe and senior cleric before making any decision."

231   "Jordan Gets It," *New York Times*, April 3, 2001.

232   "The Arabs' Road Map," *New York Times*, October 20, 2000.

233   For a less exuberant depiction of the agreement, see Charles Kernaghan, "U.S.–Jordan Free Trade Agreement Descends into Human Trafficking & Involuntary Servitude," National Labor Committee (now Institute for Global Labour & Human Rights, globallabourrights.org), May 2006. The report begins:

> It must seem so improbable, that in the year 2005 and under a U.S.–Jordan Free Trade Agreement, that workers sewing clothing for Wal-Mart and other U.S. companies could be routinely forced to work 72-hour shifts, while being paid just two cents an hour, and repeatedly beaten with belts and sticks, that at the outset we have to say that there are 65 workers in Bangladesh ready to testify as to the horrors they faced at the Al Shahaed factory in Jordan.

Friedman, on the other hand, cheerily hopes for the rest of the region to follow in Jordan's footsteps.

234   "The Hidden Victims," *New York Times*, May 1, 2002.

235   *Ibid.*

236   "Arabs Lift Their Voices," *New York Times*, April 7, 2005.

237   "There Is Hope," *New York Times*, October 27, 2002.

238   "The Fast Eat the Slow," *New York Times*, February 2, 2001.

239   *Hot, Flat, and Crowded*, p. 10. The bearer of the maybe-tattoo prompts a discussion between Friedman and the innovative crown prince about the Bahrain School, set up for Navy dependents by the U.S. Defense Dept. and defined on its website as a "Department of Defense Education Activity (DoDEA)." According to Friedman, by the 1980s "nearly 70 percent [of attendees] were tuition-paying non-Americans, primarily the sons and daughters of Bahrain's business and political elite, including the crown prince in his day," while the frightening prospect of the school's closure in 2004 and "the departure of the dependents would have brought to an end every-

thing from the American women's annual flower show in Bahrain, to American–Bahraini softball games, to young Americans competing in soccer leagues with young Bahrainis" (*Ibid.*, p. 11). Friedman faithfully reports the crown prince's confirmation that the school "was the best advertisement the Americans ever had," although it and the annual flower show presumably failed to resonate among the non-elite, non-royal majority of Bahrainis (*Ibid.*).

240   See *The World Is Flat*, p. 506.

241   See William Wallis, "Google Earth Spurs Bahraini Equality Drive," *Financial Times*, November 24, 2006.

242   "14 Big Macs Later …," *New York Times*, December 31, 1995.

243   "Tribes With Flags," *New York Times*, March 22, 2011.

244   "The Fast Eat the Slow," *New York Times*.

245   "Fathers and Sons," *New York Times*, February 12, 1999.

246   "The Sand Wall," *New York Times*, April 13, 2003.

247   He maintains the conviction, however, that Iraqi resistance to the O-word is generally illegitimate and terroristic in nature (see, for example, "Are There Any Iraqis In Iraq?," April 8, 2004).

248   "Dubai and Dunces," *New York Times*, March 15, 2006.

249   "Not So Smart," *New York Times*, July 19, 2006.

250   *Ibid.*

251   See Conal Urquhart, "Israel Planned for Lebanon War Months in Advance, PM Says," *Guardian*, March 9, 2007; and "Military Analysts Question Israeli Bombing of Civilian Targets," *Associated Press*, July 20, 2006.

252   See pulitzer.org/citation/2002-Commentary. Additionally, since 2004 Friedman has sat on the Pulitzer board.

253   "Crazier Than Thou," *New York Times*, February 13, 2002.

254   "Dubai and Dunces," *New York Times*, March 15, 2006.

255   "Tolerable or Awful: The Roads Left in Iraq," *New York Times*, November 8, 2006.

256   "The Land of Denial," *New York Times*, June 5, 2002.

257   "The Hidden Victims," *New York Times*, May 1, 2002.

258   "Drilling for Freedom," *New York Times*, October 20, 2002.

259   "B.E., Before Egypt. A.E., After Egypt," *New York Times*, February 1, 2011.

260   "They Did It," *New York Times*, February 12, 2011.

261   "The Country We've Got," *New York Times*, January 6, 2005.

262   See "Oil Pressure Rising," *The Economist* online, February 23, 2011.

263   *Hot, Flat, and Crowded*, p. 96. Egypt is specifically listed as a petrolist state.

264   "Out of Touch, Out of Time," *New York Times*, February 10, 2011. Additional validation occurs in the same article:

> I spent part of the morning in [Cairo's Tahrir] square watching and pho-tographing a group of young Egyptian students wearing plastic gloves taking garbage in both hands and neatly scooping it into black plastic bags to keep the area clean. This touched me in particular because more than once in this column I have quoted the aphorism that 'in the history of the world no one has ever washed a rented car.' I used it to make the point that no one has ever washed a rented country either—and for the last century Arabs have just been renting their countries from kings, dictators and colonial powers. So, they had no desire to wash them.

265   "Tribes With Flags," *New York Times*, March 22, 2011. "Real coun-tries" are defined as hosting "big homogenous majorities that put nation before sect or tribe and have enough mutual trust to come together like a family: 'everyone against dad.'"

266   *The Lexus and the Olive Tree*, pp. 339–40.

267   "This Is Just the Start," *New York Times*, March 1, 2011.

268   For a hilarious and spot-on rebuttal to Friedman's not-so-obvious forces, see Sarah Carr, "This Is Just the Start and It Never Fucking Ends," *Inanities*, March 2, 2011.

269   "B.E., Before Egypt. A.E., After Egypt," *New York Times*, February 1, 2011. For the "nasty job," see "The Palestine Papers," english. aljazeera.net.

270   "The Core of Muslim Rage," *New York Times*, March 6, 2002.

271   As for other instances of unexpected co-optation, these include the following announcement in *The World Is Flat*: "Indeed, reading the *Communist Manifesto* today, I am in awe at how incisively Marx detailed the forces that were flattening the world during the rise of the Industrial Revolution, and how much he foreshadowed the way these same forces would keep flattening the world right up to the present" (p. 234).

272   "This Is Just the Start," *New York Times*.

273   See "Lebanon—Amnesty International Report 2007," amnesty.org; and "Amnesty Details Gaza 'War Crimes,'" BBC News, July 2, 2009.

274   *The Lexus and the Olive Tree*, p. 71.

275   "China, Twitter and 20-Year-Olds vs. the Pyramids," *New York Times*, February 5, 2011.

276   *Ibid.*

277   *Ibid.* After arguing for years that one of the effects of the flat world is that Arabs and Muslims get their humiliation fiber-optically and can see how far behind the "caravan" they are (see, for example, "Transcript: A TimesSelect/TimesTalks Event on Globalization," *New York Times*, April 25, 2006.), Friedman declares with regard to young protesters in Jordan, Egypt, and Tunisia: "My heart aches for them. So much human potential, but they have no idea how far behind they are—or maybe they do and that's why they're revolting" (*Ibid.*). In the very next article he definitively asserts that "this revolt is primarily about a people fed up with being left behind in a world where they can so clearly see how far others have vaulted ahead" ("Up With Egypt," February 8, 2011).

278   "The $110 Billion Question," *New York Times*, March 6, 2011.

279   "China, Twitter and 20-Year-Olds vs. the Pyramids," *New York Times*, February 5, 2011.

280   See Federico Fuentes, "System's Crisis Fuels Arab Revolt," *Green Left Weekly*, March 6, 2011; and Daniel Dicker, "Food Commodity Speculation Adds to Egypt Unrest," *The Huffington Post*, January 30, 2011.

281   "Up With Egypt," February 8, 2011.

282   "They Did It," *New York Times*, February 12, 2011.

283   See Austin Mackell, "The IMF Versus the Arab spring," *Guardian*, May 25, 2011, in which Mackell addresses the "failure [in the West] to appreciate the revolutions as a rebellion not just against local dictators, but against the global neo-liberal programme they were implementing with such gusto in their countries." See also John Pilger, "Behind the Arab revolt lurks a word we dare not speak," *New Statesman*, February 24, 2011:

> The revolt in the Arab world is against not merely a resident dictator, but a worldwide economic tyranny, designed by the US Treasury and imposed by the US Agency for International Development, the IMF and the World Bank, which have ensured that rich countries such as Egypt are reduced to vast sweatshops, with 40 per cent of the population earning less than $2 a day. The people's triumph in Cairo was the first blow against what

Benito Mussolini called corporatism, a word that appears in his definition of fascism.

284 "The Whole World Is Watching," *New York Times*, June 27, 2007.

285 *Ibid.*

286 "Tommy Again," uploaded to youtube.com by "paulhinr" on
September 19, 2010.

287 "The Taxi Driver," *New York Times*, November 1, 2006.

3 THE SPECIAL RELATIONSHIP

1 "Just Knock It Off," *New York Times*, October 19, 2010.

2 "Thomas Friedman: Americans 'Fed Up' With Israel," uploaded to
youtube.com on October 25, 2010, by "israelnews" (Israeli Channel 2
News).

3 *Ibid.*

4 *Ibid.*

5 "Rooting for Bibi Is Rooting for Israel," *New York Times*, September
23, 2005. In *From Beirut to Jerusalem*, Friedman meanwhile notes
that the Labor and Likud parties "each pointed to their written platforms and said, 'Look how different we are from them,' but in daily
life they were each selling the same Puppy Chow" (p. 268).

6 "Thomas Friedman: Americans 'Fed Up' With Israel," Israeli Channel
2 News.

7 As does the delusional claim that Friedman "has always been a
militant of the Palestinian cause," levied by *Wall Street Journal* con-
tributor Giulio Meotti in "The Thomas Friedman Myth," *Ynetnews*,
May 22, 2011.

8 "Steal This Movie," *New York Times*, August 7, 2010.

9 *Ibid.*

10 "U.N. Human Rights Chief: Israel's Blockade of Gaza Strip Is Illegal,"
Fox News, August 14, 2009.

11 See "Rain of Fire: White Phosphorus in Gaza," *Human Rights Watch*,
March 25, 2009.

12 For a debunking of such myths, see Virginia Tilley, "Putting Words
in Ahmadinejad's Mouth," *CounterPunch*, August 28, 2006.

13 "Just Knock It Off," *New York Times*, October 19, 2010.

14 See Michael S. Ladah and Suleiman I. Aljouni, "Mr. Bush, What
About Israel's Defiance of UN Resolutions?," *Media Monitors
Network*, September 29, 2002.

15   See, for example, "Time for Straight Talk," *New York Times*, January 7, 1996.

16   "Hafez Answers Chris," *New York Times*, January 10, 1996.

17   "The Physics of Mideast Peace," *New York Times*, September 15, 1997.

18   "War of Ideas, Part 4," *New York Times*, January 18, 2004.

19   "Suicidal Lies," *New York Times*, March 31, 2002.

20   See Palestinian Center for Human Rights, "Israeli Forces Kill Elderly Disabled Palestinian During Demolition of 34 Homes in Khan Yunis," *Electronic Intifada*, July 12, 2004.

21   "Bibi's Playbook," *New York Times*, December 4, 1997.

22   "A Delicate Balance," *New York Times*, June 30, 1998.

23   See Liel Leibovitz, "Fibi Netanyahu," *Tablet*, July 15, 2010. Initially lauded as "nothing less than the Israeli Balfour Declaration for the Palestinians" ("Promised Land; Israel and the Palestinians See a Way to Co-Exist," *New York Times*, September 5, 1993), Oslo is gradually downgraded by Friedman to "a necessary and worthwhile test of whether Israel could produce a Palestinian partner for a secure peace" ("A Way Out of the Middle East Impasse," August 24, 2001). We thus end up in a curious situation in which Israeli-produced peace partners are responsible for psychological breakthroughs to their creators.

24   See Ethan Bronner, "As Biden Visits, Israel Unveils Plan for New Settlements," *New York Times*, March 9, 2010. For the illegality of Israeli settlements, see "Illegal Israeli Settlements," The Council for European Palestinian Relations, thecepr.org: "The 2004 ruling by the International Court of Justice declared that 'Israeli settlements ... including East Jerusalem, are illegal and an obstacle to peace.'"

25   "Driving Drunk in Jerusalem," *New York Times*, March 14, 2010.

26   "Lessons From Tahrir Sq.," *New York Times*, May 24, 2011. As *FAIR*'s Peter Hart points out, it is absurd to suggest that such a routine would draw media attention when regular nonviolent protests against the West Bank separation wall—that are regularly met with violent repression by the IDF—do not. Peter Hart, "Friedman's Bogus Advice on Palestinian Nonviolence," *FAIR*, May 25, 2011.

27   "Report of the Commission of Inquiry Into the Events at the Refugee Camps in Beirut (The Kahan Commission)," February 8, 1983, accessible at *Jewish Virtual Library*, jewishvirtuallibrary.org.

28   See Sonja Karkar, "Remembering Sabra and Shatila: On Massacres, Atrocities and Holocausts," *PULSE Media*, September 17, 2010.

29   *From Beirut to Jerusalem*, p. 164

30   *Ibid.*

31   See Robert Fisk, "Bush Is Walking Into a Trap," *Independent*, September 16, 2001.

32   *From Beirut to Jerusalem*, p. 452.

33   Ibid., p. 455–6.

34   *Ibid.*, p. 456.

35   *Ibid.*, p. 165.

36   *Ibid.*

37   *Ibid.*

38   *Ibid.*, p. 166.

39   *Ibid.*

40   "The Beirut Massacre: The Four Days," *New York Times*, September 26, 1982.

41   Robert Fisk, *Pity the Nation: The Abduction of Lebanon*, New York: Thunder's Mouth Press/Nation Books, 2002, p. 364.

42   "The Beirut Massacre: The Four Days," *New York Times*.

43   *From Beirut to Jerusalem*, p. 488.

44   *Ibid.*, pp. 164–5.

45   "Wanted: An Arab Sharon," *New York Times*, January 11, 2006.

46   Ari Shavit, "The Big Freeze," *Haaretz Magazine*, October 8, 2004.

47   "Jews, Israel and America," *New York Times*, October 24, 2004.

48   "A Hole in the Heart," *New York Times*, October 28, 2004.

49   See Ali Abunimah, *One Country: A Bold Proposal to End the Israeli–Palestinian Impasse*, New York: Metropolitan Books, 2006, p. 70. Abunimah additionally debunks the claim, regurgitated by Friedman ("Yasir Arafat's Moment," July 28, 2000), that the Palestinians did not make a counteroffer at Camp David.

50   "Fog of War," *New York Times*, August 18, 2002.

51   See "Fmr. Israeli Foreign Minister Shlomo Ben Ami Debates Outspoken Professor Norman Finkelstein on Israel, the Palestinians, and the Peace Process," *Democracy Now!*, February 14, 2006.

52   "Clinton's Last Memo," *New York Times*, January 12, 2001.

53   "Dear Ehud, Hafez and Yasir," *New York Times*, February 22, 2000.

54   "Yasir Arafat's Moment," *New York Times*, July 28, 2000.

55 Jerusalem's Arabic name. "The Real Deal," *New York Times*, May 2, 2000.

56 "If I Forget Thee, O Jerusalem," *New York Times*, September 22, 1997.

57 "Brainless in Gaza," *New York Times*, June 2, 1998.

58 "The New Mideast Paradigm," *New York Times*, March 6, 2001.

59 "Time to Choose, Yasir," *New York Times*, October 6, 2000.

60 "Arafat's War," *New York Times*, October 13, 2000.

61 *Ibid.*

62 *Ibid.*

63 "Ritual Sacrifice," *New York Times*, October 31, 2000.

64 *Longitudes and Attitudes*, p. 373.

65 "Suicidal Lies," *New York Times*, March 31, 2002. So much for Friedman's hypothetical post-9/11 missive from the desk of George W. Bush, in which Friedman-channeling-Bush warns Sharon that if Israel attempts to "use this situation" to destroy Arafat and the P.A. and is then "force[d] ... to reoccupy" the Palestinian territories, it "will be seriously undermining our coalition against bin Laden. And whoever undermines that coalition undermines us" ("Dear Ariel and Yasir," October 23, 2001).

66 *Ibid.*

67 Robert Fisk, *The Great War for Civilisation*, p. 500.

68 "Nine Wars Too Many," *New York Times*, May 15, 2002.

69 *Longitudes and Attitudes*, p. xii.

70 "War of Ideas, Part 4," *New York Times*, January 18, 2004.

71 "Suicidal Lies," *New York Times*, March 31, 2002.

72 Quoted in "Lebanon's Aftermath," *New York Times*, May 15, 1996.

73 Edward Said, "The Orientalist Express: Thomas Friedman Wraps Up the Middle East," *The Village Voice*, October 17, 1989.

74 See "Tom's Journal," PBS Online NewsHour, September 25, 2003.

75 "Lessons From Sri Lanka," *New York Times*, August 7, 2002.

76 "Israel's Goals in Gaza?," *New York Times*, January 14, 2009. He also goes as far as to issue the following threat to "The World of Order" (in this case defined as "the West" plus "countries like Russia, China, India, Egypt, Jordan and Saudi Arabia") in 2006: "This is not Israel's fight alone—and if you really want to see a 'disproportional' Israeli response, just keep leaving Israel to fight this war alone. Then you will see some real craziness" ("Order vs. Disorder," July 21, 2006).

77 As for the education of the I.D.F., Friedman takes it upon himself to meet personally with high-ranking military officers, including Chief of Staff Gabi Ashkenazi, the very same year that the education of Hamas occurs, in order to share his impressions of Arab countries: Anshel Pfeffer, "New York Times Columnist Tom Friedman Lectures IDF Brass on Visits to Arab States," Haaretz, August 11, 2009.

78 See Neil MacFarquhar, "Hezbollah's Prominence Has Many Sunnis Worried," New York Times, August 4, 2006.

79 See Robert Fisk, "Marwahin, 15 July 2006: The Anatomy of a Massacre," Independent, September 30, 2006.

80 "Buffett and Hezbollah," New York Times, August 9, 2006.

81 See Conal Urquhart, "Israel Planned for Lebanon War Months in Advance, PM says," Guardian, March 9, 2007

82 "Outsource the Cabinet?," New York Times, February 28, 2007. Friedman gleans these statistics from Israeli economics writer Sever Plocker.

83 "Israel's Goals in Gaza?," New York Times, January 14, 2009.

84 Aaron Leonard, "Norman G. Finkelstein: Israel Overreached in Gaza," History News Network, May 3, 2010.

85 "The Mideast's Ground Zero," New York Times, January 7, 2009. In his celebrated Friedman critique "Flat N All That" (New York Press, January 14, 2009), Matt Taibbi suggests rectifying the structural inconsistencies contained within the play's proposed title by re-titling it: "Who owns this hotel? And why did a person suffering from multiple personality disorder build a mosque inside it after blowing up the bar and asking if there was a room for the Jews? Why? Because his editor's been drinking rubbing alcohol!"

86 See Howard Friel, "Chronology: Which Side Violated the Israel–Gaza Ceasefire? The Bush Administration and The New York Times v. Amnesty International," CommonDreams.org, January 14, 2009. See also Rory McCarthy, "Gaza Truce Broken as Israeli Raid Kills Six Hamas Gunmen," Guardian, November 5, 2008.

87 "The Mideast's Ground Zero," New York Times, January 7, 2009.

88 Quoted in Johann Hari, "The True Story Behind This War Is Not the One Israel Is Telling," johannhari.com, December 28, 2008. See also Norman Finkelstein, "Foiling Another Palestinian 'Peace Offensive': Behind the Bloodbath in Gaza," normanfinkelstein.com, January 19, 2009, in which he notes Friedman's encouragement of civilian

casualties and discusses Israeli thwarting of Palestinian peace efforts dating back to 1981.

89 *Ibid.* Curiously, in the immediate aftermath of the Hamas victory in the Palestinian parliamentary elections of 2006 Friedman appears to be convinced of the need to respect the party's "legitimate mandate" ("The Weapon of Democracy," February 15, 2006) but later adopts the position that "democracy is not just the act of winning a free election" and that, in the Palestinian case, it requires Hamas to uphold the recognition of Israel by previous administrations ("The Hamas Dilemma," April 12, 2006).

90 "Footprints in the Sand," *New York Times*, November 7, 2004.

91 "Hobby or Necessity?," *New York Times*, March 28, 2010.

92 Noam Chomsky, *Necessary Illusions: Thought Control in Democratic Societies*, Cambridge, MA: South End Press, 1989, pp. 290–6.

93 "Ritual Sacrifice," *New York Times*, October 31, 2000.

94 "What to Do With Lemons," *New York Times*, June 18, 2011.

95 "Senseless in Israel," *New York Times*, November 24, 2000.

96 "Lessons From Sri Lanka," *New York Times*, August 7, 2002.

97 "The New Mideast Paradigm," *New York Times*, March 6, 2001.

98 "How About Sending NATO Somewhere Important?," *New York Times*, September 4, 2001.

99 *Longitudes and Attitudes*, p. 335.

100 "Three Blind Eyes," *New York Times*, January 2, 2001.

101 "One Wall, One Man, One Vote," *New York Times*, September 14, 2003.

102 *Ibid.*

103 Nationality is for Jews only. See Robin Yassin-Kassab, "Too Late for Two States," *Al Jazeera English*, November 14, 2010.

104 "Israeli in Disguise Learns the Anguish of an Arab," *New York Times*, May 5, 1986. The Israeli Or Commission, appointed in 2000 to investigate the circumstances of a demonstration in which thirteen Arab Israelis were killed by Israeli police, reported "neglectful and discriminatory" treatment of Arab citizens of Israel by the government and failure to equally allocate resources (See "Official Summary of Or Commission Report [Haaretz translation]", accessible at orwatch.org: *The First Or Commission Watch Conference*, June 24, 2004).

105 For persons who have already reached the apartheid conclusion, see

former Israeli Minister of Education Shulamit Aloni, "Yes, There Is Apartheid in Israel," *CounterPunch*, January 8, 2007.

106   "War of Ideas, Part 4," *New York Times*, January 18, 2004.

107   "A Way Out of the Middle East Impasse," *New York Times*, August 24, 2001.

108   As for Friedman's views on unilateral reversals of other occupations, Syria is unconditionally required to "get out of Lebanon" ("Roto-Rooter," April 16, 2003) but must earn an Israeli withdrawal from the Golan Heights by "privatizing and deregulating" its economy: "Israel shouldn't exit the Golan unless it sees Syria enter the world" ("Frozen in Damascus," December 5, 1999).

109   "Israel Bombs Gaza University," *BBC News*, December 28, 2008.

110   "Arafat's War," *New York Times*, October 13, 2000.

111   "What Day Is It?," *New York Times*, April 24, 2002.

112   "Sharon, Arafat and Mao," *New York Times*, February 8, 2001.

113   See Ali Abunimah and Hussein Ibish, "Debunking 6 common Israeli myths," *The Electronic Intifada*, April 14, 2002. Naturally, Friedman actively propagates all six of the myths addressed by the authors.

114   "Sharon, Arafat and Mao," *New York Times*.

115   See, for example, "Israeli Troops Shoot Arab Student Dead at Protest," *New York Times*, November 22, 1984.

116   "Sharon, Arafat and Mao," *New York Times*.

117   "It Only Gets Worse," *New York Times*, May 22, 2001.

118   "The Wrong Answer," *New York Times*, October 17, 2000.

119   "Three Blind Eyes," *New York Times*, January 2, 2001.

120   "Get Real on Kosovo," *New York Times*, March 17, 2000.

121   "As Ugly as It Gets," *New York Times*, March 25, 2010.

122   Rachel Corrie, twenty-three years of age, was killed in 2003 by an Israeli bulldozer while peacefully protecting a Palestinian home from demolition in Gaza (see rachelcorrie.org).

123   See Bill Gertz, "Report Alters Iran Nukes Outlook," *The Washington Times*, March 7, 2011. The article begins: "An annual intelligence report to Congress has dropped language stating that Iran's nuclear weapons ambitions are a future option."

124   "Cracks in Iran's Clique," *New York Times*, September 23, 2009.

125   "As Ugly as It Gets," *New York Times*.

126   See Kevin Young, "America Says No to the Militarization of Colombia's 'Drug War,'" *AlterNet*, January 7, 2011, and "End Anti-

Trade Union Violence in Colombia," justiceforcolombia.org. As any good neoliberal advocate might do, Friedman appeals to heartstrings to urge the passage of Plan Colombia in a 2000 column ridiculously titled "Saving Colombia" (April 11, 2000):

> There are two ways to think about "Plan Colombia." One way is to get wrapped up in the details—the helicopters, the training. The other way—the right way—is to step back and ask yourself what kind of courage it takes to stay in Colombia right now and be a judge who puts drug lords in jail or a politician who fights for the rule of law—knowing the criminals have millions in drug money and would kill your kids in a second.

That Friedman ten years later continues to promote the idea that the purpose of Plan Colombia was to *fight* drug trafficking suggests that he does not care about widely publicized "parapolitics" scandals confirming deep paramilitary and narco-trafficking ties to the highest echelons of the Colombian government.

127 "The Swiss Struggle," *New York Times*, September 25, 1997.

128 "The Neutrality Myth," *New York Times*, February 5, 1997.

129 See "Lebanon's Aftermath," *New York Times*, May 15, 1996, concerning the slaughter of more than one hundred civilian refugees at the U.N. compound in Qana; or Robert Fisk, "Smoke Signals From the Battle of Bint Jbeil Send a Warning to Israel," *Independent*, July 27, 2006:

> The Israelis bombed two ambulances in Qana, killing two of the three wounded inside. All the crews were injured—one with a piece of shrapnel in his neck—but what worried the Lebanese Red Cross was that the Israeli missiles had pierced the very centre of the red cross painted on the roof of each vehicle.

Or see Kim Sengupta, "Outrage as Israel Bombs UN," *Independent*, January 16, 2009; or Chris McGreal and Hazem Balousha, "Gaza's Day of Carnage – 40 Dead as Israelis Bomb Two UN Schools," *Guardian*, January 7, 2009; or "Israeli bomb kills UN observers," *BBC News*, July 26, 2006.

130 See Robert Evans, "Israel Engaged in Ethnic Cleansing With Settlement Expansion: UN Investigator," *Reuters*, March 21, 2011.

131 "Give a Little, Get a Little," *New York Times*, September 15, 2000.

132 "The Man Who Foresaw the Uprising," *Yediot Ahronot*, April 7, 1988.

133   Noam Chomsky, *Letters from Lexington: Reflections on Propaganda*, London: Pluto Press, 2004, p. 61. Friedman assumed the post of chief diplomatic correspondent shortly after this statement was made.

134   *Longitudes and Attitudes*, p. 326.

135   Noam Chomsky, *Letters from Lexington*, p. 61.

136   "Suicidal Lies," *New York Times*, March 31, 2002.

137   See *From Beirut to Jerusalem*, p. 383:

> When the uprising began, Palestinians threw stones at the Israelis, not because they had all suddenly read the teachings of Mahatma Gandhi and become nonviolent, not because they didn't want to hurt the Israelis, but because when their anger suddenly exploded, stones and clubs and kitchen knives were all that most of them found available and operationally expedient.

For a concise summary of the effects of Palestinian nonviolence, see Ramzy Baroud, "Non-Violence in Palestine," *CounterPunch*, April 17, 2009.

138   *From Beirut to Jerusalem*, p. 385.

139   *Ibid.*, pp. 407–8.

140   "Footprints in the Sand," *New York Times*, November 7, 2004.

141   "Forgive and Forget," *New York Times*, August 11, 1998.

142   *From Beirut to Jerusalem*, p. 414.

143   *Ibid.*, p. 413. Additional details of the mass nonviolent action that Friedman conveniently forgets in later years appear on this same page:

> In fact, the only time I really saw Israeli officials get truly worried during the uprising was when they felt the Palestinians might actually be disengaging from them. Israelis had faced one- and two-day commercial strikes from the Palestinians many times before, but never the kind of mass civil disobedience they witnessed in the early months of the *intifada*, when the underground Palestinian leadership ordered all shopkeepers to open only for a few hours each day; when hundreds of Palestinians who worked for the Israeli occupation administration, either as policemen or clerks, quit their jobs; when thousands of Palestinian laborers refused or were prevented from going to work in Israel; and when thousands of Palestinian merchants refused to pay their taxes or buy Israeli products.

144   "The Core of Muslim Rage," *New York Times*, March 6, 2002.

145   *From Beirut to Jerusalem*, p. 416. This policy is classified by Friedman

as "double bookkeeping," other manifestations of which include continued Palestinian attendance at Hebrew classes in Gaza and, in one case, a Palestinian purchase of a used car from the Israeli foreign ministry spokesman who is being transferred to Rio de Janeiro (*Ibid.*, pp. 416–7).

146 *The Lexus and the Olive Tree*, p. 262.

147 *Ibid.*

148 See "24. U.S. Aid to Israel Fuels Repressive Occupation in Palestine," *Project Censored*: Top 25 of 2004; and Akiva Eldar, "U.S. Taxpayers Are Paying for Israel's West Bank Occupation," *Haaretz*, November 16, 2010.

149 *The Lexus and the Olive Tree*, p. 30.

150 Friedman claims to not remember the details of "whatever her interpretation was," though he does remember the article was "on the top right corner of page 3" of the *International Herald Tribune* (*Ibid.*, pp. 30–1).

151 *Ibid.*, pp. 30–1.

152 *Ibid.*, pp. 31–3.

153 *Ibid.*, p. 37.

154 Friedman's preferred story illustrating a proper Lexus/olive tree balance is meanwhile one in which an Israeli friend has his briefcase blown up—with handheld computer inside—by the Israeli police after accidentally leaving it on the sidewalk (*Ibid.*, pp. 42–3). The handheld computer is presumably the symbol of modernity in this case, leaving the explosion to symbolize Israeli tradition.

155 *Ibid.*, p. 41.

156 "What a Mess," *New York Times*, June 6, 2007.

157 "Steal This Movie," *New York Times*, August 7, 2010.

158 See David Rose, "The Gaza Bombshell," *Vanity Fair*, April 2008, for details of the "covert initiative, approved by Bush and implemented by … Condoleezza Rice and Deputy National Security Adviser Elliott Abrams, to provoke a Palestinian civil war."

159 *The Lexus and the Olive Tree*, p. 262. In the 1980s, meanwhile, Israel is still definitively tribal, and Friedman concludes in *From Beirut to Jerusalem*, in reference to the Israelis, Lebanese, and Palestinians: "Faced with a choice between passion and modernity, they had chosen passion. Faced with a choice between expanding economies and the tribe, they had chosen the tribe" (p. 494). Two decades later

Israel is promoted to existence as "a country that is hard-wired to compete in a flat world" ("People vs. Dinosaurs," June 8, 2008) and "a perfect fit with this era of globalization" ("Israel Discovers Oil," June 10, 2007).

160   *The Lexus and the Olive Tree*, p. 345.

161   "Clinton's Last Memo," *New York Times*, January 12, 2001.

162   *The Lexus and the Olive Tree*, p. 345. Friedman defends the flight of jobs as "Israeli textile manufacturers … doing the logical thing" and determines that the sole hazard resulting from such logic is hostility to globalization, which, he threatens, "often lapses into sectarianism, violence and exclusivity. And the more noninclusive you become, the less networked you are, the more you will fall behind, and the more you fall behind, the more you will want to retreat and reject the outside world with more exclusivity" (*Ibid.*, pp. 345–6).

163   *Ibid.*, p. 344.

164   *Ibid.*

165   See pacbi.org for the text of the original, indigenous "Call for Academic and Cultural Boycott of Israel," endorsed in 2004 by the Palestinian Federation of Unions of University Professors and Employees; Palestinian General Federation of Trade Unions; Palestinian NGO Network, West Bank; Teachers' Federation; Palestinian Writers' Federation; Palestinian League of Artists; Palestinian Journalists' Federation; General Union of Palestinian Women; Palestinian Lawyers' Association; and tens of other Palestinian federations, associations, and civil society organizations.

166   "A Boycott Built on Bias," *New York Times*, June 17, 2007.

167   Friedman has yet to employ the anti-Semitic accusation against states quite familiar with apartheid, featured here: Adam Horowitz, "University of Johannesburg to Officially Sever Ties With Israel's Ben-Gurion University," *Mondoweiss*, March 23, 2011. Friedman meanwhile transcribes the smattering of Arab names he hears at the 2007 Hebrew University commencement for doctoral candidates to show that boycotting Israeli universities even harms Palestinians: "How crazy is this, I thought. Israel's premier university is giving Ph.D.'s to Arab students, two of whom were from East Jerusalem— i.e. the occupied territories—supervised by Jewish Israeli professors, all while some far-left British academics are calling for a boycott of Israeli universities" ("A Boycott Built on Bias," *New York Times*,

June 17, 2007). Friedman also manages to note that one student who receives her diploma in a headscarf would not have been able to do so in France. Obviously, the majority of Palestinians are more affected by the squelching of educational opportunities for Palestinians as a result of the occupation than by potential setbacks to doctoral programs at Hebrew University.

168   For a speech by Lebanese criminal justice expert Dr. Omar Nashabe at the London School of Economics in 2011, outlining the tribunal's biases and manipulations, see "The Special Tribunal for Lebanon (STL): Prerequisites for Injustice?," LSE Global Governance public lecture, The London School of Economics and Political Science, January 18, 2011 (accessible at www2.lse.ac.uk).

169   "A Boycott Built on Bias," *New York Times*.

170   *The Lexus and the Olive Tree*, pp. 420–1.

171   "The New Mideast Paradigm," *New York Times*, March 6, 2001.

172   "The Mideast's Ground Zero," *New York Times*, January 7, 2009.

173   *From Beirut to Jerusalem*, p. 439. In reference to a 1987 NBC documentary about Israel subtitled "A Dream Is Dying," Friedman himself remarks: "Can one imagine a documentary called *Hafez Assad's Syria: 'A Dream Is Dying'*? No, because there has to be a dream which we can all relate to before its death is worth an hour on network television" (*Ibid.*, p. 434).

174   In a first Intifada anecdote included in *From Beirut*, Friedman is eating breakfast in a London hotel and notices a photograph in the *International Herald Tribune* of an Israeli soldier grabbing a Palestinian youth. Friedman muses: "I couldn't help but say to myself, 'Let's see, there are 155 countries in the world today. Say five people grabbed other people in each country; that makes 775 similar incidents worldwide. Why was it that this grab was the only one to be photographed and treated as front-page news?'" (p. 432). Missing from Friedman's equation, of course, is that the grabbers in the 155 other countries were presumably not under government orders to break the bones of the people being grabbed (See Alex Kane, "The real Yitzhak Rabin," *Mondoweiss*, November 4, 2010). Nor does alleged media fixation on Israeli violence in this case appear to have the logical effect on media audiences, as Friedman speculates that, in regards to the Intifada, "many viewers said to themselves, 'My God, this is a war. How can the Israelis tolerate this uprising for

another day?'"—not "My God, how can the Palestinians tolerate being grabbed?" (*From Beirut to Jerusalem*, p. 442).

175   As writer Max Ajl notes, "Jews don't control 'the world's media'; Jewish people are disproportionately represented among media institutions and amongst their ownership, as the Jewish demographic disproportionately lands on the wealthy end of the spectrum." Max Ajl, "Israel Lobby? Try Again," *Jewbonics*, May 8, 2010.

176   *From Beirut to Jerusalem*, p. 441.

177   "The Focus on Israel," *New York Times Magazine*, February 1, 1987. Friedman's treatment of media coverage in *From Beirut* is summed up nicely by Edward Said in "The Orientalist Express: Thomas Friedman Wraps Up the Middle East," *Village Voice*, October 17, 1989. Said writes:

> When [Friedman] arrives finally at the vexed problem of press coverage, he warns us that the media are unfair in their relentless fixation on Israel (this from the journalist-author of a 600-page book on the subject), then he compliments the Israelis on manipulating the media brilliantly, then he blathers on about Israeli troops beating up three-year-olds, and how that vigorous form of outdoor exercise provides them with self-knowledge!

178   *Longitudes and Attitudes*, p. 336.

179   "Nine Wars Too Many," *New York Times*, May 15, 2002.

180   Robert Fisk, *The Great War for Civilisation*, p. 497.

181   "The Hard Truth," *New York Times*, April 3, 2002. On the subject of media bias during the West Bank invasion and for a scathing response to "that pseudo-pundit, the insufferably conceited Thomas Friedman," see Edward Said, "What Price Oslo?," *CounterPunch*, March 24–30, 2002.

182   "The End of Something," *New York Times*, June 30, 2002.

183   *Ibid.*

184   Turkey is incidentally a country that shares with Israel and India the honor of being had at hello by Friedman ("Letter From Istanbul," June 15, 2010), who appreciates its exemplary fusion of Islam and free-market democracy and the fact that parents of Turkish suicide bombers choose to apologize rather than glorify God following the 2003 synagogue bombings in Istanbul ("War of Ideas, Part 2," January 11, 2004). When Turkish humanitarian ships are attacked, the Israeli hello naturally trumps the Turkish one.

185　"When Friends Fall Out," *New York Times*, June 1, 2010. For the headline accrual argument, see "Israeli Government Defends Raids" (interview by Leigh Sales with Israeli government spokesman Mark Regev), Australian Broadcasting Corporation, May 31, 2010. Regarding the real motive for the flotilla attack, Chomsky offers the following passage from Israeli journalist Amira Hass: "The total separation of the Gaza Strip from the West Bank is one of the greatest achievements of Israeli politics, whose overarching objective is to prevent a solution based on international decisions and understandings and instead dictate an arrangement based on Israel's military superiority." Concludes Chomsky: "The Freedom Flotilla defied that policy and so it must be crushed." See Noam Chomsky, "The Real Threat Aboard the Freedom Flotilla," *In These Times*, June 8, 2010.

186　See "Weapons found on Mavi Marmara," uploaded to Flickr by IsraelMFA (Israeli Ministry of Foreign Affairs): "items are from between 07 Feb 2006 & 07 Jun 2010."

187　"Steal This Movie," *New York Times*, August 7, 2010. See also "Netanyahu: 'Israel Must Prepare to Fight Delegitimization,'" *Earth Times*, October 17, 2009.

188　*Ibid.*

189　*Ibid.*

190　As for the perceived overreaction of the international community to Israel's murderous blockade of Gaza, Friedman declares that international concern is "so out of balance with these other horrific cases in the region," but he does allow that having "a whole new generation grow up in Gaza with Israel counting how many calories they each get" might contribute to the erosion of Israel's "moral fabric" ("When Friends Fall Out," June 1, 2010).

191　*Longitudes and Attitudes*, p. 373.

192　*Ibid.*, p. 378.

193　*Ibid.*

194　*Ibid.*

195　"World War III," *New York Times*, September 13, 2001.

196　"Free Marriage Counseling," *New York Times*, August 2, 2009.

197　*Longitudes and Attitudes*, pp. 364–5.

198　"Passions and Interests," *New York Times*, October 2, 2003.

199　"Fathers and Sons," *New York Times*, May 11, 2003.

200 "Jews, Israel and America," *New York Times*, October 24, 2004.

201 Ari Shavit, "White Man's Burden," *Haaretz*, April 3, 2003. Friedman additionally manages to construe parallels between the Iraq war and Israel's Operation Defensive Shield in Jenin via typically patronizing language:

> Actually, the Iraq war is a kind of Jenin on a huge scale. Because in Jenin, too, what happened was that the Israelis told the Palestinians, We left you here alone and you played with matches until suddenly you blew up a Passover seder in Netanya. And therefore we are not going to leave you along any longer. We will go from house to house in the Casbah. And from America's point of view, Saddam's Iraq is Jenin. This war is a defensive shield.

The precise need for the defensive shield in Iraq continues to be unclear, given that Friedman himself admits Saddam is not a threat to the United States.

202 *Ibid.*

203 *Ibid.*

204 For the role of the Israel lobby in the war effort, see John Mearsheimer and Stephen Walt, "The Israel Lobby," *London Review of Books*, March 23, 2006:

> Pressure from Israel and the [pro-Israel] Lobby was not the only factor behind the decision to attack Iraq in March 2003, but it was critical … The war was motivated in good part by a desire to make Israel more secure. According to Philip Zelikow, a former member of the president's Foreign Intelligence Advisory Board, the executive director of the 9/11 Commission, and now a counsellor to Condoleezza Rice, the "real threat" from Iraq was not a threat to the United States. The "unstated threat" was the "threat against Israel," Zelikow told an audience at the University of Virginia in September 2002. "The American government," he added, "doesn't want to lean too hard on it rhetorically, because it is not a popular sell."

205 "Grapes of Wrath," *New York Times*, March 12, 2003.

206 Ari Shavit, "White Man's Burden," *Haaretz*, April 3, 2003. Friedman also informs Shavit: "Bush will never give in. That's not what he's made of. Believe me, you don't want to be next to this guy when he thinks he's being backed into a corner." His slogan meanwhile appears elsewhere in other forms, such as "some things are true even if a Texas cowboy believes them."

207   *Ibid.*

208   "Listening To the Future?," *New York Times*, May 5, 2002.

209   "Imbalance of Power," *New York Times*, April 21, 1998.

210   "Free Marriage Counseling," *New York Times*, August 1, 2009.

211   "The Free-Speech Bird," *New York Times*, March 27, 2002.

212   *Longitudes and Attitudes*, p. 368.

213   *Ibid.* We also learn in *Longitudes* that Bill Clinton phones Friedman
        at the Jidda Sheraton to suggest he publicize back-channel nego-
        tiations between Shimon Peres and Arafat aide Abu Ala'a (Ahmed
        Qurei) that have reportedly resulted in an outline for a land-for-
        peace deal. Friedman informs Clinton that he is in Saudi Arabia and
        thus "not in a position to sort out how solid it all was" (*Ibid.*, p. 366).
        As for the Saudi peace plan, Friedman discredits it as lacking "emo-
        tional content" when it is reiterated in 2007, and for being "basically
        faxed to the Israeli people … People don't give up land for peace
        in a deal that comes over the fax" ("Seeing Is Believing," August
        19, 2007). One can only assume that the Saudis have not read the
        Friedman column on how to achieve an "emotional breakthrough"
        with the Israelis, which involves now-King Abdullah flying to
        Jerusalem and visiting al-Aqsa mosque, the Palestinian parlia-
        ment, and the Yad Vashem Holocaust memorial before personally
        delivering his offer to the Israeli parliament ("Abdullah's Chance,"
        March 23, 2007). By 2010, however, the requirements have been
        downgraded, and Friedman "can't think of anything that would get
        [the latest round of] peace talks off to a better start" than Abdullah
        inviting Netanyahu to Riyadh and presenting his peace plan there
        ("Saudi Time," September 7 2010).

214   *Longitudes and Attitudes*, p. 379.

215   "The Democracy Thing," *New York Times*, October 30, 2002. In
        2001, by contrast, Israeli culpability is excised in a hypothetical
        memo from George W. Bush to Ariel Sharon and Yasser Arafat
        ("Dear Ariel and Yasir," October 23, 2001):

> Ariel, don't you get it? We know bin Laden didn't attack us to liberate
> Palestine. We know the roots of this story are in the anger of Arab citizens
> at their own bad regimes. We know the roots are with the fanatics who
> want to twist Islam into a religion of anger and martyrdom. These truths
> are too big to hide—unless you get in the way and make Israel the story.
> Get off the radar screen!

Israel's fundamental connection to the radar screen is however addressed in John Mearsheimer and Stephen Walt, "The Israel Lobby," *London Review of Books*, March 23, 2006:

> Saying that Israel and the US are united by a shared terrorist threat has the causal relationship backwards: the US has a terrorism problem in good part because it is so closely allied with Israel, not the other way around … There is no question that many al-Qaida leaders, including Osama bin Laden, are motivated by Israel's presence in Jerusalem and the plight of the Palestinians.

216 *Longitudes and Attitudes*, p. 379.

217 *Ibid.*, p. 380.

218 "A Way Out of the Middle East Impasse," *New York Times*, August 24, 2001.

219 See Akiva Eldar, "Palestine PM to *Haaretz*: We will have a state next year," *Haaretz*, April 2, 2010. Fayyad tells Eldar: "Of course, Palestinians would have the right to reside within the State of Palestine"—i.e., not to return to their original homes in what is now Israel. See also Iqbal Jassat, "Fayyad's Subversion of Right of Return," *Palestine Chronicle*, April 3, 2010.

220 "The New Mideast Paradigm," *New York Times*, March 6, 2001. Friedman elaborates: "Intifada II is Palestinian youths trying to emulate the Hezbollah in Lebanon, and playing out some heroic 1960's Che Guevara struggle against the 'Israeli imperialist'; it's Palestinian youths lashing out at the symbol of their failure to build a modern society—Israel; and it's Palestinian youths lashing out at the instruments of their decline—their own leaders."

221 "The Best of Enemies," *New York Times*, February 16, 2001.

222 "This Is Just the Start," *New York Times*, March 1, 2011.

223 "The Real Palestinian Revolution," *New York Times*, June 29, 2010.

224 "Green Shoots in Palestine," *New York Times*, August 5, 2009.

225 See Kevin Peraino, "Palestine's New Perspective," *Newsweek*, September 4, 2009, which specifies that Fayyad's party won "a dismal 2.4 percent of the vote" in the 2006 Palestinian legislative elections.

226 See Aisling Byrne, "Building a Police State in Palestine," *Foreign Policy* (The Middle East Channel), January 18, 2001:

> The security apparati being created, in tandem with a second-generation of monopolies and concentrations of economic power, have little to no

domestic transparency or accountability. Effectively, final control rests with Israel, the CIA and other external intelligence services. Western diplomats and officials have described the relationship between the CIA and the two Palestinian security bodies responsible for most of the torture of Hamas supporters as being "so close that the American agency appears to be supervising the Palestinians' work."

See additionally Mark Perry, "Dayton's Mission: A Reader's Guide," *Al Jazeera English* (The Palestine Papers), January 25, 2011.

227　Aisling Byrne, "Building a police state in Palestine," *Foreign Policy*.

228　*Ibid.*

229　"Beyond the Banks," *New York Times*, February 8, 2009.

230　*Ibid.*

231　"Green Shoots in Palestine II," *New York Times*, August 9, 2009.

232　"Beyond the Banks," *New York Times*.

233　Nathan Thrall, "Our Man in Palestine," *The New York Review of Books*, October 14, 2010.

234　*Ibid.*

235　"Green Shoots in Palestine II," *New York Times*.

236　*Ibid.*

237　See Mark Perry, "Dayton's Mission: A Reader's Guide," *Al Jazeera English* (The Palestine Papers), January 25, 2011.

238　See Avi Issacharoff, "IMF: Gaza's Economy Shot Up By 16% So Far in 2010," *Haaretz*, September 14, 2010.

239　For more on the myth of the West Bank economic miracle, see Ahmed Moor, "It's Time to Dismantle the Palestinian Authority," *The Huffington Post*, November 6, 2010:

> The unsustainable bubble economy [in the West Bank] fails to capture the means of production and therefore strengthens the occupation. That's because the European donor funds (that's how the Europeans remain "relevant" to the "peace process"—they pay for what Israel breaks) are meted out in salary form to sustain Fayyad's repressive police statelet … Those salaries are then spent on regular commodity goods—yogurt, laundry detergent, cellular phones—that are either produced by Israel or are subject to exorbitant import tariffs. At the same time, Israel imposes anti-market, anti-competitive, protectionist economic policies in the West Bank and Gaza to prevent the genesis or development of genuine Palestinian industry. The result is a badly developed Palestinian service economy whose primary function is to consume Israeli goods.

240   "Green Shoots in Palestine II," *New York Times*.

241   "Footprints in the Sand," *New York Times*, November 7, 2004.

242   "Half-Pregnant in Hebron," *New York Times*, January 5, 1997.

243   *Ibid*. Netanyahu's character is especially compatible with metaphors, and he stars the previous year as the Bibi who is being thrown out with the bathwater by Egyptian Foreign Minister Amr Moussa ("The Arab Burden," November 20, 1996).

244   *Ibid*.

245   *Ibid*.

246   Dayton's full keynote speech at the WINEP-hosted Soref Symposium can be accessed via the WINEP website, washingtoninstitute.org, under the heading "Peace Through Security: America's Role in the Development of the Palestinian Authority Security Services" (2009 Soref Symposium). Dayton also announces his conviction that WINEP is "the foremost think tank on Middle East issues, not only in Washington, but in the world" and emphasizes the infinite and unbreakable bond between the United States and Israel.

247   See Akiva Eldar, "Palestine PM to Haaretz: We will have a state next year," *Haaretz*, April 2, 2010.

248   Joseph Massad, "An Immaculate Conception?," *The Electronic Intifada*, April 14, 2010.

249   *From Beirut to Jerusalem*, p. 498.

250   See Shiri McArthur, "A Conservative Estimate of Total Direct U.S. Aid to Israel: Almost $114 Billion," *Washington Report on Middle East Affairs*, November 2008: pp. 10–11.

251   *From Beirut to Jerusalem*, p. 500.

252   Israel's 1967 victory is additionally credited in *From Beirut* with "enabl[ing] the Palestine issue to be reborn," while the ensuing occupation enables the "rebirth of Palestinian identity" (p. 333).

253   "Time for Radical Pragmatism," *New York Times*, June 4, 2008.

254   Gideon Levy, "There has never been an Israeli peace camp," *Haaretz*, March 7, 2010.

255   *From Beirut to Jerusalem*, p. 421.

256   "Albright's Kind Gesture," *New York Times*, September 11, 1997. According to Friedman, Clinton's Secretary of State Warren Christopher fails to realize that his diplomacy is unnecessary, and shamefully ends up babysitting regional sandbox fights.

257   "Hobby or Necessity?," *New York Times*, March 28, 2010.

258   "Call White House, Ask for Barack," *New York Times*, November 8, 2009.

259   "Passion for Peace," *New York Times*, May 28, 2003.

260   Friedman argues that, in their perennial quest for a scapegoat for their misery, the Arabs have failed to understand that "many Americans might identify with Israel not because the Israel lobby ordered them to do so, but for the same reason that they identify with Taiwan or South Korea or modern Germany—because they are free-market democracies that share our basic values and outlook on life" (*Longitudes and Attitudes*, p. 379). That Taiwan, South Korea, and Germany—which do not in their present incarnations engage in apartheid policies, democratically award nationality to a single religious group, or regularly undertake military maneuvers against civilians—do not receive the amount of U.S. aid that Israel does suggests that the issue is not one of popular identification.

261   "Call White House, Ask for Barack," *New York Times*, November 8, 2009.

262   "Just Knock It Off," *New York Times*, October 19, 2010.

263   "Thomas Friedman: Americans 'Fed Up' With Israel," uploaded to youtube.com on October 25, 2010, by "israelnews" (Israeli Channel 2 News) . Friedman's momentary harshness reportedly causes Netanyahu himself to remark: "We may have lost Thomas Friedman, but I don't think we lost America" (Natasha Mozgovaya, "Netanyahu tells Biden: Peace agreement must not be forced on us from above," *Haaretz*, November 8, 2010).

264   "Reality Check," *New York Times*, December 11, 2010.

265   As Gideon Levy points out, neither this "deal" nor any other ever presented to the Palestinians has satisfactorily addressed the refugee issue: Gideon Levy, "There Has Never Been an Israeli Peace Camp," *Haaretz*, March 7, 2010.

266   "Reality Check," *New York Times*.

267   "The Mideast's Ground Zero," *New York Times*, January 7, 2009.

268   *Ibid.*

269   "Let's Fight Over a Big Plan," *New York Times*, March 17, 2010. Grinstein is a relatively new addition to Friedman's circle of experts; the Reut Institute is the source of the infamous report calling for attacks on "delegitimizers of Israel," such as peace activists. See James

Marc Leas, "Israeli Think Tank Calls for Sabotaging 'Delegitimizers' of Israel," *CounterPunch*, May 21–3, 2010.

270   "End of Mideast Wholesale," *New York Times*, May 7, 2011.

271   "Thomas Friedman: Americans 'Fed Up' With Israel," Israeli Channel 2 News.

272   "Not-So-Strange Bedfellow," *New York Times*, January 31, 2007.

273   "Chicken à l'Iraq," *New York Times*, October 9, 2002.

CONCLUDING NOTE

1   *The World Is Flat*, p. 257.

2   "War of Ideas, Part 4," *New York Times*, January 18, 2004.

3   "An Hour With Thomas Friedman of 'The New York Times,'" *Charlie Rose*, May 30, 2003, charlierose.com.

4   *The Lexus and the Olive Tree*, p. 282.

5   Adrienne Pine, *Working Hard, Drinking Hard: On Violence and Survival in Honduras*, Berkeley and Los Angeles: University of California Press, 2008, p. 20.

6   "We Are All French Now?," *New York Times*, June 24, 2005.

7   See Norman Solomon, "Announcing the P.U.-litzer Prizes for 2006," *The Huffington Post*, December 26, 2006.

8   "Working Hard, Drinking Hard: On Violence and Survival in Honduras" (interview with Emma Lovegrove), *Upside Down World*, August 21, 2008.

9   "A Well of Smiths and Xias," *New York Times*, June 7, 2006.

10   "The Core of Muslim Rage," *New York Times*, March 6, 2002.

11   "Working Hard, Drinking Hard: On Violence and Survival in Honduras" (interview with Emma Lovegrove), *Upside Down World*, August 21, 2008.

12   "Y2K Plus 5," *New York Times*, November 21, 1999.

13   "Senseless in Seattle," *New York Times*, December 1, 1999.

14   *The World Is Flat*, pp. 552–3.

15   *Ibid.*, p. 546.

16   "30 Little Turtles," *New York Times*, February 29, 2004.

17   Adrienne Pine, "Mitch, Maquiladoras y Mujeres," lecture presented at the American Anthropological Association Meetings, Chicago, November 1999. Online version accessible at quotha. net/archives/mitch.

18   See usaid.gov, "Honduras: Economy."

19 "Don't Punish Africa," *New York Times*, March 7, 2000.

20 "Protesting for Whom?," *New York Times*, April 24, 2001.

21 See Howard Youth, "Green Awakening in a Poor Country," *World Watch*, September/October 1998.

22 Adrienne Pine, "Mitch, Maquiladoras y Mujeres."

23 Adrienne Pine, "Foosball With the Devil: Haiti, Honduras, and Democracy in the Neoliberal Era," *New Politics* 13: 1, Summer 2010.

24 Adrienne Pine, "Mitch, Maquiladoras y Mujeres."

25 Adrienne Pine, "Mercenary Justice and Masculinity in Urban Honduras," quotha.net, May 26, 2008.

26 "Israel's Goals in Gaza?," *New York Times*, January 14, 2009.

27 "The Third Bubble," *New York Times*, April 20, 2003.

28 "The Meaning of a Skull," *New York Times*, April 27, 2003.

29 "Call Your Mother," *New York Times*, May 11, 2008.

30 "Lessons From Tahrir Sq.," *New York Times*, May 24, 2011.

31 See Section III for Friedman's Gandhi musings. For Ajl's, see: "Our Western Privilege Is the Legacy of Historical Violence," *Mondoweiss*, June 19, 2010.

32 "Thomas Friedman on 'Petropolitics,' Iraq, Israel–Palestine and the 'Excuse Makers,'" *Democracy Now!*, June 7, 2006.

33 "This I Believe," *New York Times*, December 2, 2009.

34 "A Poverty of Dignity and a Wealth of Rage," *New York Times*, July 15, 2005.

35 "It's No Vietnam," *New York Times*, October 30, 2003.

36 "Goodbye Iraq, and Good Luck," *New York Times*, July 15, 2009.

37 Nir Rosen, "Western media fraud in the Middle East," *Al Jazeera*, May 18, 2011.

38 "Goodbye Iraq, and Good Luck," *New York Times*.

39 Nir Rosen, "Western media fraud in the Middle East," *Al Jazeera*.

40 *Ibid.*

41 *Ibid.*